PECKERWOOD, PLEASE

OR

(The "P" Word)

By

Eddie J. Thomas

This book is a work of fiction. Places, events, and situations in this story are purely fictional. Any resemblance to actual persons, living or dead, is coincidental.

ISBN: 1-4033-9843-7 (e-book)
ISBN: 1-4033-9844-5 (Paperback)
ISBN 1-4107-4293-8 (Dust Jacket)

This book is printed on acid free paper.

1stBooks - rev. 07/15/03

CONTENTS

PLOT SYNOPSIS

IN A WORLD WHERE THE ROLES OF THE BLACK AND WHITE RACES ARE REVERSED, YOUNG THOMAS EDWARDS JR. CHALLENGES THE MINDSET THAT SAYS BEING BLACK IS A POSITIVE WHILE BEING WHITE IS A NEGATIVE. THOMAS, AN INTELLIGENT AND OUTSPOKEN WHITE HIGH SCHOOL STUDENT, REALIZES THAT HE, HIS FAMILY AND WHITES IN GENERAL CAN NEVER ACHIEVE TRUE SELF-ACTUALIZATION WHEN A BASIC PREMISE BEHIND THEIR BELIEFS AND VALUES IS SELF-CONTEMPT.

ALTHOUGH WHITES WERE FREED FROM PHYSICAL SLAVERY IN 1865, IN 1965 THEY FIND THEMSELVES AS SOCIAL SECOND CLASS CITIZENS IN THE UNITED STATES OF NEW AFRICA. TECHNICALLY, THEY ARE FREE MEN AND WOMEN WITH THE SAME CONSTITUTIONAL RIGHTS AS BLACKS. HOWEVER, DE FACTO SEGREGATION, POVERTY, WHITE ON WHITE CRIME AND SOCIAL TRADITIONS THAT FAVOR BEING BLACK, CONSPIRE TO "KEEP WHITES IN THEIR PLACE."

THOMAS CHALLENGES THE SUBTLE SYMBOLS OF BLACK SUPREMACY FROM HAIR STYLES TO HISTORICAL EDUCATION. QUANTUM THEORY WHICH IS THE INTELLECTUAL BASIS OF THIS CHALLENGE OF THE STATUS QUO, ENABLES THOMAS TO SEE THE SUBJECTIVE NATURE OF THE BLACK PARADIGM. IT ALSO FORCES HIM TO SEE THE SUBJECTIVE AND SUBSEQUENTLY MISLEADING NATURE OF THE CONCEPT OF RACE ITSELF. THIS IS THE APEX OF HIS OWN SELF-ACTUALIZATION.

THE IRONY IS THAT IN TRANSCENDING RACE, THOMAS UNDERSTANDS THAT HIS "JUST CAUSE" OF WHITE FREEDOM FROM SELF-CONTEMPT AND THE ATTAINMENT OF WHITE PRIDE IS ITSELF ONLY A

TRANSITORY PHASE TOWARD THE FINAL REALIZATION. HE FINALLY REALIZES THAT HUMANITY (LIKE THE QUANTUM) IS ULTIMATELY BOTH A SINGULARITY AND A "WAVE OF POSSIBILITIES."

PREFACE

THIS BOOK IS DEDICATED TO THE MEMORY OF THE LATE JOHN HOWARD GRIFFIN. AS THE WHITE AUTHOR OF THE 1960'S BEST SELLER, "BLACK LIKE ME," HE UNDERSTOOD THE MEANING OF RACIAL PREJUDICE AND DISCRIMINATION. HIS WAS NOT THE UNDERSTANDING THAT COMES FROM THE INTELLECTUAL DETACHMENT OF OBJECTIVE AND SAFE OBSERVATION. HIS UNDERSTANDING WAS BASED ON THE DIRECT PERSONAL EXPERIENCE RESULTING FROM AN ACTUAL CHANGE IN SKIN COLOR.

IT WAS THIS DIRECT PERSONAL EXPERIENCE THAT GAVE HIM THE UNIQUE STATUS OF BEING AN INDIVIDUAL WHO PERSONALLY UNDERSTOOD RACIAL INJUSTICE FROM BOTH THE PERSPECTIVE OF THE DOMINATE GROUP AND THE SUBORDINATE GROUP. PHRASES LIKE "WALK A MILE IN MY SHOES" AND "DO UNTO OTHERS AS YOU WOULD HAVE THEM DO UNTO YOU," BECOME MORE THAN MERE VERBAL IDEALISM WHEN USED TO DESCRIBE THE RACIAL CROSSOVER THAT GRIFFIN REALIZED. ONLY THE MOST CALLOUS OF INDIVIDUALS WOULD REMAIN STEADFAST IN SUPPORT OF BIGOTRY WHEN THE "TABLES ARE TURNED" AND THEY BECOME THE VICTIMS.

THE PURPOSE OF THIS BOOK IS TO "TURN THE TABLES," PUT ONE IN "ANOTHER'S SHOES," AND TO ENCOURAGE SERIOUS INDIVIDUAL THOUGHT ABOUT RACE RELATIONS AND THE ROLE OF THE INDIVIDUAL IN SOCIETY. IF THAT IS ACHIEVED, THEN MAYBE SOCIETAL PROBLEMS OF RACE CAN BE MINIMIZED BY THE ACTIONS OF INDIVIDUALS WHO COME TO UNDERSTAND THE PHRASE "DO UNTO OTHERS AS YOU WOULD HAVE THEM DO UNTO YOU" FOR WHAT IT TRULY IS – THE GOLDEN RULE,

IN THE CULTURE OF THE SOUTHERN UNITED STATES (THE "OLD SOUTH") PRIOR TO THE LAST HALF OF THE 20TH CENTURY, THE WORD "PECKERWOOD" WAS A DEROGATORY TERM USED TO DESCRIBE THE POOR CLASS OF SOUTHERN WHITE FARMERS. IT IS A REVERSAL OF THE NAME FOR A BIRD (THE RED-BELLIED WOODPECKER). A NOTED CHARACTERISTIC OF THE BIRD WAS A PATCH OF RED ON THE BACK OF IT'S HEAD AND NECK. POOR SOUTHERN WHITE FARMERS WERE OFTEN SUNBURNED ON THE NECK. HENCE, THE TERMS "PECKERWOOD" AND "REDNECK" ORIGINATED AS REFLECTIONS OF THAT EXPOSURE TO TOO MUCH SUN.

THE NOVELIST STEPHEN LONGSTREET IS QUOTED AS SAYING "ANY WHITE MAN FROM THE SOUTH IS A PECKERWOOD." THIS BRIEF HISTORY OF THE WORD IS BASED ON INFORMATION FROM THE NEW DICTIONARY OF AMERICAN SLANG, BY ROBERT L. CHAPMAN PH.D (HARPER AND ROW, N.Y.,1986).

I WOULD LIKE TO MAKE A DISTINCTION BETWEEN THE USE OF RACIALLY DEROGATORY TERMS WITH THE INTENTION OF BEING DEROGATORY AND THEIR USE IN CONJUNCTION WITH A LITERARY WORK. THIS DISTINCTION BECOMES CLEAR WHEN THE PURPOSE OF THAT LITERARY WORK IS TO MINIMIZE THE NEGATIVE ATTITUDES THAT RESULT IN THE USE OF SUCH TERMS FOR THE EXPRESSED PURPOSE OF BEING DEROGATORY. THIS IS THE SPIRIT IN WHICH I USE THE WORD "PECKERWOOD" THROUGHOUT THIS BOOK.

* ANY SIMILARITY BETWEEN THE NAMES OR PERSONALITIES OF THE FICTIONAL CHARACTERS IN THIS BOOK AND ANY ACTUAL PERSONS (LIVING OR DECEASED) IS PURELY COINCIDENTAL.

PREFACE (CONTINUED)

QUANTUM THEORY?

WEBSTER DEFINES THEORY AS THE GENERAL PRINCIPLES FROM A BODY OF FACTS, AS IN SCIENCE. THESE PRINCIPLES REPRESENT CONCLUSIONS BASED ON OBSERVATION AS WELL AS PREDICTIONS BASED ON THE EXPERIENCE OF SUCH OBSERVATION. THE TERM PRINCIPLE IS NOT INTENDED TO BE SYNONYMOUS WITH "ABSOLUTE, UNCHANGING TRUTH." NEW FACTS ARE CONTINUOUSLY BEING DISCOVERED IN ALL AREAS OF SCIENCE. "FACTS" ARE OFTEN DISCOUNTED WITH THE DISCOVERY OF NEW KNOWLEDGE. THESE NEW DISCOVERIES RESULT IN ALTERATION OF AND EVEN REFUTATION OF PRINCIPLES AND THEORIES.

BEFORE THE ASTRONOMICAL OBSERVATIONS OF COPERNICUS, WESTERN SCIENCE ACCEPTED AS "FACT" THE NOTION THAT THE EARTH WAS AT THE CENTER OF THE UNIVERSE. IT WAS ALSO ACCEPTED AS "FACT" THAT THE SUN AND THE PLANETS REVOLVED AROUND THE EARTH. OBVIOUSLY, ANY PRINCIPLES OR THEORIES BASED ON THESE "FACTS" WOULD BE SEVERELY LIMITED IN MAKING CONCLUSIONS OR PREDICTIONS ABOUT THE PHYSICAL WORLD, IN LIGHT OF PRESENT-DAY KNOWLEDGE.

IN THE 18TH, 19TH, AND EARLY 20TH CENTURIES THE "PRINCIPLES" OF WHITE RACIAL SUPERIORITY AND BLACK RACIAL INFERIORITY WERE WIDELY ACCEPTED AS SOUND PREMISES FOR CONCLUSIONS ABOUT THE SOCIAL ROLES THAT SHOULD BE ASSUMED BY THE TWO RACES. THE HISTORICAL "FACTS" OF THOSE TIMES (WHAT WAS BEING TAUGHT) DISCREDITED ANY NOTION THAT THE PREHISTORIC AND ANCIENT HISTORY OF THE BLACK RACE CONTRIBUTED SIGNIFICANTLY TO THE ACCOMPLISHMENTS OF HUMANITY IN GENERAL. THIS WAS A MAJOR ARGUMENT USED BY THE PROPONENTS

OF WHITE SUPREMACY. TODAY, IN THE LAST HALF OF THE 20TH CENTURY, OLD (BUT IGNORED) KNOWLEDGE AND NEWLY DISCOVERED FACTS ARE SLOWLY BUT SURELY CHIPPING AWAY AT THE FOUNDATION OF THE PRINCIPLES THAT HAVE DISTORTED THE THINKING OF BLACKS AND WHITES. CHIEF AMONG THESE "NEW FACTS" IS THE ACKNOWLEDGEMENT THAT THE FIRST HUMAN BEINGS (HOMO SAPIENS) WERE BLACK, FROM AFRICA, AND WERE THE ORIGINATORS OF THAT GIFT TO THE EVOLUTION OF CIVILIZATION KNOWN AS ANCIENT EGYPT.

THE PRINCIPLES AND THEORIES ASSOCIATED WITH THE SCIENCE OF PHYSICS HAVE EVOLVED OVER THE AGES. THIS PROCESS INCLUDES THE EARLY SCIENTIFIC UNDERSTANDINGS OF ANCIENT EGYPTIAN MYSTICISM AND GREEK PHILOSOPHY. IT ALSO INCLUDES ISAAC NEWTON'S "LAW OF UNIVERSAL GRAVITATION" AND ALBERT EINSTEIN'S "THEORIES OF RELATIVITY." THE PROCESS HAS CONTINUED WITH DEVELOPING TENETS OF QUANTUM PHYSICS AS DERIVED FROM THE STUDY OF SUB-ATOMIC PARTICLES.

THE TERM "QUANTUM" IS DEFINED BY WEBSTER AS A SUB-ATOMIC UNIT OF ENERGY RECEIVED OR GIVEN OFF BY ATOMS OR MOLECULES. THIS PROCESS OF ENERGY FLOW IS NOT CONTINUOUS, BUT INSTEAD TAKES PLACE STEP-BY-STEP OR UNIT-BY-UNIT. THE INFINITELY SMALL DISTANCE BETWEEN EACH STEP OR UNIT GIVES THE APPEARANCE OF CONTINUOUS OR UNBROKEN FLOW.

WHEREAS EINSTEIN SHOWED THAT MASS AND ENERGY ARE DIFFERENT ASPECTS OF THE SAME THING, A BASIC TENET OF QUANTUM THEORY IS THAT ULTIMATELY MIND AND MATTER ARE DIFFERENT ASPECTS OF THE SAME THING. IN OTHER WORDS ENERGY (MATTER) CANNOT BE DESTROYED. IT CAN BE REDUCED TO INFINITELY SMALL QUANTUMS THAT CAN BE OBSERVED AS CONTINUOUS AND WAVE- LIKE OR AS DISTINCT UNITS. THE <u>ACT OF OBSERVING</u> FOCUSES IN ON THE "WAVE FUNCTION" AND REVEALS THE DISTINCTIVENESS OF THE QUANTUM UNIT. THE SAME

x

ACT OF OBSERVATION, WHEN DIRECTED AT THE UNITS AS A WHOLE REVEALS ONLY A WAVE OF POSSIBILITIES.

THUS, AT THE SUB-ATOMIC LEVEL, MIND (THE INTERPRETATION OF THE OBSERVER) DIRECTLY EFFECTS AND IS INSEPARABLE FROM THE NATURE OF THE REALITY. OUR LARGER PHYSICAL REALITY IS COMPOSED OF THE SUB-ATOMIC AND THE INFINITELY SMALL UNITS OF THE QUANTUM. COULD IT BE POSSIBLE THAT THE LARGER "REALITY" IS JUST AS AMENABLE TO FOCUSED, OBSERVING MINDS AS THAT OF THE INFINITELY SMALL? THE ANSWER TO THAT QUESTION IS A BASIC THEME OF THIS BOOK.

INTRODUCTION

A BASIC TENET OF QUANTUM THEORY IS THAT THE OBSERVER AND THE OBSERVED ARE BOTH PART OF A SYSTEM THAT MAKES THEM MUTUALLY DEPENDENT. IN OTHER WORDS, THAT WHICH IS OBSERVED HAS NO DEFINITE EXISTENCE PRIOR TO THE ACT OF OBSERVATION. IT EXISTS ONLY AS A "WAVE FUNCTION" OF INFINITE POSSIBILITIES. EACH POSSIBILITY REPRESENTS A DISTINCT REALITY OF THE UNIVERSE WHOSE EXISTENCE PARALLELS THAT WHICH YOU AND I PRESENTLY "KNOW" AS REALITY. THE ACT OF OBSERVATION CAUSES THE WAVE FUNCTION TO COLLAPSE ON ONE POSSIBLE REALITY. BUT, IF THE OBSERVER AND THE OBSERVED ARE PART OF ONE SYSTEM, THEN THE ACT OF OBSERVATION AND THE "COLLAPSE OF THE WAVE FUNCTION" PRODUCES A REALITY THAT ENCOMPASSES THE OBSERVER AS WELL AS THE OBSERVED. THE STATE OF EXISTENCE OF THE OBSERVER AND THE OBSERVED ARE MUTUALLY DEPENDENT.

IF REALITY AS WE KNOW IT IS ONLY ONE POINT ON AN INFINITE WAVE OF POSSIBILITIES THEN IT MAY BE POSSIBLE TO GAIN GREATER INSIGHT AND PERSPECTIVE ABOUT OUR OWN "REALITY" BY IMAGINING AN ALTERNATE ROUTE OF HUMAN HISTORY. THIS ALTERNATE DEVELOPMENT WOULD PROCEED FROM A CRUCIAL POINT IN HISTORY WHERE A CHANGE IN A FEW KEY EVENTS WOULD SIGNAL THE "QUANTUM LEAP" FROM ONE POSSIBLE STATE OF REALITY TO ANOTHER.

LET'S NARROW THE SCOPE OF HUMAN HISTORY TO AN AREA THAT IS A MAJOR SOURCE OF CONTROVERSY AND CONFLICT IN HUMAN SOCIETY TODAY. LET'S NARROW THE SCOPE TO RACE RELATIONS. LET'S IMAGINE A CRUCIAL POINT IN THE PAST WHERE A

QUANTUM EVENT SETS HUMAN HISTORY ON A COURSE THAT RESULTS IN A PRESENT-DAY SOCIETY IN WHICH THE CULTURAL, ECONOMIC AND POLITICAL STATUS OF THE BLACK AND WHITE RACES ARE THE REVERSE OF WHAT WE ARE FAMILIAR WITH IN OUR PRESENT STATE OF REALITY.

LET'S IMAGINE AN ANCIENT EGYPT WHOSE PREHISTORIC INHABITANTS FROM THE INTERIOR OF AFRICA RETAIN THEIR STATUS AS THE PREDOMINATE RACIAL GROUP. THE BLACK EGYPTIANS (4000 BC) RESTRICT THE MIGRATION OF SEMITIC ASIANS AND SOUTHERN EUROPEANS IN ORDER TO PRESERVE THEIR OWN RACIAL IDENTITY. AT THE SAME TIME THEY EXTEND THEIR CULTURAL INFLUENCE SOUTHWARD INTO THE HEART OF BLACK AFRICA. EVENTUALLY, SEVERAL STATES ON THE CONTINENT, RIVALING EGYPT IN SIZE AND POWER, COME INTO EXISTENCE. A LOOSE CONFEDERATION BETWEEN EGYPT AND THESE RIVAL STATES MAKES THE CONTINENT OF AFRICA THE CENTER OF WORLD CULTURAL, ECONOMIC AND POLITICAL POWER. WEAKER STATES DEVELOP IN SOUTHERN EUROPE AND THE NEAR EAST. THESE SOON FALL UNDER THE CONTROL OF THE AFRICAN CONFEDERATION. IN THE BRITISH ISLES, NORTHERN, AND CENTRAL EUROPE NO SENSE OF NATIONAL IDENTITY DEVELOPS AMONG THE BARBARIC TRIBES AND THERE IS CONSTANT WARFARE BETWEEN THEM.

IN 1500 BC, EGYPT ALLOWS A SIZEABLE NUMBER OF SEMITICS TO MIGRATE AND BECOME EGYPTIAN CITIZENS. MUCH INTERMARRIAGE TAKES PLACE BETWEEN THE SEMITICS AND THE LOCAL BLACKS. BY 1000 BC, THE POPULATION OF EGYPT IS MOSTLY THE MIXED DESCENDENTS OF BLACKS AND SEMITICS. CULTURALLY, ECONOMICALLY AND POLITICALLY THE EGYPTIANS STILL CONSIDER THEMSELVES TO BE AFRICANS. DUE TO THE CONTINUED INFLUX OF SEMITICS, BY THE YEAR 500 BC, THE EGYPTIAN POPULATION MAJORITY IS SEMITIC. THE SEMITICS LIVE MAINLY IN LOWER (NORTHERN) EGYPT. THEY

REPRESENT 70% OF THE TOTAL POPULATION. THE REMAINING 30% IN UPPER (SOUTHERN) EGYPT ARE BLACKS. THE CHANGE IN THE ETHNIC POPULATION RESULTS IN A CHANGE OF CULTURAL IDENTIFICATION. EGYPT DECLARES ITSELF A SEMITIC NATION AND WITHDRAWS FROM THE AFRICAN CONFEDERATION. THE REMAINING CONFEDERATION STATES DECLARE WAR ON EGYPT.

WITH THE MILITARY MIGHT OF THE AFRICAN CONFEDERATION DESCENDING ON EGYPT, THE SOUTHERN EUROPEANS DECLARE THEIR INDEPENDENCE FROM AFRICA. BUT THEIR OCCASION FOR JOY IS SHORT-LIVED AS THEY SOON FIND THEMSELVES BESIEGED BY INVADING TRIBES OF GERMANIC BARBARIANS FROM NORTH-CENTRAL EUROPE. LACKING THE POLITICAL AND MILITARY SOPHISTICATION OF THE AFRICANS, THE SOUTHERN EUROPEANS FIND THEMSELVES ON THE VERGE OF DEFEAT AT THE HANDS OF THE SUPERIOR NUMBERS OF BARBARIANS.

THE REBELLIOUS SEMITIC EGYPTIANS ARE SOON SUBDUED BY THE COMBINED MILITARY POWER OF THE AFRICAN CONFEDERATION STATES. A COLONIAL TYPE OF GOVERNMENT IS PUT IN PLACE, HEADED BY BLACK EGYPTIAN AFRICANS. HAVING REGAINED CONTROL OF EGYPT, THE AFRICANS TURNED THEIR ATTENTION TO SOUTHERN EUROPE. FACING CERTAIN DESTRUCTION AT THE HANDS OF THE BARBARIC GERMANS, THE SOUTHERN EUROPEANS WELCOMED THE "RESCUING" AFRICANS WITH OPEN ARMS. THE EUROPEANS ACCEPTED THE "LESSER OF TWO EVILS" AND FOUGHT SIDE BY SIDE WITH THEIR FORMER BLACK MASTERS. TOGETHER THEY DROVE THE GERMAN INVADERS OUT OF SOUTHERN EUROPE AND ATTACKED THE GERMAN HOMELAND ITSELF. THOUSANDS OF CAPTIVE GERMANS WERE TAKEN TO SOUTHERN EUROPE AND AFRICA AS SLAVES.

THE AFRICANS LEAVE SEVERAL BATTALIONS OF BLACK TROOPS AT THE NORTHERNMOST BOUNDARIES

OF SOUTHERN EUROPE TO PREVENT FUTURE GERMAN INVASIONS. WHITE SOUTHERN EUROPEANS ARE INTEGRATED INTO THE BATTALIONS TO AID IN DEFENDING THEIR OWN LAND. REALIZING THAT A GERMAN OCCUPATION OF SOUTHERN EUROPE WOULD LEAVE NORTH AFRICA VULNERABLE TO A MAJOR INVASION BY EUROPEANS, THE AFRICANS OFFERED POLITICAL AUTONOMY TO THE SOUTHERN EUROPEANS. THIS GIFT OF INDEPENDENCE WAS SUPPORTED BY AN AFRICAN MILITARY DEFENSIVE PRESENCE. WITH THE THREAT OF GERMAN INVASION CHECKED BY THE NEW RELATIONSHIP WITH THE SOUTHERN EUROPEANS AND SEMITIC RULE OUSTED FROM EGYPT, THE SECURITY OF AFRICA APPEARED TO BE WELL IN PLACE.

IN 1492 AD SAILORS FROM THE WEST COAST OF AFRICA DISCOVER A LAND MASS 4000 MILES OUT INTO THE UNEXPLORED OCEAN. DURING THIS SAME TIME PERIOD A MAJOR TRADE ROUTE DEVELOPS BETWEEN THE EAST COAST NATIVES OF THE "NEW CONTINENT" AND THE WEST COAST AFRICANS. GRADUALLY, AFRICANS BEGIN TO SETTLE ALONG THE EAST COAST OF THE NEW LAND, BRINGING WITH THEM GERMANIC SLAVES. FREQUENT MILITARY EXPEDITIONS INTO GERMANY TO SQUASH ATTEMPTS TO INVADE SOUTHERN EUROPE HAD RESULTED IN THOUSANDS OF GERMANIC CAPTIVES. IT BECAME OBVIOUS THAT THESE CAPTIVES COULD BE A SOURCE OF CHEAP LABOR FOR AFRICANS WHO SETTLED IN THE NEW LANDS ACROSS THE OCEAN.

AS THE NUMBER OF AFRICANS SETTLING IN THE NEW LAND INCREASED, SO DID THE DEMAND FOR GERMAN SLAVES. TO MEET THE DEMAND, AFRICAN DEFENSIVE FORCES ON THE NORTHERN BORDERS OF SOUTHERN EUROPE BEGAN TO MAKE RAIDS DEEP INTO GERMANY STRICTLY FOR CAPTIVES TO BE USED AS SLAVES. ASSISTING THE AFRICANS IN THESE INCURSIONS WHERE MILITARY UNITS OF SOUTHERN EUROPEANS WHO SAW THESE INVASIONS AS AN OPPORTUNITY TO

KEEP THEIR OLD GERMAN ENEMIES FROM EVER POSING A THREAT TO SOUTHERN EUROPE.

TO OBTAIN A CLEAR DISTINCTION BETWEEN WHITE SLAVES AND WHITE FREE MEN, ONLY THE FAIREST SKINNED GERMANS WERE TAKEN. BLONDE HAIR BECAME AN OBVIOUS SYMBOL FOR SLAVE. THE BUYING AND SELLING OF FAIR SKINNED GERMANS BECAME A GLOBAL TRADE FROM SOUTHERN EUROPE TO WEST AFRICAN, AND FINALLY TO THE NEW LAND ACROSS THE OCEAN. MANY AFRICANS AND SOUTHERN EUROPEANS OBTAINED GREAT WEALTH FROM THE SLAVE TRADE. THE HUMAN PRICE FOR SUCH WEALTH WAS THE DEHUMANIZATION OF THE GERMAN PEOPLE AND A FALSE SENSE OF BLACK RACIAL SUPERIORITY.

BY 1600 AD, THE NATIVE PEOPLES OF THE NEW LAND HAD BEEN EITHER SUBJUGATED OR EXTERMINATED BY AFRICAN SETTLERS. THE AFRICANS NOW CALLED THE NEW LAND "NEW AFRICA." AS SETTLEMENTS GREW INTO TOWNS AND CITIES, GEOGRAPHIC DIVISIONS PROMPTED THE UNIFICATION OF TOWNS AND CITIES INTO STATES RIVALING THOSE OF THE AFRICAN MOTHER LAND IN SIZE AND POPULATION. IT WAS ONLY NATURAL THAT THESE STATES WOULD UNIFY TO FORM A CONFEDERATION SIMILAR TO THAT EXISTING IN THE MOTHERLAND. THE NEW ENTITY CALLED ITSELF THE "UNITED STATES OF NEW AFRICA."

IN THE YEAR AD 1776, THE UNITED STATES OF NEW AFRICA DECLARED ITSELF TO BE POLITICALLY INDEPENDENT OF THE MOTHERLAND. THIS CAUSED LITTLE CONCERN IN AFRICA WHICH FOUND ITSELF CONFRONTED WITH THE MOST SERIOUS THREAT TO THE CONTINENT'S SECURITY SENSE THE SEMITIC CONTROL OF EGYPT IN 500 BC.

THE SLAVE TRADE HAD WIDENED. IT WAS VICTIMIZING NOT ONLY GERMANS, BUT ALSO OTHER FAIR SKINNED PEOPLE THROUGHOUT EUROPE AND THE BRITISH ISLES. A CONTINENT WIDE MOVEMENT TO END THE WHITE SLAVE TRADE UNITED THE EUROPEANS FROM THE NORTH TO THE SOUTH. WITH THIS NEW

SENSE OF UNITY THROUGHOUT EUROPE AND REVIVED NATIONALISM AMONG THE SEMITIC MAJORITY IN EGYPT, THE AFRICANS FOCUSED THEIR ATTENTION ON BUILDING UP THE DEFENSES OF THE NORTHERN COAST AND NEAR EASTERN BOUNDARIES OF THEIR CONTINENT.

BY THE BEGINNING OF THE 19TH CENTURY AD, THE EUROPEAN SLAVE TRADE HAD ENDED AND SLAVERY WAS OUTLAWED IN EUROPE AND AFRICA. IN NEW AFRICA SLAVERY WAS NOT ONLY LEGAL, BUT CONSIDERED TO BE THE NATURAL SOLUTION IN A SOCIETY THAT WAS 90% BLACK AND 10% WHITE. IT WAS ONLY A WORLD WIDE TRADE EMBARGO THAT FINALLY FORCED THE NEW AFRICANS TO FREE THEIR WHITE SLAVES IN AD 1865.

THE END OF SLAVERY FOR THE WHITE MAN IN NEW AFRICA WAS ONLY THE BEGINNING OF 100 YEARS OF RACIAL SEGREGATION, NEGATIVE RACIAL STEREOTYPING, LYNCHING, AND SELF-CONTEMPT. THE WHITE MAN WAS A SECOND CLASS CITIZEN WHO WAS CONSTANTLY REMINDED OF HIS POSITION BY THE CONTEMPTUOUS WORD USED BY BLACKS AND WHITES THEMSELVES OUT OF SELF-CONTEMPT. THAT INFAMOUS WORD WAS "**PECKERWOOD**".

PHASE ONE

BLACK IS BEAUTIFUL

THOMAS EDWARDS JR. SAT STARING AT HIS REFLECTION IN HIS BEDROOM DRESSER MIRROR. FOR A YOUNG MAN OF 17, HIS THOUGHTS TAKE ON THE SERIOUSNESS OF A PHILOSOPHER CONTEMPLATING THE ULTIMATE MEANING OF EXISTENCE ITSELF. SUCH PENETRATING AND FOCUSED THOUGHT CAUSE HIM TO FAIL TO NOTICE THE REFLECTION OF HIS MOTHER AS SHE QUIETLY APPROACHES AND STANDS BY HIS SIDE.

MRS. EDWARDS: SON, WHAT ARE YOU THINKING SO HARD ABOUT?

THOMAS JR.: MOM, WHY DID I HAVE TO BE BORN WHITE?

MRS. EDWARDS: THOMAS, THAT IS THE COLOR GOD WANTED FOR YOU.

THOMAS JR.: BUT MOM, THERE DOES NOT SEEN TO BE ANYTHING GOOD ABOUT BEING WHITE. A DARK-SKINNED WHITE KID CALLED ME A STRINGY, YELLOW-HAIRED PECKERWOOD. MY HAIR IS STRINGY, MY LIPS ARE THIN, AND MY NOSE IS LONG.

MRS. EDWARDS: DON'T YOU EVER LET ME HEAR YOU TALK THAT WAY ABOUT YOURSELF! YOU ARE A NICE LOOKING BOY. GOD MADE ALL TYPES OF PEOPLE. HE MADE SOME WHITE, SOME BLACK AND

1

A LOT IN BETWEEN. EVERYTHING THAT HE MADE IS GOOD. THAT DARK SKINNED BOY IS NO BETTER THAN YOU ARE. JUST BECAUSE HIS FAMILY BACKGROUND INCLUDES SOME AFRICANS, THAT DOESN'T MEAN ANYTHING. BLACK PEOPLE CALL ALL OF US PECKERWOODS.

THOMAS JR.:   MOM, IF WHAT YOU SAY IS TRUE, WHY DO YOU AND OTHER WHITE WOMEN CURL YOUR HAIR SO THAT IT LOOKS LIKE BLACK PEOPLE'S HAIR? WHY DO SOME WHITE PEOPLE GET SUNTANS? WHY DID JACKIE MICHAELS GET PLASTIC SURGERY AND DARKEN HIS SKIN?

MRS. EDWARDS: JACKIE MICHAELS IS A RICH ENTERTAINER. RICH FOLKS SOMETIMES FORGET ABOUT THEIR ROOTS. TAKE AWAY HIS MONEY, AND HE'S NOTHING BUT ANOTHER DARK SKINNED PECKERWOOD TRYING TO PASS FOR BLACK! WHITE WOMEN HAVE BEEN CURLING THEIR HAIR FOR AS LONG AS I CAN REMEMBER. IT'S JUST TRADITION.

THOMAS JR.:   BUT, MOM, HOW CAN WE EXPECT TO GET RESPECT FROM BLACK PEOPLE, WHEN WE DON'T RESPECT OURSELVES?

MRS. EDWARDS: SON, TRADITION AND HABITS ARE HARD TO CHANGE. NOW, GET DOWNSTAIRS TO BREAKFAST. YOUR DAD IS WAITING ON US.

THOMAS SR.: THOMAS, WERE YOU UPSTAIRS READING ANOTHER ONE OF THOSE SCIENCE FICTION BOOKS? THE LAST THING A PECKERWOOD NEEDS TO DO IS WASTE HIS TIME READING NONSENSE. BOY, IF YOU WANT TO GET AHEAD IN THE BLACK MAN'S WORLD, THERE ARE TWO THINGS YOU DON'T NEED. LONG STRINGY HAIR AND FICTION!

THOMAS JR.: THEY ARE NOT FICTION BOOKS. THEY ARE BOOKS ON QUANTUM THEORY, AND I LIKE TO WEAR MY HAIR LONG AND STRINGY.

THOMAS SR.: WELL I THINK YOU NEED A HAIR CUT. AND, WHAT IS QUANTUM THEORY ANYWAY?

THOMAS JR.: IT'S A SET OF PRINCIPLES ABOUT NATURE THAT COME FROM THE STUDY OF SUB-ATOMIC PARTICLES. ONE OF THE BASIC PRINCIPLES IS THAT AN OBSERVER AND WHAT HE OBSERVES ARE MUTUALLY DEPENDENT AND PART OF ONE SYSTEM. IT ALSO SUGGESTS THAT BECAUSE OF THIS, WE CAN NEVER "OBJECTIVELY" KNOW THE NATURE OF THE OBSERVED. BEFORE OBSERVATION, THE OBSERVED EXISTS ONLY AS A SERIES OF INFINITE POSSIBILITIES. EACH POSSIBILITY IS ITSELF A DISTINCT REALITY THAT......

THOMAS SR.: WAIT A MINUTE! THAT SOUNDS LIKE FICTION TO ME.

3

THOMAS JR.: BUT DAD, THE STUDY OF ELECTRONS AND OTHER SUB-ATOMIC PARTICLES HAS PROVEN THAT......

THOMAS SR.: SUB-ATOMIC! SON, WE LIVE IN THE REAL WORLD. THE ONE AND ONLY REAL WORLD. THIS WORLD IS CONTROLLED BY THE BLACK MAN, AND PECKERWOODS ARE NOT GOING TO CHANGE IT BY DREAMING ABOUT WORLDS THAT DON'T EXIST.

THOMAS JR.: DAD, IS GOD INFINITE?

THOMAS SR.: WELL, I GUESS SO.

THOMAS JR.: THEN HE COULD HAVE AN INFINITE NUMBER OF REAL POSSIBILITIES OF ONE "REAL" THING.

THOMAS SR.: WELL, I GUESS....

THOMAS JR.: THEN DAD, DON'T YOU SEE?! QUANTUM THEORY APPLIES TO THE WORLD AS WE SEE IT BECAUSE THE WORLD IS MADE FROM THINGS THAT WE CANNOT SEE. THESE ARE THINGS THAT EXIST AS POSSIBILITIES. WHAT WE CALL REALITY IS NOT NECESSARILY THE WAY THAT THINGS REALLY HAVE TO BE.

THOMAS SR.: OKAY, THAT'S ENOUGH OF THIS FOOLISHNESS. FINISH YOUR BREAKFAST AND DON'T BE LATE FOR SCHOOL. IF WE WHITES REALLY WANT TO CHANGE THINGS IN THIS COUNTRY, THEN WE HAD BETTER GET AN EDUCATION TO COMPETE WITH

Peckerwood, Please or (The "P" Word)

THE BLACK MAN. QUANTUM THEORY! PECKERWOOD, PLEASE!

PHASE 2

WHITE HISTORY

   THOMAS JR. DREADED THE DAILY WALK TO HIGH SCHOOL. IT USUALLY SERVED ONLY TO REMIND HIM OF THE INEQUITIES OF LIFE IN THE UNITED STATES OF NEW AFRICA FOR WHITE PEOPLE. THE POVERTY OF HIS GHETTO NEIGHBORHOOD WAS A PRIME EXAMPLE OF THAT INEQUITY. THERE WERE MONOTONOUS AND DECAYING THREE STORY APARTMENT BUILDINGS. THERE WERE SIDEWALKS LITTERED WITH TRASH, DISCARDED BEER CANS AND LIQUOR BOTTLES. PROSTITUTES AND PIMPS WAITED IN FANCY CARS FOR BLACK JOHNS FROM THE SUBURBS. THERE WAS THE HOPELESS EXPRESSION ON THE FACES OF OLD WHITE MEN STANDING ON STREET CORNERS IDLING AWAY THE TIME. THERE WAS ALSO THE DEFIANT EXPRESSION AND HAND SIGNS OF TEENAGE GANG MEMBERS AS THEY CRUISED THE STREETS IN THEIR LOW RIDING CARS. FINALLY, THERE WAS THE MOST PAINFUL REMINDER OF ALL. AS THOMAS JR. APPROACHES THE ENTRANCE TO HIS SCHOOL, A BUS FULL OF BLACK STUDENTS PASSES ALONG THE STREET ON IT'S WAY TO A HIGH SCHOOL IN THE AFFLUENT BLACK SUBURBS.

MS. MAYFIELD: CLASS, COULD I HAVE YOUR ATTENTION PLEASE? TODAY IN U.S. HISTORY WE WILL BEGIN OUR STUDY OF THE EARLY PERIOD OF OUR NATION'S HISTORY. THIS IS THE TIME PERIOD WHEN LARGE NUMBERS OF AFRICANS BEGIN TO SETTLE ON THE EAST COAST. THESE AFRICANS LEFT

THE MOTHERLAND OF THE AFRICAN
CONFEDERATION HOPING TO....

THOMAS JR.:　　EXCUSE ME MS. MAYFIELD.

MS. MAYFIELD:　　YES, THOMAS?

THOMAS JR.:　　WHY DON'T WE EVER STUDY
EUROPEAN HISTORY. YOU KNOW. THE
HISTORY OF OUR OWN PEOPLE.
WHITE PEOPLE. WE LIVE IN THIS
COUNTRY TOO.

MS. MAYFIELD:　　WE WILL GET TO THE CHAPTER ON
SLAVERY DURING THE NEXT
SEMESTER.

THOMAS JR.:　　SLAVERY! OUR HISTORY IS MORE
THAN SLAVERY. WHAT ABOUT
EUROPE? WE CAME FROM EUROPE.

REGGIE:　　SPEAK FOR YOURSELF YOU STRINGY
YELLOW HAIRED PECKERWOOD.

THOMAS JR.:　　DON'T CALL ME A PECKERWOOD. I'M
PROUD OF MY WHITE ANCESTRY. ALL
OF US SHOULD BE PROUD OF BEING
WHITE.

REGGIE:　　I MAY BE WHITE. BUT I'M DARKER
THAN YOU AND PROUD OF THAT. MY
GREAT-GREAT GRANDFATHER WAS
BLACK!

JASON:　　YEAH MAN, A LOT OF US ARE DARK.
AND BESIDES, HAVEN'T YOU HEARD
THAT OLD SAYING? "IF YOU'RE BLACK,
YOU'RE ON THE RIGHT TRACK. IF

YOU'RE BROWN, STICK AROUND. IF YOU'RE WHITE, GET OUT OF SIGHT!"

THOMAS JR.: BUT, IF WE THINK LIKE THAT…IF WE THINK OF OURSELVES AS "PECKERWOODS," HOW CAN WE EVER BE EQUAL TO BLACKS?

MS. MAYFIELD: CLASS! CLASS! THAT'S ENOUGH ARGUING. I WILL NOT TOLERATE NAME CALLING IN HERE AND I DEFINITELY DON'T WANT TO HEAR THE "P" WORD IN HERE AGAIN. THOMAS, YOU'RE A TROUBLE MAKER. EVER SINCE YOU STARTED WEARING YOUR HAIR LONG, YOU'VE HAD A CHIP ON YOUR SHOULDER. I WANT YOU TO GO TO THE PRINCIPAL'S OFFICE. I THINK YOUR HAIR IS TOO LONG!

THOMAS JR.: WELL…AT LEAST I'M PROUD OF MY HAIR AND PROUD OF WHAT I AM. YOU SHOULD TRY WEARING YOUR HAIR NATURAL.

MS. MAYFIELD: NOW THAT'S GOING TOO FAR. YOU WILL NOT INSULT ME IN FRONT OF THE CLASS. GO TO THE PRINCIPAL, IMMEDIATELY!

PRINCIPAL JACKSON: HAVE A SEAT THOMAS. WHAT IS THIS ABOUT YOU DISRUPTING THE CLASS AND DISRESPECTING MS. MAYFIELD?

THOMAS JR.: I ONLY WANTED THEM TO UNDERSTAND WHY IT WAS

IMPORTANT THAT WE LEARN ABOUT OUR OWN WHITE HISTORY.

PRINCIPAL JACKSON: WHITE HISTORY, HUH?

THOMAS JR.: TOO MANY WHITES THINK OF THEMSELVES AS LESS THAN BLACKS.

PRINCIPAL JACKSON: HOW IS THAT?

THOMAS JR.: WE CALL EACH OTHER PECKERWOODS. WE CURL OUR HAIR TO BE LIKE BLACKS. WE EVEN TAN OUR SKINS TO BE DARKER. JACKIE MICHAELS EVEN HAD SURGERY TO MAKE HIMSELF LOOK BLACK.

PRINCIPAL JACKSON: AND YOU THINK THAT TEACHING WHITE HISTORY WILL CHANGE ALL OF THAT?

THOMAS JR.: I THINK IT WOULD HELP.

PRINCIPAL JACKSON: SON, YOU'RE A STUDENT. YOU ARE NOT HERE TO MAKE CURRICULUM DECISIONS. THE SCHOOL BOARD MAKES THOSE DECISIONS. AND THEY ARE ALL BLACK PEOPLE. BLACKS HAVE THE POWER IN THIS COUNTRY. THEY CAN MAKE US, AND THEY CAN BREAK US. IF I TRIED TO PUSH FOR WHITE HISTORY, THEY WOULD BREAK ME.

THOMAS JR.: WHAT WOULD THEY DO?

PRINCIPAL JACKSON: WELL, FOR STARTERS, I'D PROBABLY BE OUT OF A JOB.

THOMAS JR.: SO YOUR JOB IS MORE IMPORTANT THAN WHITE HISTORY OR HOW WHITE KIDS FEEL ABOUT THEMSELVES.

PRINCIPAL JACKSON: YES. NOW, LOOK SON, YOU HAVE GOT TO LEARN TO ACCEPT REALITY. YOU START GETTING PEOPLE ALL STIRRED UP OVER BLACK AND WHITE AND IT WILL ONLY LEAD TO TROUBLE. I WON'T HAVE IT AT THIS SCHOOL. I'M GOING TO NIP THIS IN THE BUD BY FIRST DEMANDING THAT YOU GET A HAIRCUT. WHEN WHITE KIDS LET THEIR HAIR GROW LONG, THAT'S THE FIRST SIGN OF REBELLION.

THOMAS JR.: AND WHAT IF I REFUSE?

PRINCIPAL JACKSON: THOMAS, YOU'RE A SMART YOUNG MAN. YOU HAVE MADE THE HONOR ROLL SINCE YOU HAVE BEEN A STUDENT HERE. I KNOW THAT YOU ARE INTERESTED IN PHYSICS AND WANT TO BECOME A SCIENTIST.

THOMAS JR.: SO YOU ARE SAYING THAT YOU WILL PUT ME OUT OF SCHOOL?

PRINCIPAL JACKSON: EXACTLY.

PHASE 3

B.G.M.S

DECISIONS, DECISIONS! SHOULD ONE CUT HIS HAIR AND CONFORM TO A SYSTEM THAT DENIES HIS OWN PRINCIPLES? SHOULD ONE REVOLT AGAINST THE SYSTEM BY REFUSING TO GET A HAIRCUT AND STAND UP FOR HIS PRINCIPLES? SHOULD ONE RISK THE LOST OF SOMETHING AS IMPORTANT AS AN EDUCATION? SUCH ARE THE THOUGHTS GOING THROUGH THE MIND OF THOMAS JR. AS HE LEAVES THE SCHOOL BUILDING AT THE END OF THE DAY.

EDUCATION IS ONE OF THE MOST IMPORTANT THINGS FOR THE IMPROVEMENT OF THE LIVES OF WHITE PEOPLE. THOSE THAT VALUE IT KNOW THAT THE CHANCE OF IMPROVING THEIR STATUS IS GREATLY IMPROVED BY THE OBTAINMENT OF AS MUCH EDUCATION AS POSSIBLE. WHAT DIFFERENCE WILL A HAIRCUT MAKE? PROBABLY NOT MUCH OF A DIFFERENCE WILL BE MADE FOR ONE WHO TRULY KNOWS WHAT IS RIGHT. BESIDES, IT DOESN'T HURT TO OCCASIONALLY SWALLOW ONE'S PRIDE. THE MAIN THING IS TO KNOW IN ONE'S MIND AND HEART WHAT THE TRUTH REALLY IS. MAYBE WHEN ALL WHITES ACCEPT THE TRUTH AND LEARN TO VALUE THEMSELVES, THEY WILL TRULY BE FREE AND EQUAL IN NEW AFRICA.

BLUE GANG MEMBER #1: HEY, HOMEBOY! WHAT ARE YOU CLAIMING?

THOMAS JR.:   I'M WHITE AND PROUD OF IT.

B.G.M. #2:   DON'T GET SMART PECKERWOOD. I DON'T SEE ANY **BLUE** OR **RED**. NOW, WHAT ARE YOU CLAIMING?

THOMAS JR.:   LOOK, I DON'T BELONG TO ANY GANG. JUST LEAVE ME ALONE.

B.G.M. #1:   LEAVE YOU ALONE? **MOTHERFUCKER**, YOU DON'T TELL US WHAT TO DO. WE RUN THIS NEIGHBORHOOD. THIS IS **BLUE** TERRITORY.

THOMAS JR.:   I DON'T CARE ABOUT BLUE OR RED. YOU GANG BANGERS ARE JUST KILLING EACH OTHER AND MAKING WHITE PEOPLE LOOK LIKE FOOLS. LOOK AROUND. CAN'T YOU SEE. YOU ARE DESTROYING OUR NEIGHBORHOOD. JUST THINK OF ALL OF THE PROBLEMS WE WHITES HAVE. YOU GUYS ARE MAKING IT WORST.

B.G.M. #1:   DON'T TRY TO PREACH TO US PECKERWOOD. YEAH, I SAID **PECKERWOOD**! YOU'RE A PECKERWOOD. I'M A PECKERWOOD. SOME PECKERWOODS WEAR BLUE AND SOME WEAR RED. BUT, THE WORST PECKERWOODS ARE THOSE WHO ARE NOT CLAIMING. THE NEXT TIME I SEE YOU ON THE STREETS, IF YOU'RE NOT WEARING BLUE, I'M GOING TO KICK YOUR ASS. IF YOU'RE WEARING RED, I'M GOING TO PUT A **CAP** IN YOUR ASS.

THOMAS JR.:   MAN, YOU ARE SICK!

B.G.M. #1: I'M GOING TO KICK YOUR ASS RIGHT NOW PECKER...

BEFORE B.G.M. #1 CAN FINISH THE WORD, HE IS INTERRUPTED BY THE SOUND OF SQUEALING CAR TIRES AS A LOW RIDING CAR FULL OF **RED** BALL CAP WEARING TEENAGE BOYS, RACES TOWARD HE AND B.G.M. #2. TWO SHOTS RING OUT FROM THE CAR. THOMAS JR. AND THE TWO GANG MEMBERS ALL FALL TO THE GROUND. AS THE CAR SPEEDS OUT OF RANGE AND SIGHT, EVERYONE BUT B.G.M. #2 SLOWLY RISES FROM THE GROUND. B.G.M. #2 LIES IN A POOL OF BLOOD. FOR A FEW MINUTES THOMAS JR. AND B.G.M. #1 STAND IN A MOTIONLESS EERIE SILENCE, STARING AT THE BODY OF B.M.G. #2. FINALLY, THE SILENCE IS BROKEN BY THOMAS JR.

THOMAS JR.: NOW, CAN YOU SEE? HE'S DEAD JUST BECAUSE HE WAS WEARING BLUE. HE WAS WHITE. THE GUY THAT SHOT HIM WAS WHITE.

B.G.M. #1: THAT IS RIGHT. AND, THE NEXT PECKERWOOD THAT GETS **CAPPED** WILL BE WEARING **RED**!

THOMAS JR.: THIS CANNOT BE REAL. THIS IS CRAZY.

THE EDWARDS FAMILY GATHER AROUND THE TELEVISION WATCHING THE 6 P.M. NEWS. NEWS REPORTS ON GANG SHOOTINGS ARE NOT NEW. THEY HAVE BECOME AN ALL TOO FREQUENT OCCURRENCE. THIS ONE IS OF SPECIAL SIGNIFICANCE. ONE OF THEIR OWN FAMILY MEMBERS WAS A NEAR FATALITY.

MRS. EDWARDS: THOMAS, THAT COULD HAVE BEEN YOU KILLED THIS AFTERNOON.

THOMAS SR.: AS IF WE DO NOT HAVE ENOUGH PROBLEMS AS A RACE OF PEOPLE. THESE YOUNG WHITE THUGS ARE DOING A MORE EFFECTIVE JOB OF DESTROYING WHITE PEOPLE THAN BLACKS EVER HAVE.

THOMAS JR.: WHAT IS WRONG WITH WHITE PEOPLE? WHY CAN WE NOT GET ALONE WITH EACH OTHER? WHY IS THERE SO MUCH SELF-CONTEMPT AND SELF-HATE? WE COMPLAIN ABOUT BLACKS NOT TREATING US AS EQUALS, BUT AT THE SAME TIME WE CALL EACH OTHER PECKERWOODS. WE VALUE BEING DARK-SKINNED AND MIXED-RACE OVER BEING FAIR-SKINNED AND WHITE. WE ARE ASHAMED OF OUR STRINGY HAIR, OUR LONG NOSES AND OUR THIN LIPS. BLACK IS BEAUTIFUL! WHITE IS UGLY!

THOMAS SR.: BOY, THERE YOU GO AGAIN. YOU AND YOUR OUT-OF-THIS-WORLD IDEAS.

MRS. EDWARDS: THOMAS, IT TAKES TIME FOR PEOPLE TO CHANGE. WHITE PEOPLE HAVE NOT BECOME THIS WAY OVER NIGHT.

THOMAS JR.: BUT, WE HAVE TO START SOMEWHERE, SOMETIME.

MRS. EDWARDS: SOMETIMES, STARTING WITH SOMETHING SMALL CAN LEAD TO BIG CHANGES. YOU HAVE TO CHANGE THE

WAY PEOPLE THINK A LITTLE AT A TIME.

THOMAS SR.: I WISH WE COULD CHANGE THE WAY THAT SOME BLACK PEOPLE THINK. WE ARE NOT SLAVES ANY MORE, BUT THEY DO EVERYTHING THEY CAN TO MAKE US FEEL LIKE SECOND CLASS CITIZENS. A GOOD EXAMPLE IS AT MY JOB. THE WHITES NEVER SEEM TO BE ABLE TO ADVANCE. I'M TIRED OF SEEING YOUNG BLACK GUYS BEING PROMOTED OVER WHITES THAT HAVE BEEN ON THE JOB LONGER. TOMORROW, I'M GOING TO GO HAVE A TALK WITH MR. JOHNSON AND I'M GOING …. THOMAS! BOY, YOU ARE NOT EVEN LISTENING TO ME. WHAT ARE YOU DOING? LET ME GUESS, DREAMING ABOUT THAT QUANTUM STUFF AGAIN.

THOMAS JR.: I WAS THINKING ABOUT SOMETHING THAT MOM SAID. YOU KNOW, STARTING WITH SOMETHING SMALL TO PRODUCE SOMETHING BIG. QUANTUM THEORY OPERATES LIKE THAT.

THOMAS SR.: HERE WE GO AGAIN. BOY, IF YOUR QUANTUM CAN SOLVE THE RACE PROBLEM, TEACH IT TO ME. LORD KNOWS, I'LL NEED MORE THAN THEORY WHEN I GO IN TO TALK TO MR. JOHNSON.

THOMAS JR.: WHAT COULD BE SOMETHING THAT IS TAKEN FOR GRANTED….SOMETHING THAT ONCE ALTERED COULD LEAD TO

A CHANGE IN ATTITUDE ABOUT THE MEANING OF BEING WHITE?

THOMAS SR.: **PECKERWOOD, PLEASE!** GET OUT OF THE CLOUDS. COME DOWN TO EARTH AND GET THAT LONG STRINGY HAIR CUT. IF I WENT INTO MR. JOHNSON'S OFFICE LOOKING LIKE THAT, HE WOULD PROBABLY FIRE ME. ASKING FOR A PROMOTION WOULD BE A JOKE. I COULD JUST HEAR HIM SAY, "**PECKERWOOD, PLEASE**"!

THOMAS JR.: DO YOU HAVE TO SAY "PECKERWOOD"? I AM TIRED OF THAT WORD. BLACKS CALL US....

THOMAS SR.: OKAY. OKAY. JUST GET A HAIRCUT.

PHASE 4

PRETTY BOY

BARBER SHOPS CAN BE A YOUNG MAN'S INTRODUCTION TO THE TYPE OF WORLDLY KNOWLEDGE THAT FORMAL CLASSROOM INSTRUCTION SELDOM PROVIDES. THEY CAN ALSO BE PROVIDERS OF INSIGHT INTO THE WORKINGS OF HUMAN PSYCHOLOGY. SURELY, THEY ARE PLACES WHERE VARIETIES OF CHARACTERS CONGREGATE. QUITE DEFINITELY THIS IS A PLACE WHERE THOMAS JR. DOES NOT WANT TO BE.

ON FIRST OBSERVATION, HIS RELUCTANCE SEEMS TO HAVE NOTHING TO DO WITH THE PRESENCE OF "WORLDLY KNOWLEDGE," "HUMAN PSYCHOLOGY," OR "CHARACTERS." IT SIMPLY SEEMS THAT HIS DISINCLINATION IS OVER A HAIRCUT. BUT, HE KNOWS THAT "WORLDLY KNOWLEDGE," "HUMAN PSYCHOLOGY," AND "CHARACTER" HAVE JUST AS MUCH TO DO WITH THIS AS THE SCISSORS AND CLIPPERS USED BY THE BARBER.

BARBER: THOMAS, BOY I HAVEN'T SEEN YOU IN HERE IN A LONG TIME. AND FROM THE LOOK OF YOUR HAIR, IF COULD EASILY BE A YEAR. WELL, I'VE GOT THREE AHEAD OF YOU. HAVE A SEAT.

CHARACTER. WEBSTER DEFINES IT AS "A PERSON HAVING NOTABLE TRAITS OR CHARACTERISTICS." THAT DESCRIPTION ADEQUATELY DESCRIBES THE VARIETY OF INDIVIDUALS THAT ONE ENCOUNTERS IN A BARBER SHOP. EACH ONE IS UNIQUE, YET POSSESSING A COMMON AURA THAT ACCENTUATES THE FACT THAT ALL HAVE A COMMON RACIAL HEREDITY.

ALL SEEM TO HAVE ADJUSTED THEIR PERSONALITIES IN RESPONSE TO THE STATUS OF RACE RELATIONS IN THE LARGER SOCIETY. WHAT THE NATURE OF THESE PERSONALITIES MIGHT HAVE BEEN UNDER DIFFERENT SOCIAL CIRCUMSTANCES, COULD BE ANYONE'S GUESS. IN A SOCIETY IN WHICH ALL RACES OF MEN ARE GIVEN EQUAL RESPECT AND JUSTICE, SURELY THEIR PERSONAL DEVELOPMENTS WOULD HAVE TAKEN MUCH MORE REWARDING PATHS.

PRETTY BOY SAT IN THE BARBER'S CHAIR WITH A COCKY EXPRESSION ON HIS FACE AND A CIGARETTE HANGING FROM THE CORNER OF HIS MOUTH. PRETTY BOY WAS A RATHER DARK SKINNED WHITE PERSON. HE MAY HAVE EVEN HAD SOME BLACK ANCESTRY. IN THE UNITED STATES OF NEW AFRICA BEAUTY WAS MEASURED IN TERMS OF BLACK AFRICAN STANDARDS. EVEN THE MOST MILITANT OF EURO-CENTRIC WHITES EXHIBITED SOCIAL HABITS THAT REVEALED THIS SUBCONSCIOUS MENTALITY.

PRETTY BOY WAS HAVING HIS HAIR CURLED. THE BARBER WAS FINISHING THE ATTACHMENT OF THE LAST ROLLER TO HIS HAIR. IT WAS COMMON PRACTICE FOR WHITE WOMEN TO HAVE THEIR HAIR CURLED. THE NATURAL STRAIGHT HAIR OF WHITES WAS LOOKED UPON AS BEING UNDESIRABLE AS FAR AS BEAUTY STANDARDS GO. HAIR STYLES THAT APPROACHED THE KINKY APPEARANCE OF BLACKS WHERE WORN BY MOST WHITE WOMEN AND A SMALL PERCENTAGE OF WHITE MEN.

MOST WHITE MEN PREFERRED TO WEAR THEIR HAIR IN A CREW-CUT OR MILITARY STYLE. LONG STRAIGHT HAIR AMONG MEN WAS A SIGN OF UNTIDINESS AND NONCONFORMITY. STREET GANGS OFTEN WORE THEIR HAIR LONG. EURO-CENTRIC WHITE MALES AND FEMALES DID SO AS A FORM OF PROTEST AGAINST THE NORMS OF A BLACK DOMINATED SOCIETY AND AS A

MANIFESTATION OF PRIDE IN THEIR WHITE EUROPEAN HERITAGE. THIS LATTER GROUP WAS INDEED A MINORITY WITHIN A MINORITY. THOMAS JR. CONSIDERED HIMSELF TO BE A MEMBER OF THIS GROUP.

PRETTY BOY: NOW, DON'T MESS UP THIS CURL. I WANT TO MAKE A GOOD IMPRESSION ON MY DATE TONIGHT.

BARBER: PRETTY BOY, YOU ARE THE LADY'S MAN. HOW MANY DO YOU HAVE ON THE STRING NOW?

PRETTY BOY: MAN, I HAVE LOST COUNT. BUT, I TREAT ALL MY WOMEN RIGHT. AND, ALL OF THEM ARE JUST AS PRETTY AS I AM. SO, DON'T MESS UP THIS CURL AND RUIN MY IMAGE.

BARBER: YOU HEAR THAT THOMAS? PRETTY'S GOT MORE WOMEN THAN HE CAN COUNT. HOW ARE YOU MAKING IT WITH THE WOMEN?

THOMAS JR.: WELL, I GUESS I'M DOING OKAY.

BARBER: OKAY? WHAT DOES THAT MEAN?

PRETTY BOY: IN OTHER WORDS, HE AIN'T GETTING NO PUSSY.

AS THE LAUGHTER IN THE SHOP BEGINS TO SUBSIDE, THOMAS JR. SLOWLY RISES TO HIS FEET. COULD THIS BE THE QUANTUM INSTANCE WHERE THE COURSE OF HISTORY MAKES A CHANGE THAT RESULTS IN A NEW REALITY?

THOMAS JR.: PRETTY BOY, YOU ARE **UGLY**!

PRETTY BOY: PECKERWOOD, PLEASE! YOU CALLING ME UGLY? YOU? YOU STRINGY, YELLOW-HAIRED, PALE-FACE MOTHERFUCKER.

BARBER: GENTLEMAN, THE SIGN ON THE WALL SAYS NO PROFANITY.

THOMAS JR.: I DIDN'T USE PROFANITY. I SAID HE WAS UGLY. BY WHITE STANDARDS HE IS UGLY. MOST WHITE PEOPLE HAVE NATURAL STRAIGHT HAIR AND FAIR COMPLEXIONS. WHY SHOULD WE MEASURE OURSELVES BY BLACK STANDARDS? I'M NOT SAYING THAT PRETTY BOY SHOULD NOT BE PROUD OF HOW HE LOOKS, BUT NEITHER SHOULD ANY OF THE REST OF US. NO MATTER HOW FAIR-SKINNED OR STRAIGHT-HAIRED WE ARE, WE SHOULD BE PROUD OF WHAT WE ARE.

THE SILENCE IN THE SHOP THAT FOLLOWS THOMAS' SPEECH SEEMS TO LAST A LIFE TIME. THE SPELL IS FINALLY BROKEN BY PRETTY BOY.

PRETTY BOY: OKAY MAN. YOU'VE MADE YOUR POINT. NOW, LET ME MAKE MINE. THIS AIN'T EUROPE. THIS COUNTRY IS THE BLACK MAN'S WORLD. "IF YOU'RE BLACK, YOU'RE ON THE RIGHT TRACK. IF YOU'RE BROWN, STICK AROUND. IF YOU'RE WHITE, GET OUT OF SIGHT." I DIDN'T MAKE THE RULES, AND YOU CAN'T CHANGE THEM. CAN YOU?

THOMAS JR.: I SURE CAN TRY! AND, IF ALL OF US TRIED, MAYBE WE CAN CHANGE THINGS.

PRETTY BOY: WHAT CAN ANY PECKERWOOD IN HERE DO? YOU'RE JUST ONE UPPITY, MILITANT PECKERWOOD. AND YOU CAN'T DO A DAMN THING!

THOMAS JR.: YOU'RE WRONG PRETTY BOY. THERE IS ONE THING THAT I'M GOING TO DO AND THAT EVERYONE IN HERE CAN DO. I'M NOT GETTING MY HAIR CUT TODAY. I'M LEAVING IT LONG AND NATURAL. EVERYONE IN HERE SHOULD DO THE SAME.

BARBER: NOW, WAIT A MINUTE BOY. DON'T BE RUNNING MY CUSTOMERS OFF. IF YOU WANT TO BE LONG AND STRINGY, THAT'S YOUR BUSINESS. BUT DON'T RUIN MY BUSINESS.

PRETTY BOY: DON'T WORRY. THE ONLY ONE WALKING OUT OF THAT DOOR IS THIS CRAZY PECKERWOOD.

THOMAS JR.: IS PRETTY BOY RIGHT? AM I THE ONLY ONE IN HERE WHO THINKS THAT BEING WHITE IS JUST AS GOOD AS BEING BLACK? AM I THE ONLY WHITE MAN IN HERE?!

THOMAS JR. LEAVES THE SHOP. THE REMAINING CUSTOMERS ONE AT A TIME, SLOWLY STAND AND LEAVE. THAT IS, ALL EXCEPT PRETTY BOY. FOR A FEW SECONDS PRETTY BOY AND THE BARBER STARE AT EACH OTHER IN BEWILDERMENT.

BARBER: WELL, I'LL BE DAMNED. THAT BOY JUST MIGHT BE ON TO SOMETHING.

PRETTY BOY: IT DON'T MEAN A THING. THIS IS STILL THE BLACK MAN'S WORLD. NOW, FINISH MY CURL. I HAVE A DATE TONIGHT, REMEMBER.

PHASE 5

EQUAL OPPORTUNITY

DURING THE HISTORICAL ERA OF WHITE SLAVERY IN NEW AFRICA IT WAS CUSTOMARY FOR WHITES NOT TO LOOK DIRECTLY INTO THE EYES OF A BLACK PERSON, WHEN TALKING TO THE BLACK PERSON. INSTEAD, OUT OF RESPECT, THE WHITE WOULD LOOK TOWARD THE FEET OF THE BLACK PERSON. TODAY, THOMAS EDWARDS SR. HAD TO MAKE A DECISION. WHICH WOULD BE THE BEST APPROACH? SHOULD HE LOOK THE BOSS DIRECTLY IN THE EYES WHEN CHALLENGING HIM ABOUT JOB PROMOTIONS FOR WHITES OR SHOULD HE "RESPECTFULLY" GLANCE DOWN TOWARDS MR. JOHNSON'S FEET?

AS THOMAS SR. APPROACHES MR. JOHNSON'S OFFICE, HE FINALLY SETTLES ON LOOKING THE MAN SQUARE IN HIS EYES. HE REMEMBERS HIS OWN WORDS TO HIS SON. "WE ARE NOT SLAVES ANYMORE".

THOMAS SR.: MR. JOHNSON, COULD I TALK TO YOU FOR A FEW MINUTES?

MR. JOHNSON: CERTAINLY, THOMAS. COME IN AND HAVE A SEAT. HOW IS THE FAMILY?

THOMAS SR.: THEY ARE ALL DOING JUST FINE.

MR. JOHNSON: AND THAT SON OF YOURS, THOMAS JR., THE LAST TIME I SAW HIM HE WAS ONLY FIVE YEARS OLD.

THOMAS SR.: YES SIR, HE'S A SENIOR IN HIGH SCHOOL NOW. HE WANTS TO GO TO

COLLEGE TO BECOME A PHYSICS MAJOR.

MR. JOHNSON: PHYSICS! HE'S NOT BITING OFF MORE THAN HE CAN CHEW, IS HE?

THOMAS SR.: WHEN THAT BOY MAKES UP HIS MIND TO DO SOMETHING, HE DOES IT. HE'S ALWAYS TALKING ABOUT QUANTUM THIS AND QUANTUM THAT. IT ALL SOUND LIKE FOOLISHNESS TO ME. BUT, HE SEEMS TO NOW WHAT HE IS TALKING ABOUT.

MR. JOHNSON: WE NEED MORE WHITE BOYS WITH AMBITION LIKE THAT.

THOMAS SR.: UH, MR. JOHNSON, SPEAKING OF AMBITION, I HAVE A CONCERN THAT I WOULD LIKE TO DISCUSS WITH YOU.

MR. JOHNSON: AND, WHAT MIGHT THAT BE?

THOMAS SR.: MR. JOHNSON, I'VE WORKED FOR YOU THE PAST 23 YEARS. I'VE DONE THE SAME JOB, ON THE ASSEMBLY LINE, FOR ALL OF THOSE YEARS. I'VE SEEN DOZENS OF YOUNG BLACK GUYS PROMOTED FROM ASSEMBLY LINE TO FOREMAN. AND, I TRAINED MOST OF THOSE GUYS ON THE ASSEMBLY LINE. BUT, I HAVE NEVER BEEN PROMOTED TO A HIGHER POSITION. I DESERVE TO BECOME A FOREMAN.

MR. JOHNSON: WELL, IT SEEMS AS THOUGH YOUR SON ISN'T THE ONLY ONE IN THE FAMILY WITH AMBITION. THOMAS, WE HAVE NEVER HAD A WHITE FOREMAN

IN THE HISTORY OF THIS COMPANY. OUR BLACK EMPLOYEES MIGHT NOT WORK WELL UNDER THE SUPERVISION OF A WHITE MAN. I KNOW THAT THE WORLD IS SLOWLY CHANGING. I KNOW THAT WHITES ARE BEGINNING TO SOCIALLY ADVANCE THEMSELVES. YOUR SON, THOMAS JR., IS A GOOD EXAMPLE. I NEVER HEARD OF A WHITE KID WANTING TO BE A PHYSICIST. BUT, SOMETIMES THINGS CAN CHANGE TOO FAST. IT'S BETTER TO GO SLOW AND BE CAUTIOUS ABOUT SOME THINGS.

THOMAS SR.: ARE YOU TELLING ME THAT I CANNOT GET THE PROMOTION?

MR. JOHNSON: THOMAS, I LIKE YOU. YOU'RE A GOOD MAN. YOU ARE A HARD WORKER. YOU PROBABLY KNOW MORE ABOUT THIS BUSINESS THAN ANY EMPLOYEE I'VE GOT.

THOMAS SR.: DO I GET THE PROMOTION?

MR. JOHNSON. I HAVE TO LOOK AT THIS FROM A BUSINESS STANDPOINT. HAVING A WHITE FOREMAN COULD AFFECT THE MORALE OF THE BLACK WORKERS. POOR MORALE COULD MEAN POOR PRODUCTION. POOR PRODUCTION MEANS POOR PROFITS. AND, YOU KNOW WHAT POOR PROFITS MEANS.

THOMAS SR.: YOU GO OUT OF BUSINESS. I GUESS THAT ANSWERS MY QUESTION.

MR. JOHNSON: STARTING NEXT MONTH, YOU ARE THE FOREMAN IN YOUR DEPARTMENT.

THOMAS SR.:   I KNEW THIS WOULD BE A WASTE OF TIME. I….WHAT? DID YOU SAY FOREMAN?

MR. JOHNSON: YES. NOW, GET BACK TO WORK. WE BOTH HAVE BUSINESS TO TEND TO.

THE "COLLAPSE OF THE WAVE FUNCTION" BRINGS INTO FOCUS A "REALITY" THAT IS A QUANTUM STEP IN A NEW DIRECTION. MR. JOHNSON'S AFFIRMATIVE RESPONSE TO THOMAS SR.'S QUESTION HAS SET INTO MOTION A NEW CHAIN OF EVENTS. THESE WILL PROVE TO BE MORE CHALLENGING TO THOMAS SR. THAN THE ACTUAL MEETING WITH MR. JOHNSON. INDEED, THOMAS SR. WILL SOON WONDER WHETHER THE REWARDS OF THIS NEW DIRECTION ARE WORTHY OF THE TRIALS AND TRIBULATIONS THAT HE WILL ENCOUNTER ALONG THE WAY.

PHASE 6

PRINCIPLE OR PRINCIPAL

THERE COMES A TIME IN EVERYONE'S LIFE WHEN THEY ARE PUT IN A POSITION WHERE THEY MUST EITHER STAND UP FOR WHAT THEY BELIEVE OR COMPROMISE ON THEIR PRINCIPLES. THOSE WHO CHOOSE THE FORMER COURSE OF ACTION ARE INTERNALLY SELF-ACTUALIZED IF THEY ARE VICTORIOUS. THERE CAN EVEN BE SOME SELF-SATISFACTION IN THE FACE OF DEFEAT. BUT, THOSE WHO COMPROMISE OUT OF FEAR OR COWARDICE FIND THEMSELVES WITH A LOWERED SELF-ESTEEM.

THOMAS JR. UNDERSTANDS CLEARLY THE CHOICES BEFORE HIM, LEAVING HIS HAIR LONG MAY BE DEFIANT OF SCHOOL AUTHORITY, BUT IT IS ALSO A SYMBOL OF WHITE PRIDE. THE IRONY OF THE DILEMMA IS THAT LONG HAIR IS A SYMBOL OF REBELLION FOR SOMEONE AS SOCIALLY CONSCIOUS AS THOMAS JR. AND ALSO FOR GANG MEMBERS WHOSE ACTIONS THREATEN WHAT LITTLE GAINS WHITES HAVE MADE IN SOCIETY. SURELY, THOMAS DOES NOT WANT TO JOIN THE RANKS OF THE "REDS" AND "BLUES." THE GANGS HAVE AS MUCH NEED FOR WHITE PRIDE AS THOSE WHITE SCHOOL OFFICIALS AND OTHERS WHO HAVE UNQUESTIONABLY ACCEPTED BLACK STANDARDS FOR WHAT IS ACCEPTABLE AND WHAT IS UNACCEPTABLE.

AS THOMAS JR. TAKES HIS SEAT IN HIS HISTORY CLASS, ALL EYES ARE ON HIM. BEHIND EACH SET OF EYES ARE SPECULATIVE THOUGHTS ABOUT THE EVENTS THAT WILL FOLLOW HIS BOLD ENTRANCE.

MS. MAYFIELD: THOMAS, I SEE THAT YOU HAVE DECIDED TO CHALLENGE THE

27

SCHOOL ON THE ISSUE OF YOUR HAIR.

THOMAS JR.: YES, MS. MAYFIELD, I AM STANDING UP FOR WHAT I BELIEVE IS RIGHT.

MS. MAYFIELD: IS IT RIGHT TO BREAK SCHOOL RULES?

THOMAS JR.: YOU'VE TAUGHT US ABOUT THE HISTORY OF THE EARLY BLACKS IN THIS COUNTRY. YOU TAUGHT US HOW THEY BROKE THE RULES OF AFRICA AND FORMED THEIR OWN COUNTRY HERE IN NEW AFRICA. YOU TAUGHT US THAT THIS WAS THE RIGHT THING TO DO.

MS. MAYFIELD: ARE YOU GOING TO COMPARE YOUR HAIR WITH THE CAUSE OF THE NEW AFRICAN REVOLUTION?

THOMAS JR.: NOT JUST "MY" HAIR! BUT, THAT OF EVERY STRINGY HAIRED WHITE PERSON WHO HAS EVER CUT IT OR CURLED IT TO CONFORM TO BLACK STANDARDS.

REGGIE: RIGHT ON!

MS. MAYFIELD: WHAT DID YOU SAY?

JASON: HE SAID, "RIGHT ON!"

BETTY: AND, SO DO I!

SARAH: ME TOO!

REGGIE: THOMAS, I'M LETTING MY HAIR GROW LONG TOO. IF YOU GET SUSPENDED, THEN THE SCHOOL WILL HAVE TO SUSPEND A LOT MORE OF US. IT IS TIME THAT WE START RESPECTING OURSELVES. WE ARE WHITE. WE SHOULD BE PROUD OF IT.

BETTY: WE GIRLS NEED TO STOP CURLING OUR HAIR AND PUSHING OUR LIPS OUT TO MAKE THEM LOOK LIKE BLACK'S.

SARAH: I'M WITH YOU SISTER.

MS. MAYFIELD: ENOUGH! ENOUGH! THOMAS, GO TO THE OFFICE IMMEDIATELY!

PRINCIPAL: THOMAS EDWARDS JR.! YOU KNOW, THAT NAME HAS A RING TO IT. ONE OF THESE DAYS YOU MIGHT BECOME FAMOUS. ALREADY AROUND HERE YOU ARE BECOMING "INFAMOUS" AS A REBEL AND A RABBLE-ROUSER. I HEARD ABOUT HOW YOU GOT THOSE STUDENTS WORKED UP IN YOUR HISTORY CLASS. I CANNOT HAVE THAT KIND OF DISRESPECT FOR AUTHORITY. IF BLACK PEOPLE CAME IN HERE AND SAW YOU KIDS WITH LONG STRINGY HAIR....

THOMAS JR.: BLACK PEOPLE! MR. JACKSON, WHY DOES EVERYTHING THAT WE DO HAVE TO BE EVALUATED IN TERMS OF BLACKS? WHY CAN'T YOU BE A MAN

AND MAKE THIS SCHOOL RELEVANT TO WHAT WHITE KIDS NEED TO KNOW.

PRINCIPAL: WHAT WHITE KIDS NEED TO KNOW?! WHO ARE YOU TO JUDGE ME, AN ADULT, A TRAINED PROFESSIONAL? LET ME TELL YOU WHAT YOU WHITE KIDS NEED TO KNOW. YOU NEED TO KNOW THAT BLACKS ARE THE MAJORITY IN THIS COUNTRY. THEY MAKE UP 90% OF THE POPULATION. THEY REPRESENT POWER. THAT'S WHAT YOU WHITE KIDS NEED TO KNOW.

THOMAS JR.: YOU CALL YOURSELF AN ADULT....A PROFESSIONAL?! YOU'RE JUST A FRIGHTENED LITTLE MAN. YOU ARE AFRAID TO STAND UP FOR WHAT IS RIGHT.

PRINCIPAL: THOMAS, I'M SUSPENDING YOU FOR FIVE DAYS. BUT, IF YOU GET YOUR HAIR CUT BEFORE THAT TIME, YOU MAY COME BACK SOONER. LET ME WARN YOU. IF YOU RETURN TO SCHOOL AFTER THE FIVE DAYS, AND YOU HAIR HAS NOT BEEN CUT, I WILL IMMEDIATELY SUSPEND YOU FOR ANOTHER FIVE DAYS. SON, YOU'RE A SENIOR. THIS COULD PREVENT YOU FROM GRADUATING. IF YOU DON'T GRADUATE FROM HIGH SCHOOL, YOU MAY AS WELL FORGET ABOUT COLLEGE. NOW, GO HOME AND THINK ABOUT THIS. I DON'T WANT THIS REBELLIOUS ATTITUDE TO SPREAD TO ANY MORE STUDENTS.

PHASE 7

REBELLION

THE "REBELLIOUS ATTITUDE" IS ALREADY SPREADING AMONG MORE STUDENTS. AS WORD GETS AROUND THAT THOMAS HAS BEEN SUSPENDED, STUDENTS BEGIN TO INFORMALLY DISCUSS TACTICS FOR PROTESTING MR. JACKSON'S DECISION. SIX FEMALE STUDENTS DECIDE TO COME TO SCHOOL WEARING THEIR HAIR IN IT'S NATURAL LONG STRINGY STATE. AN EQUAL NUMBER OF MALES DECIDE TO WEAR LONG HAIR PIECES UNTIL THEIR HAIR HAS GROWN SUFFICIENTLY ENOUGH.

IN SUMMARY FASHION, MR. JACKSON SUSPENDS THE TWELVE NEW REBELS. BUT, LIKE A GROWING CANCER, TWELVE ADDITIONAL STUDENTS APPEAR, PROUDLY DISPLAYING THEIR LONG STRINGY HAIR. AND, TO FURTHER ADD TO MR. JACKSON'S DISMAY, THESE STUDENTS ARE ACCOMPANIED BY ANGRY PARENTS WHO DEMAND AN END TO THE SUSPENSIONS.

PRINCIPAL JACKSON KNOWS THAT BLACK POWER IS A REALITY THAT WHITES MUST ALWAYS BE AWARE OF. BUT NOW, HE IS JUST BEGINNING TO BE CONSCIOUS OF THE POTENTIAL OF WHITE POWER. WHITE POWER, AS REPRESENTED BY THESE PARENTS AND STUDENTS, IS THE IMMEDIATE PRIORITY. FORTUNATELY, THE FUSE ON THIS EXPLOSIVE MIXTURE IS EXTINGUISHED BY THE AGREEMENT TO HAVE AN EVENING COMMUNITY MEETING FOR A DISCUSSION AND PEACEFUL RESOLUTION OF THE PROBLEM.

FROM A HISTORICAL PERSPECTIVE, A MEETING WITH DOZENS OF IRATE WHITE PARENTS AND STUDENTS MAY

NOT BE AS LIFE THREATENING AS A LYNCH MOB OF BIGOTED BLACKS. BUT, BOTH GROUPS DEFINITELY HAVE THE POWER TO DEMAND ONE'S ATTENTION, IF NOT ONE'S RESPECT. PRINCIPAL JACKSON KNOWS THAT THE GROUP HE IS ABOUT TO ADDRESS THIS EVENING WILL SETTLE FOR NOTHING LESS THAN HIS ATTENTION AND HIS RESPECT.

PRINCIPAL: PLEASE, COULD I HAVE YOUR ATTENTION, PLEASE! ....THANK YOU. UNDERSTANDABLY, EMOTIONS MAY BE HEATED THIS EVENING. BUT, I MUST INSIST ON CIVIL BEHAVIOR. NOTHING WILL BE ACCOMPLISHED BY LOUD, BOISTEROUS, AND DISRESPECTFUL BEHAVIOR!

MRS. EDWARDS: MR. JACKSON, NO ONE HAS BEEN BOISTEROUS OR DISRESPECTFUL. I RESENT THE IMPLICATION THAT A GATHERING OF WHITE PEOPLE CANNOT BEHAVE IN A CIVIL MANNER. IF THAT IS WHAT THIS SCHOOL IS TEACHING OUR CHILDREN, THEN WE DO HAVE A SERIOUS PROBLEM. YOU'RE SAYING THAT WE ARE DISRESPECTFUL?! IF YOU PREJUDGE ADULTS AS DISRESPECTFUL, THEN I KNOW WHAT THESE KIDS MUST BE GOING THROUGH. I THINK WE HAD BETTER START WITH DISCUSSING JUST WHAT IS AND WHAT IS NOT DISRESPECTFUL. THAT SEEMS TO BE THE ROOT OF THIS SUSPENSION MESS ANYWAY.

PRINCIPAL: YOU'RE RIGHT MRS. EDWARDS. THIS DOES BOIL DOWN TO THE DIFFERENCE BETWEEN RESPECT AND

DISRESPECT. SINCE, YOUR SON HAS TAKEN A LEADERSHIP ROLE IN CHALLENGING THE STATUS QUO, I WOULD LIKE TO START WITH HIS EXPLANATION OF THIS SITUATION.

THOMAS JR.: MR. JACKSON, IF WE DON'T RESPECT OURSELVES, HOW CAN WE HONESTLY SAY WHAT IS RIGHT OR WHAT IS NOT RIGHT?

PRINCIPAL: I HAVE NOT SAID THAT YOU SHOULD NOT RESPECT YOURSELF. I WANT ALL THE STUDENTS AT THIS SCHOOL TO BECOME HONEST AND RESPECTFUL CITIZENS.

THOMAS JR.: BUT, MR. JACKSON, DON'T YOU SEE? BEING WHITE IS PART OF WHAT WE ARE. STRINGY HAIR, FAIR SKIN. LONG NOSES AND THIN LIPS. WE MUST RESPECT WHAT WE ARE. GOD MADE US THE WAY WE ARE. NONE OF US HAD A CHOICE ABOUT THAT. IF WE CAN'T ACCEPT AND RESPECT OURSELVES FIRST, HOW CAN THE SCHOOL TEACH US TO BE "HONEST AND RESPECTFUL" CITIZENS?

PRINCIPAL: WE MUST HAVE RULES. I CANNOT RUN THIS SCHOOL WITHOUT RULES. ONE OF THE RULES IS THAT STUDENTS WILL NOT WEAR THEIR HAIR LONG AND STRINGY. PERSONAL APPEARANCE IS IMPORTANT FOR SCHOOL MORALE.

MRS. EDWARDS: PRINCIPAL JACKSON! ARE YOU SAYING THAT THERE IS SOMETHING

WRONG WITH HAVING LONG STRINGY HAIR?

PRINCIPAL: WELL…YES AND NO.

MRS. EDWARDS: PRINCIPAL JACKSON, YOU'RE SUPPOSE TO BE AN EDUCATED MAN. ARE YOU GOING TO STAND THERE AND TELL US WHITE FOLKS THAT THERE IS SOMETHING WRONG WITH THE WAY GOD MADE US? PECKERWOOD, PLEASE! YOU'RE JUST AS WHITE AS THE REST OF US!

PRINCIPAL: OKAY! OKAY! LET ME EXPLAIN MYSELF.

AS THE GROUP QUIETS ITSELF IN ANTICIPATION OF WHAT PRINCIPAL JACKSON IS ABOUT TO SAY, FIVE, BLACK SKIN, SOLEMN, AND FORMALLY DRESSED INDIVIDUALS ENTER THE AUDITORIUM. THEY STAND QUIETLY AT THE REAR OF THE ROOM. ALTHOUGH, NEITHER SO MUCH AS UTTER A WORD, THEIR FACIAL EXPRESSIONS ANNOUNCE THEM AS AUTHORITY FIGURES. THESE ARE MEN WHO REPRESENT BLACK POWER. THESE ARE THE BOARD OF EDUCATION.

THE QUIET BECOMES DEATHLY QUIET, AS WHITE HEADS TURN TOWARD THESE BLACK MEN. BUT, NONE REACT IN THE FEARFUL MANNER OF PRINCIPAL JACKSON, WHO MOMENTARILY TAKES ON FACIAL EXPRESSIONS OF A MAN IN SHOCK. THE SILENCE IN THE AUDITORIUM IS FINALLY BROKEN BY ONE OF THE DARK FIGURES THEMSELVES.

MR. NILES: OH, DON'T MIND US. WE'RE JUST HERE AS OBSERVERS. WE LIKE TO KNOW WHAT CONCERNS COMMUNITY

PEOPLE HAVE. JUST CARRY ON WITH YOUR MEETING. JACKSON, I BELIEVE YOU WERE ABOUT TO RESPOND TO WHAT THE LADY SAID.

PRINCIPAL: UH...UH...YES. I WANT TO SAY THAT THE RULES ARE NOT INTENDED TO DISRESPECT WHITE PEOPLE. MRS. EDWARDS IS RIGHT. THERE IS NOTHING WRONG WITH THE WAY GOD MADE US.

THOMAS JR.: THEN CHANGE THE RULES.

PRINCIPAL: I CAN'T CHANGE THE RULES MYSELF. THAT IS SOMETHING THAT THE SCHOOL BOARD WILL HAVE TO CONSENT TO.

THOMAS JR.: WELL, THEY'RE HERE NOW. LET'S HERE WHAT THEY HAVE TO SAY.

MR. NILES: THIS IS NOT THE PROPER SETTING FOR US TO MAKE A RULING ON SCHOOL POLICY. I NEED TO DISCUSS THIS MATTER WITH PRINCIPAL JACKSON...PRIVATELY. JACKSON!

PRINCIPAL: YES, SIR?

MR. NILES: I WILL BE IN YOUR OFFICE TOMORROW MORNING. YOU AND I WILL THEN DISCUSS THIS MATTER.

THOMAS JR.: WHILE YOU'RE DISCUSSING THAT, WHY DON'T YOU TALK ABOUT TEACHING WHITE HISTORY IN THIS SCHOOL. WE WANT TO LEARN ABOUT OUR HISTORY.

MR. NILES: WHITE HISTORY?! YOUNG MAN,
                HAVEN'T YOU TAKEN THE COURSE ON
                NEW   AFRICAN   HISTORY...THE
                HISTORY OF THIS GREAT NATION.

THOMAS JR.:   I'M TAKING THAT COURSE NOW. BUT,
                ALL THAT WE LEARN ABOUT WHITE
                PEOPLE IS THAT WE WERE SLAVES.
                WHAT ABOUT THE HISTORY OF
                EUROPE? WE WERE NOT ALWAYS
                SLAVES!

MR. NILES   YOUNG MAN, FOR SOME REASON, I
                SENSE THAT YOU ARE BEHIND ALL OF
                WHAT IS HAPPENING HERE THIS
                EVENING. DO OTHERS SHARE YOUR
                DESIRE FOR LONG HAIR AND WHITE
                HISTORY?

REGGIE: YES, WE DO! HE SPEAKS FOR ALL OF
                US.

MR. NILES: JACKSON!

PRINCIPAL: YES SIR!

MR. NILES: ANY   STUDENTS   PRESENTLY
                SUSPENDED BECAUSE OF THEIR HAIR,
                WILL BE ALLOWED TO RETURN TO
                SCHOOL. NO MORE WILL BE
                SUSPENDED PENDING AN OFFICIAL
                SCHOOL BOARD RESOLUTION OF THIS
                MATTER.

PRINCIPAL: YES SIR!

PHASE 8

UNCLE TOM

PRINCIPAL JACKSON IS A MAN WHO LEARNED LONG AGO THAT SURVIVAL AND ADVANCEMENT IN BLACK NEW AFRICA, FOR WHITES, MEANT SWALLOWING ONE'S PRIDE AND DISPLAYING AN ATTITUDE OF RESPECTFUL SUBORDINATION, BASED ON NOTHING BUT SKIN COLOR. YES, FEAR ALSO PLAYS A MAJOR ROLE IN THIS TYPE OF POSTURING. PRINCIPAL JACKSON REMEMBERS, AS THOUGH IT WERE ONLY YESTERDAY, THE SCENES OF BLACK AGGRESSION AGAINST WHITES WHO SOUGHT TO CHALLENGE THE RACIAL SEGREGATION LAWS OF THE COUNTRY. MOST OF THE MORE BLATANTLY RACIST OF THOSE LAWS HAVE SINCE BEEN REPEALED. BUT, THIS OCCURRED ONLY AFTER THE SHEDDING OF MUCH WHITE BLOOD.

PRINCIPAL JACKSON UNDERSTANDS THAT THOSE DAYS OF OPEN BLACK PHYSICAL AGGRESSION AGAINST WHITES IS A THING OF THE PAST. BUT, HE ALSO UNDERSTANDS THAT POLITICALLY, ECONOMICALLY, AND SOCIALLY BLACKS ARE STILL THE DOMINANT RACIAL GROUP IN NEW AFRICA. WITH THAT ASPECT OF REALITY FIRMLY PLANTED IN HIS MIND, PRINCIPAL JACKSON NERVOUSLY AWAITS THE ARRIVAL OF THE SCHOOL BOARD PRESIDENT.

PRINCIPAL: COME RIGHT IN MR. NILES. IT IS A PLEASURE TO HAVE YOU VISIT OUR SCHOOL.

MR. NILES: LET'S HOPE THAT THE MATTER BEFORE US CAN BE SOLVED IN

AS PLEASURABLE A WAY AS POSSIBLE FOR ALL INVOLVED.

PRINCIPAL JACKSON: YES SIR.

MR. NILES: NOW LET'S DROP THE ASS-KISSING "YES SIRS" AND GET DOWN TO BUSINESS.

PRINCIPAL JACKSON: YES S....ER...OKAY.

MR. NILES: JACKSON, WE'VE GOT A PROBLEM HERE. THIS EDWARDS BOY SEEMS TO BE A TROUBLE MAKER. HE HAS MANAGED TO BECOME SOMEWHAT OF A HERO IN THE EYES OF THE WHITE COMMUNITY.

PRINCIPAL JACKSON: MAYBE IF WE SEND HIM TO ANOTHER SCHOOL, THE OTHERS WILL SOON FORGET ABOUT THIS MILITANT WHITE NONSENSE.

MR. NILES: NO, IT'S TOO LATE FOR THAT. NOW THINGS ARE ABOUT TO GET OUT OF CONTROL. ONE CONCESSION LEADS TO ANOTHER. FIRST LONG HAIR, THEN THE DEMAND IS FOR WHITE HISTORY. WHAT WILL IT BE NEXT, A WHITE SCHOOL BOARD MEMBER? IF THIS MILITANT WHITE ATTITUDE CONTINUES TO GROW, IT WILL RUN HEAD ON INTO BLACK RESISTANCE. AND JACKSON, DO YOU KNOW WHAT THAT MEANS?

PRINCIPAL: YES SIR.

MR. NILES: YOU'RE DAMN RIGHT THAT YOU KNOW! YOU'VE SEEN IT IN YOUR LIFE TIME. IT'S NOT A PRETTY SIGHT WHEN BLACKS TURN AGAINST WHITES. YOU PEOPLE HAVE COME A LONG WAY. YOU DON'T WANT TO LOOSE WHAT LITTLE GAINS YOU HAVE MADE?

PRINCIPAL: NO SIR, WE DON'T. WHAT SHOULD I DO SIR?

MR. NILES: WELL, WE HAVE TO BE CAREFUL WITH THIS THING, JACKSON. IF WE COME DOWN TOO HARD, IT WILL ONLY MAKE THEM ALL THAT MORE DETERMINED TO CHALLENGE US. LET THEM HAVE LONG HAIR. BESIDES, IT'S PROBABLY A FAD THAT THE KIDS WILL SOON GET TIRED OF. BUT, THIS WHITE HISTORY THING, NOW THAT IS A DIFFERENT MATTER.

PRINCIPAL: THE DAMN EDWARDS KID, MAYBE I SHOULD JUST TRANSFER HIM TO ANOTHER SCHOOL.

MR. NILES: NO! THAT WOULD ONLY MAKE MATTERS WORST. HOW SERIOUS ARE THE OTHERS ABOUT WHITE HISTORY?

PRINCIPAL: STUDENTS ARE BEGINNING TO CHALLENGE TEACHERS IN OTHER CLASSES ABOUT IT. BUT, THOMAS IS THE LEADER.

MR. NILES:	THE LEADER. THAT'S IT! CHANGE THE DIRECTION OF THE LEADER, AND THE FOLLOWERS WILL CHANGE TOO.
PRINCIPAL:	HE IS A VERY DETERMINED YOUNG MAN. IT WON'T BE THAT EASY TO CHANGE HIM.
MR. NILES:	WE'LL JUST HAVE TO MAKE HIM AN OFFER THAT HE CANNOT REFUSE.
PRINCIPAL:	WHAT DO YOU MEAN?
MR. NILES:	I'M TOLD THAT HE IS A VERY BRIGHT YOUNG MAN. HE HAS AMBITION TO BECOME A PHYSICIST. THAT MEANS HE WANTS TO GO TO COLLEGE.
PRINCIPAL:	I HAVE ALREADY THREATENED HIM WITH NOT GRADUATING.
MR. NILES:	WELL JACKSON, IF THE STICK DOESN'T WORK, TRY THE CARROT. IT TAKES MONEY TO GO TO COLLEGE. WITH MY CONNECTIONS, I'M SURE THAT WE CAN FIND A SCHOLARSHIP SOMEWHERE THAT WOULD PAY HIS COLLEGE TUITION. A MODEST WORKING CLASS FAMILY LIKE HIS WOULD BE HARD PRESSED TO PAY FOR FOUR YEARS OF COLLEGE.

PRINCIPAL: I DON'T KNOW. ANY OTHER STUDENT WOULD PROBABLY JUMP AT AN OFFER LIKE THAT AND NOT GIVE A SECOND THOUGHT. BUT, THIS BOY IS DIFFERENT. HE IS NOT ONLY INTELLIGENT, HE IS PRINCIPLED TOO. I THINK HE LOOKS AT THIS WHITE HISTORY THING AS THE DIFFERENCE BETWEEN RIGHT AND WRONG.

MR. NILES: JACKSON, I HOPE FOR YOUR SAKE THAT YOU ARE WRONG.

PRINCIPAL: WHAT DO MEAN SIR?

MR. NILES: I MEAN THAT IF THIS WHITE HISTORY, WHITE MILITANT MESS CONTINUES, YOU MAY BE LOOKING FOR ANOTHER JOB. I WANT YOU TO MAKE THE SCHOLARSHIP PROPOSAL. DON'T DISAPPOINT ME!

PRINCIPAL: YES SIR…I MEAN NO SIR.

PHASE 9

RED BLOOD

"BETWEEN THE ROCK AND THE HARD PLACE." "DAMNED IF YOU DO - DAMNED IF YOU DON'T." "YOU CAN'T WIN FOR LOSING." EACH OF THESE PHRASES CAPTURES THE SENSE OF ANXIETY THAT PRINCIPAL JACKSON NOW FINDS HIMSELF PLAGUED WITH. IF HE OUTRIGHT FORBIDS THE TEACHING OF WHITE HISTORY, HE SURELY WILL BE LABELED AS A LACKEY FOR THE BLACK ESTABLISHMENT. WHITE STUDENTS AND THEIR PARENTS WILL UNDOUBTEDLY FEEL THAT HE IS NOT CONCERNED ABOUT THEIR NEEDS. THE STUDENTS WILL FEEL JUSTIFIED IN CHALLENGING THE AUTHORITY OF TEACHERS AND THE ADMINISTRATION. SUCH UNREST COULD RESULT IN VIOLENCE. THAT COULD LEAD TO HIMSELF BEING REPLACED BY SOMEONE WHOM THE SCHOOL BOARD FEELS WOULD DO A BETTER JOB OF UPHOLDING THE STATUS QUO.

ON THE OTHER HAND, IF HE GIVES IN TO STUDENT AND COMMUNITY PRESSURE, THE SCHOOL BOARD AND THE BLACK POLITICAL ESTABLISHMENT WILL FEEL THREATENED BY WHAT COULD EASILY GROW INTO A COMMUNITY-WIDE ATTITUDE OF MILITANCY AMONG WHITES TOWARDS BLACKS. INEVITABLY, OTHER WHITE CHALLENGES TO THE STATUS QUO COULD RESULT. WITHOUT QUESTION, HE WOULD BE REPLACED.

THE ONLY OTHER OPTION IS TO PERSUADE THOMAS EDWARDS JR., THE LEADER, TO USE HIS INFLUENCE TO DISCOURAGE STUDENT AGITATION FOR WHITE HISTORY. MR. NILES' OFFER OF A SCHOLARSHIP IS THE HAND THAT HAS TO BE PLAYED NOW. MAYBE BENEATH THE EXTERIOR SHOW OF PRIDE AND PRINCIPLE, THOMAS IS JUST LIKE HIMSELF. MAYBE THOMAS WILL

PUT PRIDE AND PRINCIPLE ASIDE IN FAVOR OF OPPORTUNISTIC SELF-GAIN.

PRINCIPAL JACKSON NOW FEELS SLIGHTLY MORE UPBEAT AS HE PRESSED THE INTERCOM BUTTON FOR THE SENIOR HISTORY CLASSROOM.

PRINCIPAL: EXCUSE ME MS. MAYFIELD. IS THOMAS EDWARDS PRESENT?

MS. MAYFIELD: YES, MR. JACKSON. THOMAS IS HERE.

PRINCIPAL: WOULD YOU PLEASE SEND HIM TO MY OFFICE?

THOMAS JR.: NOW, WHAT?

REGGIE: HEY THOMAS, MAYBE HE WANTS YOU TO GET A SUNTAN.

JASON: OR MAYBE, HE HAS AN AFRO-WIG FOR YOU TO WEAR.

REGGIE: WHATEVER IT IS, THE OLD "UNCLE TOM" HAS GOT TO SAY SOMETHING ABOUT BEING MORE BLACK-LIKE.

MS. MAYFIELD: THAT'S ENOUGH! I'LL HAVE NONE OF THAT DISRESPECT IN HERE. THOMAS, GO SEE WHAT MR. JACKSON WANTS.

PRINCIPAL: THOMAS, COME ON IN SON AND HAVE A SEAT. THOMAS, YOU'VE MANAGED TO MAKE QUITE A REPUTATION FOR YOURSELF AT THIS SCHOOL. MANY OF THE STUDENTS CONSIDER YOU A HERO AND A LEADER.

THOMAS JR.:   I JUST BELIEVE IN STANDING UP FOR WHAT'S RIGHT.

PRINCIPAL: I KNOW YOU DO. AND, I ADMIRE YOU FOR THAT. MAYBE OUR RULES ABOUT HAIR WERE NOT EXACTLY "RIGHT."

THOMAS JR.:   THEN, YOU AGREE WITH ME.

PRINCIPAL: WELL, THE SCHOOL BOARD IS WILLING TO BE LIBERAL ABOUT HAIR APPEARANCE.

THOMAS JR.:   THE SCHOOL BOARD! THE ALL-BLACK SCHOOL BOARD HAD TO SAY THAT IT WAS OKAY FOR WHITE KIDS TO WEAR THEIR HAIR NATURALLY! WHAT ABOUT YOU, MR. JACKSON? DO YOU THINK IT'S OKAY?

PRINCIPAL: NOW, LOOK SON. I TAKE MY ORDERS FROM THE SCHOOL BOARD. IT'S NOT MY JOB TO QUESTION THEIR POLICIES.

THOMAS JR.:   I'M JUST ASKING FOR YOUR OPINION. AS A WHITE PERSON, YOU SHOULD HAVE AN OPINION ABOUT YOUR OWN KIND OF HAIR.

PRINCIPAL: NOW, LOOK BOY, THAT'S ENOUGH. I DIDN'T BRING YOU IN HERE TO GIVE ME THE "THIRD DEGREE." I'LL GET TO THE POINT. YOU HAVE WON ON THIS LONG HAIR THING. BUT, WHITE HISTORY IS SOMETHING THAT THE SCHOOL BOARD WILL NOT ALLOW. YOU ARE A SENIOR. YOU ARE A

PRETTY SMART ONE AT THAT. I KNOW THAT YOU ARE INTERESTED IN SCIENCE AND WOULD LIKE TO GO TO COLLEGE. I'M OFFERING YOU A FOUR - YEAR SCHOLARSHIP TO COLLEGE. YOU AND YOUR FAMILY WOULD NOT HAVE TO PAY A CENT.

THOMAS JR.: WHAT YOU MEAN TO SAY IS THAT THE SCHOOL BOARD IS OFFERING ME A SCHOLARSHIP. YOU DON'T HAVE TO TELL ME WHAT THE CATCH IS! THEY WANT ME TO STOP TRYING TO GET WHITE HISTORY TAUGHT AT THIS SCHOOL.

PRINCIPAL: I SAID THAT YOU WERE SMART. I HOPE THAT YOU'RE SMART ENOUGH TO MAKE THE RIGHT DECISION. IF YOU WANT TO THINK ABOUT IT BEFORE.......

BEFORE PRINCIPAL JACKSON CAN FINISH HIS SENTENCE, A TERRIFYING VOICE COMES THROUGH THE INTERCOM IN THIS OFFICE. MS. MAYFIELD SCREAMS FOR HELP IN HER ROOM. A STUDENT HAS BEEN SHOT. ALMOST SIDE -BY- SIDE THOMAS AND PRINCIPAL JACKSON RACE DOWN THE HALL AND THROUGH THE CLASSROOM DOOR. LYING ON THE FLOOR, IN A POOL OF BLOOD, IS JASON REEVES.

ONLY MOMENTS BEFORE, HE HAD MADE SEVERAL UNFLATTERING REMARKS ABOUT PRINCIPAL JACKSON.

JASON REEVES. THOMAS JR. HAD KNOWN HIM SINCE JUNIOR HIGH SCHOOL. HE WAS A BIT OF A REBEL WHO WAS RUMORED TO BE A MEMBER OF THE "RED" STREET GANG. HE ALWAYS WORE SOMETHING THAT WAS RED IN COLOR. NOW, HE LAY IN A POOL OF CRIMSON. THE SIGHT CAUSES THOMAS TO VISUALIZE THE SCENE FROM A FEW WEEKS EARLIER WHEN HE WITNESSED

THE DRIVE-BY SHOOTING DEATH OF A "BLUE" GANG MEMBER. THE LIFE-LESS BODY OF JASON REEVES REPRESENTS THE FULFILLMENT OF A PREDICTION MADE BY ONE OF THE SURVIVING "BLUE" GANG MEMBERS.

YES, THE MADNESS HAS STARTED AGAIN. ANOTHER SENSELESS GANG KILLING HAD OCCURRED. BUT, THIS TIME THE "KILLING FIELD" WAS NOT THE USUAL TURF OF THE NEIGHBORHOOD STREETS. THIS TIME THE GANG WAR HAD ENTERED THE NEUTRAL SPACE OF A PUBLIC SCHOOL CLASSROOM. THIS INDEED WAS AN OMINOUS EVENT.

THE FACES STARING IN SHOCK AT THE BODY OF JASON REEVES, ALL SEEM TO GASP THE OMINOUS NATURE OF THE MOMENT. BUT OF ALL THE FACES, THE FACE OF PRINCIPAL JACKSON, SEEMED TO REGISTER THE MOST DREAD. HIS IS THE FACE OF A MAN WHO KNOWS THAT ACCOUNTABILITY IF NOT RESPONSIBILITY FOR THIS WILL REST SQUARELY ON HIS SHOULDERS.

PRINCIPAL: OH MY GOD! WHAT HAPPENED?!

MS. MAYFIELD: THERE WERE TWO OF THEM. THEY HAD THEIR FACES COVERED WITH BLUE BANDANNAS. THEY JUST WALKED IN AND SHOT HIM. IT HAPPENED SO FAST.

THOMAS JR.:   NO! NO! NOT AGAIN. WE CAN'T GO ON KILLING EACH OTHER LIKE THIS!

PRINCIPAL: GOD DAMN IT! STUDENTS WEARING LONG HAIR! DEFIANCE! DISRESPECT! AND NOW THIS! WHAT WILL THE SCHOOL BOARD THINK ABOUT THIS?! PECKERWOODS! THAT'S WHAT THEY WILL THINK. IGNORANT, SAVAGE PECKERWOODS, STRAIGHT OUT OF

THE CAVES OF EUROPE. IF I DON'T LOOSE MY JOB OVER THIS, IT WILL BE A MIRACLE. GOD DAMN IT!

MS. MAYFIELD: MR. JACKSON! PLEASE, NOT IN FRONT OF THE STUDENTS.

THOMAS JR.: IS THAT ALL THAT YOU THINK ABOUT? THE SCHOOL BOARD AND YOUR JOB. JASON IS DEAD. WHY? BECAUSE WHITE KIDS DON'T HAVE ENOUGH PRIDE IN THEMSELVES TO SEE BEYOND RED AND BLUE GANG SYMBOLS. CAN'T YOU SEE! WE NEED WHITE PRIDE. WE NEED WHITE HISTORY!

PRINCIPAL: PECKERWOOD, PLEASE! YOU KIDS NEED DISCIPLINE!

MS. MAYFIELD: PLEASE, BOTH OF YOU STOP! THIS IS NO TIME TO ARGUE. JASON IS DEAD. NOTHING THAT EITHER OF YOU CAN SAY WILL CHANGE THAT.

PHASE 10

WHITE PRIDE

JASON REEVES IS DEAD. NOTHING THAT ANYONE CAN SAY OR DO WILL CHANGE THAT. THE EMOTIONAL FUNERAL WORDS OF THE MINSTER WILL NOT CHANGE THAT. THE RED COLOR TIES WORN BY THE TEENAGE PALLBEARERS WILL NOT CHANGE THAT FACT.

IT NOW APPEARS THAT THE VICIOUS CIRCLE OF GANG KILLINGS IS OTHER FACT THAT WILL NOT CHANGE. THESE HAVE NOW CAPTURED THE ATTENTION OF BOTH THE WHITE AND BLACK COMMUNITIES. SOMETHING HAS TO BE DONE. EVEN BEFORE THE LAST SHOVEL OF DIRT HAD BEEN SPREAD OVER JASON REEVE'S GRAVE, RUMORS HAD ENGULFED BOTH THE SCHOOL AND THE WHITE COMMUNITY THAT REEVE'S KILLING WOULD SOON BE AVENGED BY THE "REDS." STUDENTS WHO PREVIOUSLY STAYED CLEAR OF GANG INVOLVEMENT, WERE BEGINNING TO TAKE SIDES IN THE DISPUTE. SOME EVEN STARTED WEARING THE APPROPRIATE COLOR OF CLOTHING TO EXPRESS THEIR SENTIMENTS. HALLWAY FISTFIGHTS HAD GROWN TO BE WEEKLY OCCURRENCES BETWEEN STUDENTS TAKING ONE SIDE OR THE OTHER.

PRINCIPAL JACKSON FOLLOWED THROUGH WITH HIS THREAT OF MORE DISCIPLINE. STUDENTS WERE FORBIDDEN TO WEAR THE GANG COLOR OF RED OR BLUE. BOTH STUDENTS AND PARENTS OBJECTED TO THIS RULE, BASED ON THE COMMONALITY OF THE TWO COLORS. RELUCTANTLY, PRINCIPAL JACKSON NARROWED THE RULING TO BANDANNAS AND BALL CAPS. SECURITY GUARDS WERE HIRED TO PATROL THE SCHOOL HALLWAYS. METAL DETECTORS WERE ROUTINELY USED TO PERFORM RANDOM CHECKS FOR

WEAPONS. THE SCHOOL BEGAN TO TAKE ON THE ATMOSPHERE OF A PRISON.

THE DISCIPLINE CRACKDOWN DID PREVENT WEAPONS FROM ENTERING THE SCHOOL. AS A RESULT, NO MORE SHOOTINGS OCCURRED IN THE SCHOOL. BUT, THE GENERAL LEVEL OF STUDENT CLASSROOM DISRUPTIONS, AND STUDENT DISRESPECT FOR AUTHORITY INCREASED ALONG WITH FIGHTS, CLASSROOM DISRUPTIONS, AND STUDENT SUSPENSIONS. TEACHERS BEGIN TO COMPLAIN ABOUT GROWING STUDENT NEGATIVE ACADEMIC ATTITUDES AND A GENERAL LACK OF SELF-RESPECT. THE WORD "PECKERWOOD" SEEMS TO FIND ITSELF COMING OUT OF THE MOUTHS OF MORE STUDENTS, MORE FREQUENTLY.

AS THE SCHOOL TENSION STEADILY INCREASED, PRINCIPAL JACKSON ONCE AGAIN FOUND HIMSELF BETWEEN THE PROVERBIAL "ROCK AND THE HARD PLACE." BLAME FOR THE DETERIORATING SITUATION WAS PLACED SQUARELY ON HIS SHOULDER BY THE WHITE COMMUNITY AND THE BLACK SCHOOL BOARD. THOMAS EDWARDS JR. COULDN'T BE USED AS A SCAPEGOAT FOR THIS PROBLEM. THE CAUSE OF THIS PROBLEM COULDN'T BE RATIONALIZED IN TERMS OF WHITE MILITANT AGITATION FOR WHITE HISTORY AND WHITE PRIDE. THIS LACK OF STUDENT SELF-RESPECT IN ONE SENSE HAD NOTHING TO DO WITH WHITE PRIDE, AND YET IN ANOTHER SENSE IT HAD EVERYTHING TO DO WITH IT!

THOMAS SR.: WHAT THE HELL IS WRONG WITH THESE KIDS? ALL OF THIS KILLING AND GANG STUFF IS CRAZY. WHO EVER HEARD OF KILLING SOMEONE JUST BECAUSE THEY'RE WEARING RED OR BLUE?

MRS. EDWARDS: THEY SHOT THAT REEVES' BOY RIGHT THERE IN THE CLASSROOM, IN FRONT

OF STUDENTS AND THE TEACHER. THESE WHITE GANGS ALMOST MAKE A PERSON ASHAMED OF BEING WHITE.

THOMAS SR.: WHITE FOLKS HAVE BEEN STRUGGLING FOR YEARS TRYING TO GET RESPECT FROM THE BLACK MAN. NOW, THESE KIDS ARE MAKING US ALL LOOK BAD. I HAVE STARTED WORKING AS FOREMAN IN MY DEPARTMENT. IT'S BAD ENOUGH THAT I HAVE TO SUPERVISE A LOT OF PREJUDICE BLACKS WHO HAVE NEVER TAKEN ORDERS FROM A WHITE MAN BEFORE. BUT NOW, WITH ALL OF THIS WHITE GANG KILLING IN THE NEWS, THEY SURELY WILL RESENT THE FACT THAT I'M THE BOSS. DAMN THESE KIDS!

THOMAS JR.: IT'S NOT JUST THE KIDS FAULT, DAD.

THOMAS SR.: YEAH, THE PARENTS SHOULD BE ARRESTED ALONG WITH THE KIDS.

THOMAS JR.: IT'S LIKE WHAT I TRIED TO TELL MR. JACKSON. WE WHITES HAVE ALWAYS BEEN TAUGHT THAT BLACK WAS GOOD AND THAT WHITE WAS BAD. WHAT THEY TEACH US IN SCHOOL, IN HISTORY, BASICALLY SAYS THE SAME THING. BLACKS WERE THE CIVILIZED PEOPLE RESPONSIBLE FOR HUMAN PROGRESS AND WHITES WERE THE SAVAGE SLAVES. THAT'S ONE OF THE REASONS THAT SOME WHITE KIDS ACT THE WAY THAT THEY DO.

THOMAS SR.: WHATEVER HAPPENED TO THAT WHITE HISTORY STUFF THAT YOU WERE TRYING TO GET IN THE SCHOOL?

THOMAS JR.: MR. JACKSON SAYS THAT THE SCHOOL BOARD DOESN'T THINK IT IS A GOOD IDEA. THEY THINK THAT TEACHING ABOUT WHITE HISTORY MIGHT MAKE WHITES TOO PROUD AND CAUSE THEM TO BECOME MILITANT.

MRS. EDWARDS: MILITANT?! THAT COWARDLY PECKERWOOD! KIDS ARE KILLING EACH OTHER AND ACTING LIKE FOOLS IN HIS SCHOOL AND HE'S WORRIED ABOUT WHITE MILITANTS. THOSE KIDS NEED SOME SELF-RESPECT. THIS IS WHY WE NEED A WHITE PERSON ON THE SCHOOL BOARD!

THOMAS SR.: THOMAS, MAYBE YOU SHOULD TALK TO JACKSON AGAIN ABOUT WHITE HISTORY.

THOMAS JR.: IT WON'T DO ANY GOOD. HE EVEN TRIED TO BRIBE ME WITH A SCHOLARSHIP TO GET ME TO STOP ASKING FOR WHITE HISTORY.

MRS. EDWARDS: THAT PECKERWOOD! TRYING TO BRIBE MY CHILD! I'M GOING TO THAT SCHOOL TOMORROW AND TELL HIM....

THOMAS SR.: WAIT A MINUTE. I'VE GOT A BETTER IDEA. YOU SAID IT. YOU SAID THAT WE NEED A WHITE PERSON ON THE SCHOOL BOARD. WHY DON'T YOU RUN

FOR THE SCHOOL BOARD. THERE IS AN ELECTION COMING UP IN NOVEMBER.

MRS. EDWARDS: NO WHITE PERSON HAS EVER RUN FOR SCHOOL BOARD.

THOMAS JR.: MOM, YOU COULD BE THE FIRST. TALKING ABOUT WHITE HISTORY! THAT WILL BE HISTORY. WITH A WHITE PERSON ON THE BOARD, JUST MAYBE "UNCLE" JACKSON MIGHT START ACTING LIKE A MAN.

THOMAS SR.: SON, IF YOU WANT TO GO TO COLLEGE, YOU'LL HAVE TO WORK TO HELP PAY YOUR WAY. I CANNOT AFFORD TO PAY FOR ALL OF IT MYSELF.

THOMAS JR.: I KNOW DAD. MR. JACKSON AND THE SCHOOL BOARD CANNOT KEEP ME OUT OF COLLEGE.

THOMAS SR.: THAT'S EXACTLY RIGHT! IT'S TIME THAT BLACK PEOPLE ACCEPT THE FACT THAT SLAVERY ENDED OVER 100 YEARS AGO IN THIS COUNTRY. WE'RE ALL NEW AFRICANS, BLACK AND WHITE. YOU ARE GOING TO COLLEGE. YOUR MOM WILL BE ELECTED TO THE SCHOOL BOARD. AND, I'M GOING TO CONTINUE AS FOREMAN ON MY JOB.

PHASE 11

RESPECT

QUANTUM THEORY PLACES AS MUCH IMPORTANCE ON MIND AS IT DOES ON MATTER. THE TWO ARE INTERRELATED AND MUTUALLY DEPENDENT. FOR HUMAN BEINGS THIS IS ESPECIALLY POIGNANT. THOUGHTS AND IDEAS GIVE RISE TO HUMAN ACTIONS. ALTHOUGH THE PHYSICAL DIMENSIONS OF THOUGHTS AND IDEAS ARE AS INCONSPICUOUS AS THE QUANTUM, THEIR IMPACT ON THE PHYSICAL WORLD IS OFTEN SO CONSPICUOUS THAT THE RESULT IS SOMETIMES CALLED A NEW REALITY.

THOMAS EDWARDS SR. MAY NOT KNOW AS MUCH ABOUT QUANTUM THEORY AS HIS SON, BUT HE DOES REALIZE THE IMPORTANCE OF THE IDEA OF WHITE SELF-RESPECT. HE KNOWS THAT IT IS IMPORTANT FOR HIMSELF AND HIS FAMILY. HE ALSO UNDERSTANDS IT'S IMPORTANCE FOR WHITE PEOPLE IN GENERAL AS THEY CONFRONT THE REMAINING OBSTACLES TO RACIAL JUSTICE IN THIS COUNTRY. THE ONE OBSTACLE THAT THOMAS SR. IS DETERMINED TO OVERCOME, IS THE PREJUDICE OF THOSE CO-WORKERS WHO NOW HAVE TO WORK WITH HIM AS SUBORDINATES.

PETTY SQUABBLES ON THE JOB, BETWEEN ADULTS, CAN BE AS FREQUENT AS THOSE IN A SCHOOL BETWEEN KIDS. AS WE HAVE SEEN, SCHOOL SQUABBLES CAN BECOME DEADLY, ESPECIALLY WHEN GANG MENTALITY IS INVOLVED. THE SAME POTENTIAL FOR VIOLENCE EXISTS ON THE JOB AND IS ACCENTUATED WHEN RACE IS INVOLVED. THOMAS SR. FINDS HIMSELF ACTING AS THE REFEREE BETWEEN A BLACK SUBORDINATE AND A WHITE ONE. BOTH CLAIM OWNERSHIP OF A WRENCH.

SAM: I SEE WHY YOUR KIDS ARE SHOOTING EACH OTHER ALL THE TIME. YOU PEOPLE CAN'T BE TRUSTED. I LAY MY WRENCH DOWN FOR A MINUTE, AND ONE OF YOU TAKE IT.

THOMAS SR.: YOU SAY IT'S YOUR WRENCH. MAXWELL SAYS THAT IT IS HIS. I'M NOT ACCUSING ANYONE OF TAKING ANYTHING. I JUST WANT YOU BOTH TO CALM DOWN SO WE CAN GET THIS THING RESOLVED.

SAM: IT SEEMS TO ME THAT YOU'RE TAKING MAXWELL'S SIDE. I TOLD YOU THAT IT WAS MY WRENCH. BUT, YOU'RE DOUBTING MY WORD AGAINST THIS PECKER....

MAXWELL: I SWEAR EDWARDS. IF HE CALLS ME A PECKERWOOD ONE MORE TIME. I'M GOING TO....

THOMAS SR.: BOTH OF YOU, SETTLE DOWN NOW! SAM, THAT'S ENOUGH OF THAT PECKERWOOD TALK FROM YOU. YOU USE THAT WORD IN HERE AGAIN AND I'M GOING TO GIVE YOU A WRITTEN REPRIMAND. YOU KNOW THAT TWO OF THOSE WILL GET YOU FIRED.

SAM: YOU THREATENING TO WRITE ME UP FOR THAT. YOU'RE GETTING PRETTY "UPPITY" SINCE YOU GOT THIS FOREMAN JOB. GIVE YOU AN INCH AND YOU TAKE A MILE. WELL PECKERWOODS, YOU'RE NOT PUSHING ME AROUND!

THOMAS SR.:	OKAY, THAT'S IT. REPRIMAND! AND, WE'RE GOING TO SEE MR. JOHNSON.
SAM:	THAT'S FINE WITH ME EDWARDS. MAYBE OLD MAN JOHNSON WILL PUT YOU IN YOUR PLACE.

MR. JOHNSON:	COME IN THOMAS. IS THERE A PROBLEM?
THOMAS SR.:	YES SIR. WE HAVE TWO PROBLEMS.
SAM:	TWO PROBLEMS?
THOMAS SR.:	SAM AND MAXWELL BOTH CLAIM TO BE THE RIGHTFUL OWNER OF A WRENCH THAT MAXWELL HAS. THAT'S THE FIRST PROBLEM.
MAXWELL:	THAT IS THE ONLY PROBLEM I'VE GOT SIR. I HAD THAT WRENCH FROM THE FIRST DAY I STARTED WORK ON THIS JOB.
SAM:	THAT PECKERWOOD IS LYING MR. JOHNSON.
THOMAS SR.:	THAT IS THE SECOND PROBLEM. I TOLD HIM NOT TO USE THAT WORD "PECKERWOOD" ON THE JOB AGAIN OR I WOULD GIVE HIM A WRITTEN REPRIMAND.
SAM:	MR. JOHNSON, YOU MADE A MISTAKE BY MAKING HIM FOREMAN. THESE PEOPLE DON'T HAVE ANY BUSINESS

TRYING TO TELL BLACK PEOPLE WHAT TO DO.

MAXWELL: MR. JOHNSON, I DON'T WANT TO CAUSE ANY TROUBLE. JUST LET HIM HAVE THE WRENCH. I CAN BUY ANOTHER ONE.

MR. JOHNSON: THAT WON'T BE NECESSARY MAXWELL. SAM WAS USING AN OLD PLOY. IT'S CALLED "USING ONE WHITE MAN AGAINST ANOTHER." THOMAS DID NOT FALL FOR IT. HE STOOD HIS GROUND AND ACTED ON HIS AUTHORITY LIKE A FOREMAN SHOULD. THINGS ARE SLOWLY BEGINNING TO CHANGE IN THIS COUNTRY. BLACK PEOPLE WILL HAVE TO LEARN TO RESPECT WHITES. THEY ARE NOT SLAVES ANYMORE.

SAM: YOU MEAN YOU'RE GOING TO SIDE WITH THESE PECKERWOODS?!

MR. JOHNSON: NOT ONLY THAT, BUT I'M FIRING YOU.

SAM: HEY. IT WAS ONLY A JOKE. I WAS JUST PLAYING WITH THEM.

MR. JOHNSON: WE DIDN'T HIRE YOU TO STIR UP RACIAL PROBLEMS ON THE JOB WITH YOUR "JOKES." BESIDES, YOU LIED AND WASTED COMPANY TIME. NOW, GET ALL OF YOUR PERSONAL ITEMS AND LEAVE. MAXWELL, YOU CAN GO BACK TO WORK. THOMAS, STAY FOR A FEW MORE MINUTES.

THOMAS SR.: YOU FIRED HIM?

MR. JOHNSON: YES. AND I WOULD FIRE YOU IF YOU BEHAVED LIKE THAT. THOMAS, I THINK YOU'RE GOING TO MAKE A GOOD FOREMAN. TOMORROW MORNING IM GOING TO MEET WITH ALL OF THE EMPLOYEES. IT'S TIME THAT I SET SOME STANDARDS FOR CONDUCT AROUND HERE. I ESPECIALLY NEED TO STATE WHAT WILL NOT BE TOLERATED AS FAR AS RACE AND COLOR IS CONCERNED. YES, TIMES ARE CHANGING. FOR THE BUSINESSMAN, THE GREEN COLOR OF MONEY IS MORE IMPORTANT THAN THE COLOR OF EMPLOYEES. IT'S GOING TO TAKE BOTH BLACK AND WHITE IN ORDER FOR THIS COUNTRY TO PROGRESS. NOW, GET BACK TO WORK. REMEMBER, DON'T WASTE COMPANY TIME.

A BIG STEP FORWARD? NO. A "QUANTUM LEAP" FORWARD AS FAR AS RACE RELATIONS ON THE JOB IS CONCERNED. THAT IS THE BEST WAY TO DESCRIBE HOW THOMAS SR. FEELS ABOUT WHAT HAS JUST TRANSPIRED. THOMAS SR. IS THANKFUL FOR HAVING A BOSS LIKE MR. JOHNSON. THERE ARE HUNDREDS OF OTHER BOSSES WHO WOULD HAVE FIRED THOMAS AND MAX RATHER THAN RISK PROVOKING THE RESENTMENT OF BLACK EMPLOYEES.

THIS WAS SIMPLY ONE CONTEST IN THE LONG TERM EFFORT OF WHITES TO BE TREATED AS EQUALS TO BLACKS. THOMAS SR. VERY WELL UNDERSTANDS THE REALITY OF WHAT HE, HIS SON, HIS WIFE AND WHITE PEOPLE IN GENERAL ARE UP AGAINST. BUT, NOW HE FEELS JUST A LITTLE MORE CONFIDENT ABOUT THE FUTURE.

PHASE 12

MEANING

HAVING OTHERS COME AROUND TO AGREE WITH YOUR POINT OF VIEW CAN BE A GRATIFYING EXPERIENCE. THOMAS EDWARDS JR. IS EXPERIENCING JUST THAT. AND, WHAT IS EVEN MORE GRATIFYING IS HAVING ONE'S OWN PARENT'S SUPPORT IN SOMETHING THAT ONE FEELS DEDICATED TO. BUT, THOMAS IS KEEPING HIS FEELINGS OF GRATIFICATION IN CHECK. LIKE HIS FATHER, HE TOO VERY WELL UNDERSTANDS THE REALITY OF WHAT WHITE PEOPLE ARE FACED WITH. HE KNOWS THAT IT WILL NOT BE AN EASY TASK TRYING TO CHANGE THE WAY THAT BLACK AND WHITE PEOPLE THINK.

THESE THOUGHTS OCCUPY THOMAS' MIND AS HE WALKS TOWARD THE BARBER SHOP. THE BARBER SHOP! OF ALL PLACES, WHY IS THOMAS EDWARDS JR. ON HIS WAY TO THE BARBER SHOP? THOMAS, WHO HAS BECOME, IN THE EYES OF HIS PEERS, A "REBEL WITH A CAUSE." THIS PROUD, IF NOT MILITANT WHITE REBEL, HAD WORE HIS LONG STRINGY HAIR AS A BADGE OF PROTEST AND SYMBOL OF WHITE PRIDE. WHY WOULD HE BE ON HIS WAY TO THE BARBER?

CALL IT PRAGMATISM. THOMAS IS STILL JUST AS PROUD OF WHO AND WHAT HE IS. BUT, EVEN TOO MUCH OF A GOOD THING CAN BE BAD. THOMAS' NEAR SHOULDER-LENGTH HAIR HAS SIMPLY BECOME DIFFICULT TO COMB AND CARE FOR. EAR LOBE LENGTH WOOD BE MUCH MORE PRACTICAL. EVEN, EAR LOBE LENGTH MAY COME AS A SHOCK TO THOSE WHO HAD GROWN ACCUSTOMED TO A THOMAS JR. WITH HAIR HANGING CLOSE TO HIS SHOULDERS.

BARBER: WELL I'LL BE A.... IS THIS THOMAS EDWARDS JR. COMING INTO MY SHOP?

THOMAS JR.: YEAH, IT'S ME. IT'S BEEN A LONG TIME.

BARBER: YOU'RE DAMN RIGHT. IT HAS BEEN A LONG TIME. IT'S BEEN A LONG TIME FOR YOU AND ABOUT A DOZEN OTHER CUSTOMERS OF MINE. BOY, WHEN YOU WALKED OUT OF HERE THE LAST TIME WITHOUT GETTING A HAIRCUT, YOU TOOK A LOT OF MY PAYING CUSTOMERS WITH YOU. SOME OF THEM HAVE NOT BEEN BACK SINCE. IT SEEMS LIKE EVERYONE WANTS TO WEAR THEIR HAIR LONG AND STRINGY. IT MIGHT BE GOOD FOR WHITE PRIDE, BUT IT SURE IS BAD FOR BUSINESS.

THOMAS JR.: WELL, TODAY I'M GOING TO GIVE YOU SOME BUSINESS. I WANT TO GET MY HAIR TRIMMED TO MY EAR LOBES.

BARBER: BOY, I DON'T KNOW WHETHER TO LAUGH OR CRY. WITH YOUR INFLUENCE, WHEN THE OTHER YOUNG REBELS SEE THAT YOU HAVE GOTTEN YOU HAIR CUT, MAYBE THEY WILL DECIDE TO DO THE SAME. MAYBE MY BUSINESS WILL PICK UP AGAIN.

THOMAS JR.: THAT'S UP TO THEM. MY HAIRCUT IS MY DECISION. HOW LONG BEFORE MY TURN?

BARBER:	WELL, NOT TOO LONG. THAT GUY SEATED OVER THERE IS WAITING FOR HIS BUDDY. I'M SHAMPOOING HIS BUDDY RIGHT NOW. I BET YOU DON'T RECOGNIZE WHO HE IS WITH THIS LONG HAIR AND BEARD.
PRETTY BOY:	YEAH. IT'S ME. PRETTY BOY.
THOMAS JR.:	PRETTY BOY?! MAN, WHAT HAPPENED TO YOUR CURL?!
PRETTY BOY:	PECKERWOOD PLEASE, I HAVEN'T HAD A CURL IN WEEKS. LONG HAIR IS IN THANKS TO YOU.
THOMAS JR.:	I CAN'T BELIEVE MY EYES! PRETTY BOY WITH LONG STRINGY HAIR AND A BEARD! THE LAST TIME I SAW YOU, YOU WERE....
PRETTY BOY:	I WAS PRETTY. I'M STILL PRETTY. CURLY OR STRAIGHT, THE WOMEN STILL WANT ME.
THOMAS JR.:	SAME OL' PRETTY. BUT MAN, DON'T YOU CARE ABOUT WHITE PRIDE, ABOUT THE GANG PROBLEM, OR ABOUT WHAT THEY TEACH US IN SCHOOL?
PRETTY BOY:	PECKERWOOD, THERE YOU GO AGAIN. STILL PREACHING. MAN, I CARE ABOUT PRETTY BOY. I'M PROUD OF WHAT I AM. I DON'T GIVE A SHIT ABOUT CRAZY GANG-BANGERS. I DROPPED OUT OF SCHOOL A LONG TIME AGO. MY WOMEN TAKE CARE OF ME. NOW, YOU'RE THE BIG HERO. YOU

GO OUT AND SAVE THE WORLD. ME?
WELL, I'M GOING TO SAVE THIS
PRETTY HAIR WITH SOME SHAMPOO.

AS THE BARBER PUTS PRETTY BOY'S HAIR UNDER THE FAUCETS, THOMAS' MIND BEGINS TO PONDER THE MEANING OF IT ALL. THE WHOLE BLACK AND WHITE ISSUE. ULTIMATELY, WHAT DOES IT MEAN ANYWAY? BLACK SKIN OR WHITE SKIN. CURLY HAIR OR STRAIGHT HAIR. WHITE HISTORY OR BLACK HISTORY.

"ALL IS VANITY" IS THE WAY THE MUCH QUOTED PHRASE GOES. IS PRETTY BOY'S ATTITUDE THE MOST PRACTICAL ONE? ULTIMATELY, IS THOMAS EDWARDS JR. JUST AS VAIN AS PRETTY BOY? SURELY THERE IS A SIGNIFICANT DIFFERENCE BETWEEN WHAT IT REPRESENTS FOR PRETTY BOY AND WHAT IT REPRESENTS FOR THOMAS EDWARDS JR.

THOMAS KNOWS THAT THE SYMBOLS OF HAIR AND COLOR, AS WELL AS HISTORY AND POLITICS, HAVE LITTLE MEANING AS ISOLATED REALITIES. BUT, TAKEN TOGETHER IN THE CONTEXT OF WHAT CAN BE UNDERSTOOD AS A GENERAL REALITY, THEY EACH REPRESENT MUCH MORE THAN SIMPLE VANITY. THEY HELP TO GIVE MEANING AND SIGNIFICANCE TO THE GENERAL REALITY. MAKING THAT REALITY BETTER FOR THOSE WHO HAVE NOT HAD IT SO GOOD IS A WORTHY GOAL THAT THOMAS IS DETERMINED TO PLAY A ROLE IN.

MAYBE PRETTY BOY CAN'T SEE THAT BIG PICTURE. MAYBE A LOT OF PEOPLE CANNOT SEE BEYOND THE SYMBOLS. THOMAS JR. CAN AND HE IS DETERMINED TO CHANGE THINGS.

BARBER: OKAY THOMAS, I'M FINISHED WITH PRETTY BOY. IT'S YOUR TURN.

THOMAS JR.: NO. ON SECOND THOUGHT, I THINK I WILL PASS. I'LL COME BACK ANOTHER DAY. THIS JUST ISN'T THE RIGHT TIME.

BARBER: GODDAMN! BOY, THIS WILL MAKE THE SECOND TIME THAT YOU HAVE WALKED OUT OF HERE WITHOUT GETTING YOUR HAIR CUT. CAN'T YOU MAKE UP YOUR MINE?

THOMAS JR.: I WILL. BUT, I'VE GOT THINGS TO DO FIRST.

BARBER: DON'T DO THIS AGAIN. IT'S BAD FOR BUSINESS.

THOMAS JR.: DON'T WORRY. I WON'T COME BACK UNTIL IT'S REALLY TIME TO GET MY HAIR CUT.

BARBER: BOY, IF YOU WAIT ANY LONGER YOU'RE GOING TO END UP LOOKING LIKE THE "MISSING LINK."

THOMAS JR.: IF THE MISSING LINK HAD HAD THE BRAINS, HE PROBABLY WOULDN'T BE MISSING....LONG HAIR AND ALL.

PRETTY BOY: PECKERWOOD, PLEASE.

PHASE 13

FAMILY

YOU MAY CALL IT AN OATH. YOU MAY CALL IT A VOW. YOU MAY SIMPLY CALL IT A PROMISE. WHATEVER YOU CALL IT, IT HAS REACHED THE LEVEL OF NEAR SACREDNESS AS FAR AS THOMAS JR. IS CONCERNED. INDEED, THE BETTERMENT OF PEOPLE WHO HAPPEN TO BE WHITE IS A MATTER OF UTTERMOST IMPORTANCE IF NOT SACREDNESS. THOMAS JR. HAS MADE UP HIS MIND THAT HE WILL NOT GET HIS HAIR CUT UNTIL THE COMMUNITY GANG VIOLENCE HAS STOPPED, UNTIL WHITE HISTORY IS TAUGHT IN THE SCHOOL, AND UNTIL A WHITE PERSON IS ON THE SCHOOL BOARD.

THERE IS AN OLD SAYING CALLED "BITING OFF MORE THAN ONE CAN CHEW." IT IS A PHRASE THAT RAISES SERIOUS DOUBT ABOUT ONE PERSON BEING ABLE TO RESOLVE THE ISSUES THAT THOMAS HAS TAKEN ON. OUR HERO IS NOT SO NAÏVE AS TO BELIEVE THAT ONLY HIS SELF-SACRIFICE WILL SOLVE THESE PROBLEMS. THERE ARE OTHERS WHO WANT TO IMPROVE THE WELL-BEING OF THE WHITE COMMUNITY. THOMAS IS FORTUNATE TO COUNT AMONG THOSE OTHERS, HIS OWN PARENTS.

THERE HAS NEVER BEEN A WHITE PERSON ON THE SCHOOL BOARD. AND NOW, THE EDWARDS FAMILY IS DETERMINED THAT ONE OF THEIR OWN WILL BE THE FIRST. THIS DETERMINATION, IN ITSELF, MAY BE A FIRST. ANYONE WOULD BE HARD PRESSED TO FIND ANOTHER EXAMPLE OF A WHITE FAMILY COOPERATING ON AN AGENDA THAT GOES BEYOND THE FAMILY NUCLEUS AND SEEKS TO HAVE A MAJOR IMPACT ON THE LARGER COMMUNITY ITSELF.

MRS. EDWARDS HAS ALWAYS THOUGHT OF HERSELF AS PRIMARILY A MOTHER, WIFE, AND HOUSEKEEPER. RUNNING FOR THE SCHOOL BOARD IS SOMETHING THAT PLACES HER IN A ROLE THAT IS NOT ONLY UNFAMILIAR, BUT DOWN RIGHT FRIGHTENING. THIS CHALLENGE GOES BEYOND HOUSEWIFE VS. SCHOOL BOARD MEMBER. SINCE NO WOMAN HAS EVER SERVED ON THE BOARD, THAT CHALLENGE CAN BE VIEWED AS MALE VS. FEMALE. THE RACIAL ISSUE EVEN PUTS IT IN THE CONTEXT OF BLACK VS. WHITE.

ON FIRST GLANCE, THE MAGNITUDE OF MRS. EDWARDS CHALLENGE SEEMS TO BE MORE THAN WHAT ONE HOUSEWIFE CAN SHOULDER. BUT, LIKE HER SON, SHE TOO IS COMFORTED BY THE KNOWLEDGE THAT HER FAMILY IS BEHIND HER. AND IN TRUTH, IT IS THAT SUPPORT SYSTEM WHICH PROVIDES HER WITH ANY CONFIDENCE THAT SHE CAN BECOME THE FIRST WOMAN....THE FIRST WHITE TO SERVE ON THE SCHOOL BOARD.

MRS. EDWARDS: THOMAS, I'M SCARED.

THOMAS SR.: SCARED OF WHAT?

MRS. EDWARDS: YOU KNOW. RUNNING FOR THE SCHOOL BOARD.

THOMAS SR.: LOOK HONEY. I CAN UNDERSTAND YOU BEING A LITTLE NERVOUS. BUT TRUST ME, THERE IS NOTHING TO BE AFRAID OF. A HUNDRED YEARS AGO WHITE PEOPLE HAD GOOD REASON TO BE AFRAID. THE VERY LAWS IN THIS COUNTRY WERE AGAINST US THEN. NOW, NO ONE IS GOING TO LYNCH YOU OR BURN A CROSS IN OUR YARD.

MRS. EDWARDS: THAT'S NOT WHAT I MEAN. IT'S THE WAY SOME BLACK PEOPLE LOOK AT US. THEY HAVE THAT HATEFUL EXPRESSION ON THEIR FACES. THAT SCARES ME. I DON'T KNOW IF I CAN PUT UP WITH THEIR UPPITY ATTITUDES. DO YOU REMEMBER WHEN THOSE BOARD MEMBERS CAME TO THE COMMUNITY MEETING AND STOOD AT THE BACK OF THE ROOM? THEY JUST LOOKED DOWN THEIR NOSES AT US. THEY DIDN'T SAY A WORD AT FIRST, BUT YOU COULD TELL BY THE LOOK ON THEIR FACES THAT THEY THOUGHT WE WERE TRASH.

THOMAS SR.: THAT'S THE POINT HONEY. IT'S ALL PSYCHOLOGICAL. IT'S A MIND GAME. SOME BLACKS WANT TO KEEP AN UPPER HAND ON US. THEY CAN'T USE THE OLD METHODS. THAT'S AGAINST THE LAW. WE FALL RIGHT INTO THEIR HANDS WHEN WE GO ALONG WITH THE GAME. A BLACK WORKER TRIED IT ON THE JOB WITH ME. FORTUNATELY, MY BOSS DOESN'T TOLERATE THAT KIND OF CRAP.

MRS. EDWARDS: THERE WON'T ALWAYS BE A MR. JOHNSON AROUND.

THOMAS SR.: THAT'S EVEN MORE REASON FOR US TO LEARN TO STAND UP TO PREJUDICE. WE CAN'T ALWAYS DEPEND ON OTHERS TO DO IT FOR US.

MRS. EDWARDS: YOU'RE BEGINNING TO SOUND LIKE YOUR SON.

THOMAS SR.: YOU KNOW WHAT THEY SAY, "LIKE FATHER, LIKE SON." IT IS IRONIC. I'VE RIDICULED THOMAS FOR ALL OF THAT SCIENCE FICTION QUANTUM STUFF, AND HERE I AM TALKING ABOUT PSYCHOLOGY AND MIND GAMES. I GUESS IT'S ALL "MIND OVER MATTER." IF WE CAN'T BELIEVE THAT WE CAN DO SOMETHING...IF WE THINK OF OURSELVES AS LESS THAN BLACKS...THEN, WE ARE OUR OWN WORST ENEMY. IF WE ACCEPT THE WORST NEGATIVE STEREOTYPES FOR WHAT IT MEANS TO BE WHITE, THEN....HONEY. WAKE UP. DID I PUT YOU TO SLEEP?

MRS. EDWARDS: HUH? OH, I'M SORRY, THOMAS. I'M JUST TIRED. I'VE GOT TO GET UP IN THE MORNING AND GO DOWN TO THE COURT HOUSE TO REGISTER AS A CANDIDATE IN THE SCHOOL BOARD ELECTION.

THOMAS SR.: WE BOTH NEED TO BE GETTING TO SLEEP. I'VE GOT TO GET UP FOR WORK TOMORROW. IT'S 1 A.M. AND WE'RE LYING IN BED DISCUSSING PSYCHOLOGY, POLITICS, AND QUANTUM....WHATEVER.

MRS. EDWARDS: THAT'S QUANTUM "THEORY," SWEETHEART.

THOMAS SR.: RIGHT. GOOD NIGHT.

MRS. EDWARDS: GOOD NIGHT.

PHASE 14

MIND OVER MATTER

THE SUPPORT OF FAMILY AND FRIENDS CAN INDEED BE THE DIFFERENCE BETWEEN OVERCOMING AN OBSTACLE AND BEING OVERCOME BY AN OBSTACLE. THE NEW FOUND UNITY OF THE EDWARDS FAMILY HAS EMBOLDENED EACH OF IT'S MEMBERS. BUT, INDIVIDUALS ARE NOT ALWAYS IN THE PHYSICAL PRESENCE OF EACH OTHER. THE FORCE OF UNITY HAS TO GO BEYOND MERE PHYSICAL NEARNESS. LIKE THE QUANTUM, IN IT'S INFINITELY DECREASING SCALE OF MEASURE, TRUE UNITY EXTENDS BEYOND THE BOUNDS OF MERE MATTER. IT ENTERS A REALM OF THE NONPHYSICAL, THE METAPHYSICAL, THE SPIRITUAL AND THE MIND.

IT IS THIS LATTER DIMENSION OF UNITY THAT IS THE ULTIMATE SOURCE FOR ANY PHYSICAL MANIFESTATION OF IT'S PROPERTIES. "MIND OVER MATTER." THE PHASE SEEMS TO INFER THAT OF THE TWO, MIND IS SUPERIOR. THIS NON-SUBSTANCE IS GIVEN PRECEDENCE OVER EVEN THE MOST MASSIVE OF PHYSICAL SUBSTANCES. IDEAS, THOUGHTS, BELIEFS, PERCEPTIONS, CONCEPTIONS, REASONING AND ALL THE OTHER MANIFESTATIONS OF MIND ARE AWARDED A STATUS ABOVE THAT OF THE MATERIAL. BUT, HOW CAN THAT BE? SURELY A ROCK, A FLESH AND BLOOD CREATURE, A HUMAN BRAIN, ARE TANGIBLE THINGS THAT HAVE EXISTENCE IN AND OF THEMSELVES. IT IS POSSIBLE TO TOUCH OR TO SEE EACH FOR WHAT IT IS. WHERE IS THE TOUCHING OR SEEING THAT GIVES FORM TO MIND? CAN MIND EXIST INDEPENDENTLY OF PHYSICAL THINGS? FOR THAT MATTER, CAN PHYSICAL THINGS EXIST INDEPENDENTLY OF MIND?

67

THIS CIRCLE OF QUESTIONS IS REMINISCENT OF THE OLD "CHICKEN OR THE EGG" PROBLEM. THE EXISTENCE OF BOTH SEEM TO BE MUTUALLY DEPENDENT. WITHOUT MIND (PERCEPTIONS AND CONCEPTION) THE PHYSICAL WORLD LACKS THE QUALITY THAT ALLOWS FOR THE VERIFICATION OF IT'S EXISTENCE. AND, IF THE MIND ASPECT OF PERCEPTION ITSELF DOES NOT EXIST, THEN LOGICALLY THAT WHICH DEPENDS ON PERCEPTION FOR IT'S EXISTENCE HAS NO BASIS FOR EXISTENCE. LIKEWISE, MIND AND PERCEPTION CANNOT EXIST IN A VOID. IF THERE IS NOTHING TO OBSERVE...IF ALL IS TRULY A VOID, THEN THE EXISTENCE OF THE OBSERVER ITSELF IS PRECLUDED. A TRUE VOID, IS THE ESSENCE OF NON-EXISTENCE. IF THERE IS NOTHING THAT POSSESSES THE POSSIBILITY FOR DETECTION, THEN MIND WHICH MUST MANIFEST ITSELF THROUGH THE PHYSICAL, IS PRECLUDED.

MIND AND MATTER APPEAR TO BE MUTUALLY DEPENDENT AS FAR AS FUNDAMENTAL EXISTENCE IS CONCERNED. BUT, IN INTERACTIONS OF THE TWO, MIND DEFINITELY MANIPULATES MATTER MORE SO THAN MATTER MANIPULATES MIND. THE INTELLIGENCE AND CREATIVITY OF MIND (AS WITNESSED IN THE ACCOMPLISHMENTS OF MAN HIMSELF) MAKES IT ULTIMATELY SUPERIOR TO MATTER IN THEIR MUTUALLY DEPENDENT RELATIONSHIP. IT WAS MIND THAT ENVISIONED THE WHEEL AND MADE IT AN INDISPENSABLE PART OF CIVILIZATION. IT WAS MIND THAT RELEASED AND HARNESSED THE ENERGY OF THE ATOM. IT WAS MIND THAT GAVE RISE TO THE ENTITIES CALLED NATIONS. IT IS MIND THAT UNIFIES INDIVIDUALS IN THE EMOTIONALLY BOUND UNITS OF FAMILY.

"THE FAMILY THAT PRAYS TOGETHER, STAYS TOGETHER." PRAYER CAN BE ONE OF THE MOST FOCUSED FORMS OF MEDITATION. WHEN PERFORMED BY A GROUP, IT CAN RESULT IN A SINGLE-MINDEDNESS

THAT ENABLES ACCOMPLISHMENTS THAT THE LONE INDIVIDUAL COULD NOT HOPE TO ACHIEVE. MRS. EDWARDS IS RELYING ON THAT DEGREE OF MENTAL AND EMOTIONAL UNITY TO PROVIDE HER WITH THE COURAGE TO DO WHAT NO WOMAN IN THE COMMUNITY HAS EVER DONE. SHE WILL NEED COURAGE TO ENTER ONE OF THE DOMAINS OF THE BLACK POWER SOCIAL STRUCTURE AND EXERCISE HER RIGHT TO ATTEMPT TO BECOME PART OF IT. SHE WILL NEED COURAGE TO REGISTER AS A CANDIDATE FOR THE UPCOMING SCHOOL BOARD ELECTION. SHE WILL BE THE LONE WHITE FACE AMONG BLACK FACES THAT DEFINITELY WILL NOT BE FRIENDLY.

CLERK: MAY I HELP YOU?

MRS. EDWARDS: I WANT TO REGISTER AS A CANDIDATE IN THE SCHOOL BOARD ELECTION.

CLERK: I BEG YOUR PARDON!

MRS. EDWARDS: I SAID I WANT TO REGISTER AS A CANDIDATE IN THE SCHOOL BOARD ELECTION.

A DEAD SILENCE ENGULFS THE OFFICE AREA. EMPLOYEES WHO BEFORE WERE PREOCCUPIED WITH THE ROUTINE PAPER SHUFFLE, FOCUSED THEIR SILENCE AND ATTENTION ON MRS. EDWARDS. IT IS AS THOUGH SHE WAS THE ULTIMATE SAGE WHO HAD JUST UTTERED WORDS EXPLAINING THE MEANING OF EXISTENCE ITSELF. MRS. EDWARDS IS NO SAGE. IN THE MINDS OF THE GLARING BLACK FACES HER PRESENCE AND WORDS MIGHT JUST AS WELL HAVE COME FROM SOME BIBLICAL PROPHET OF DOOM. IN THE MINDS OF SOME, A WHITE PERSON RUNNING FOR THE SCHOOL BOARD PORTENDS DOOM FOR THE STATUS QUO OF AN ALL BLACK SCHOOL BOARD.

CLERK: ARE YOU SURE?

MRS. EDWARDS: YES, I AM SURE.

CLERK: OKAY. YOU NEED TO FILL OUT THESE
                 FORMS AND PAY THE REGISTRATION
                 FEE. YOU MAY TAKE THE FORMS WITH
                 YOU AND BRING THEM BACK.

MRS. EDWARDS: I WOULD LIKE TO FILL THE FORMS
                 OUT RIGHT HERE.

CLERK: HERE?

MRS. EDWARDS: YES. IS THAT A PROBLEM?

CLERK: YES...I MEAN NO! HAVE A SEAT AT
                 THAT TABLE. HERE IS A PEN.

MRS. EDWARDS: THANK YOU. BUT, I HAVE MY OWN
                 PEN.

"IF LOOKS COULD KILL," MRS. EDWARDS WOULD BE PROSTRATE ON THE OFFICE FLOOR. THE INTENSITY OF THE STARES ALONE WOULD BE UNNERVING TO MANY INDIVIDUALS. FEW WOULD SIT AND TAKE TIME TO FILL OUT SEVERAL FORMS KNOWING THAT THEIR EVERY MOVE WAS BEING SCRUTINIZED BY DOZENS OF HOSTILE FACES. FORTUNATELY, LOOKS ALONE WILL NOT KILL. THE THOUGHTS IN THE "MINDS" OF THESE DISAPPROVING BLACK FACES DO NOT "MATTER." MRS. EDWARDS HAS FOUND THE COURAGE TO OVERCOME THE WORST FEAR. SHE HAS CONQUERED "THE FEAR OF FEAR" ITSELF!

PHASE 15

RED, WHITE AND BLUE

THE SECRET OF SAMSON'S STRENGTH WAS IN HIS HAIR. WHEN IT WAS CUT, HE WAS DEFEATED. THOMAS JR.'S HAIR CERTAINLY DOESN'T POSSESS THE MYTHICAL POWER OF SAMSON'S. BUT, IN HIS MIND IT HAS BECOME SYMBOLIC OF STRENGTH OF CONVICTION. IT REPRESENTS HIS RESOLVE TO CORRECT WHAT HE SEES AS DETRIMENTS TO THE WHITE COMMUNITY. ONE OF THESE DETRIMENTS IS SO DESTRUCTIVE AND LIFE THREATENING THAT FEW THINGS SHOULD BE OVERLOOKED FOR USE IN COMBATING IT. IF LONG HAIR GIVES ONE AN ADVANTAGE OR PSYCHOLOGICAL EDGE, THEN BY ALL MEANS IT SHOULD BE USED IN COMBATING THIS PARTICULAR DETRIMENT.

THE GANG PROBLEM CERTAINLY IS DESTRUCTIVE AND LIFE THREATENING. SINCE MANY GANG MEMBERS WEAR THEIR HAIR LONG, THIS COULD BE ONE POINT OF COMMONALITY BETWEEN THEM AND ANYONE ATTEMPTING TO DEVELOP A RATIONAL DIALOGUE WITH THEM. THOMAS JR. WILL ATTEMPT TO DEVELOP A RATIONAL DIALOGUE WITH HIS LONG-HAIRED COUNTERPARTS. THOMAS KNOWS THAT THE BEGINNING OF SUCH DIALOGUE MUST BE A ONE ON ONE CONVERSATION WITH THE GANG LEADERS. HE HAS ALREADY ENCOUNTERED B.G.M #1 OF THE BLUE GANG. ALTHOUGH, THE ENCOUNTER WAS SOMEWHAT ANTAGONISTIC, AT LEAST IT WAS A FIRST STEP.

B.G.M. #1 LIVES IN ONE OF THE TOUGHEST AREAS IN THE WHITE COMMUNITY. THE BLOCK WHERE HIS APARTMENT BUILDING IS LOCATED IS KNOWN FOR DRUGS AND SHOOTINGS. ANYONE WEARING AN OBVIOUS DISPLAY OF THE COLOR RED WOULD BE AT RISK WALKING THROUGH THE AREA. THE AREA HAS A

REPUTATION AS "BLUE" TERRITORY. THE ONLY RED GANG MEMBERS WHO VENTURE INTO THIS AREA ARE THOSE WHO DRIVE AT A HIGH RATE OF SPEED AS THEY FIRE SHOTS AT THEIR BLUE CLAD RIVALS.

THOMAS JR. IS WEARING WHITE AS HE WALKS DOWN THE SIDEWALK LEADING TO B.G.M. #1'S APARTMENT BUILDING. HE DOESN'T HAVE TO LOOK FAR TO FIND THE LEADER OF THE BLUES. NUMBER ONE AND THREE OTHER BLUES ARE SEATED ON THE FRONT STEPS OF THE APARTMENT BUILDING.

B.G.M. #1: WELL, LOOK WHO'S HERE! IF IT ISN'T "MR. I AIN'T CLAIMING" HIMSELF. HE STILL AIN'T WEARING RED OR BLUE. HE'S WEARING WHITE!

B.G.M. #3: MAYBE HE'S STARTING A NEW GANG.

B.G.M. #4: YEAH. MAYBE THEY CALL THEMSELVES THE WHITE-PECKERWOODS.

B.G.M. #1: OKAY, PECKERWOOD. WHY ARE YOU WALKING AROUND HERE IN OUR TERRITORY? I TOLD YOU ONCE BEFORE THAT THE NEXT TIME I SAW YOU, YOU HAD BETTER BE WEARING BLUE.

THOMAS JR.: I'M STILL NOT WEARING RED OR BLUE. IF YOU WANT TO SHOOT ME BECAUSE OF THAT, GO RIGHT AHEAD. I'M HERE BECAUSE I WANT TO TALK TO YOU.

B.G.M. #1: TALK? IF THIS HAS ANYTHING TO DO WITH THE SHOOTING OF JASON REEVES, YOU CAN FORGET IT. WE'VE TOLD THAT POLICE ALL THAT WE

KNOW. WE DON'T KNOW NOTHING. IT'S JUST ONE LESS RED-PECKERWOOD.

THOMAS JR.: YOU AND I BOTH KNOW THAT THERE IS MORE TO IT THAN THAT. THAT'S WHAT I WANT TO TALK ABOUT. THIS WHITE KILLING WHITE HAS GOT TO STOP.

B.G.M. #1: AND, WHO IS GOING TO STOP IT? YOU?!

THOMAS JR.: ME AND YOU! WE CAN START. IF WE CAN GET THE BLUES TO STOP, THEN WE SHOULD BE ABLE TO CONVINCE THE REDS TO STOP ALSO.

B.G.M. #1: DAMN. YOU'VE GOT A LOT OF NERVE, PECKERWOOD! WHY IN THE HELL SHOULD I HELP YOU?

THOMAS JR.: BECAUSE WE WOULD BE HELPING OUR PEOPLE. WHITE PEOPLE. IF WE KEEP KILLING EACH OTHER, THERE WON'T BE ANY OF US LEFT. THE NEXT ONE KILLED COULD BE YOU OR ANY OF US HERE NOW. NUMBER ONE, THAT'S WHY YOU SHOULD HELP ME.

B.G.M. #1: MAN, I AIN'T AFRAID OF DYING. AS LONG AS I'M PACKING THIS .45 UNDER MY BELT, I DON'T INTEND TO DIE. IF I DO DIE, I INTEND TO TAKE A RED WITH ME. BESIDES, THIS BLUE AND RED STUFF HAS BEEN GOING ON FOR SO LONG THAT IT PROBABLY NEVER WILL STOP.

THOMAS JR.:   YOU'RE RIGHT. IT WON'T STOP UNTIL ONE SIDE MAKES THE FIRST MOVE TOWARD PEACE. IT WILL JUST GO ON AND ON. LET'S ALL JUST BE PROUD OF BEING WHITE AND FORGET ABOUT THIS RED AND BLUE NONSENSE.

B.G.M. #1:   PROUD OF BEING WHITE?! WHAT DOES ANY PECKERWOOD HAVE TO BE PROUD OF? LOOK AROUND. LOOK AT THIS NEIGHBORHOOD. YOU'VE HEARD THAT OLD SAYING:
        "IF YOU'RE BLACK, YOU'RE ON THE RIGHT TRACK.
        IF YOU'RE BROWN, STICK AROUND.
        IF YOU'RE WHITE, GET OUT OF SIGHT."

THOMAS JR.:   BUT, WE CAN CHANGE ALL OF THAT. WE HAVE TO BEGIN WITH KNOWING OUR HISTORY.

B.G.M. #1:   MAN, WE KNOW ALL ABOUT THAT SLAVERY STUFF. BEING A PECKERWOOD MEANS NOTHING, AND HAS ALWAYS MEANT NOTHING. BEING A BLUE GIVES US SOMETHING TO BE PROUD OF.

THOMAS JR.:   BUT, THERE IS MORE TO OUR HISTORY THAN SLAVERY. THERE IS A LOT TO BE PROUD OF. THERE IS MUCH ABOUT BEING WHITE AND FROM EUROPE THAT THEY ARE JUST NOT TEACHING US IN SCHOOL. INSTEAD OF FIGHTING EACH OTHER, WE SHOULD BE WORKING TOGETHER TO GET THE SCHOOLS TO TEACH THE TRUTH ABOUT OUR HISTORY.

DIVISION HAS ALWAYS BEEN THE THING THAT HAS HURT US THE MOST. HOW DO YOU THINK OUR ANCESTORS WERE ENSLAVED IN THE FIRST PLACE? IT WAS DIVISION BETWEEN THOSE OF US WHO ARE FAIR SKINNED AND THOSE WHO WERE DARKER COMPLEXIONED. EVEN TODAY, SOME OF US YET BELIEVE THAT DARKER MEANS BETTER, AND THAT CURLY HAIR IS BETTER THAN STRAIGHT HAIR. LOOK AT JACKIE MICHAELS.

B.G.M. #3: WHAT HE SAYS, MAKES SENSE, NUMBER ONE.

THOMAS JR.: BUT, IT DOESN'T MAKE SENSE TO LET SOMETHING AS PETTY AS RED AND BLUE DIVIDE US. WE'RE ALL BROTHERS, MAN! WHITE BROTHERS. NOT RED AND BLUE. NOT FAIR AND DARK.

B.G.M. #1: YEAH, IT DOES MAKE SENSE.

THOMAS JR.: THEN, ARE YOU GUYS WITH ME?

B.G.M. #1: WE NEED TO THINK ABOUT IT. WHAT ABOUT THE REDS? IF WE LET OUR GUARDS DOWN, THEY MIGHT TAKE ADVANTAGE OF THE SITUATION.

B.G.M. #3: RIGHT. YOU CAN'T TALK TO THEM DAMN REDS. ALL THEY UNDERSTAND IS THE GUN.

THOMAS JR.: THEY PROBABLY FEEL THE SAME WAY ABOUT YOU GUYS. IF IT MAKES YOU

FEEL BETTER, I'LL MEET WITH THE REDS JUST AS I HAVE WITH YOU.

B.G.M. #1:   LIKE I SAID, WE'LL THINK ABOUT IT. YOU GO TALK TO THE REDS. IF THEY WON'T STOP SHOOTING AT US, THEN WE SURE AS HELL ARE GOING TO SHOOT BACK AND THE BANGING WON'T EVER END!

PHASE 16

LIBERAL

A LIBERAL: "ONE WHO IS OPEN-MINDED OR NOT STRICT IN THE OBSERVANCE OF ORTHODOX OR TRADITIONAL FORMS." THAT DEFINITION CERTAINLY SEEMS TO FIT THOMAS SR.'S BOSS, MR. JOHNSON.

IN THE UNITED STATES OF NEW AFRICA, THE AVERAGE BLACK CITIZEN ONLY GRUDGINGLY ACCEPTS WHITES AS FELLOW CITIZENS. OVERT DENIAL OF CIVIL RIGHTS TO WHITES IS VIEWED AS IMPROPER BY ALL BUT THE MOST CONSERVATIVE OF BLACKS. HOWEVER, AN UNWRITTEN STATUS QUO JUSTIFIES AN ATMOSPHERE OF SOCIAL PREJUDICE THAT CAUSES BOTH RACES TO INTERACT ON A BASIS THAT IS ANYTHING BUT EQUAL. THIS RELATIONSHIP GENERALLY GIVES BLACKS A SOCIAL ADVANTAGE. THUS, BLACKS HAVE AN INCLINATION TO BEHAVE IN A DOMINANT MANNER IN THE COMPANY OF WHITES. WHITES TEND TO BE SOMEWHAT SUBMISSIVE.

MR. JOHNSON IS ONE OF THE SLOWLY INCREASING NUMBERS OF BLACKS WHO REFUSE TO CONFORM TO THE TRADITIONAL BLACK CONSERVATIVE MOLD. THESE INDIVIDUALS FORESEE THE NEED FOR HONEST SOCIAL EQUALITY BETWEEN THE RACES. THEY ARE OF THE OPINION THAT IN THE LONG RUN, THE COUNTRY WILL BENEFIT FROM A CITIZENRY WHERE ALL CAN DEVELOP TO THE MAXIMUM OF THEIR INDIVIDUAL TALENTS. LIBERAL IS THE "POLITICALLY CORRECT" TERM FOR THESE PROGRESSIVE MINDED BLACK NEW AFRICANS. "PECKERWOOD-LOVER" IS THE "POLITICALLY INCORRECT" TERM.

BEING CALLED A PECKERWOOD-LOVER DOES NOT DETER MR. JOHNSON. HE ADAMANTLY SUPPORTS THOMAS SR. IN HIS NEW ROLE AS JOB FOREMAN. HE

DOES THIS DESPITE THE GOSSIP AND PETTY ACTS OF PREJUDICE FROM SOME OF HIS BLACK EMPLOYEES. IN FACT, THESE THINGS ONLY SERVE TO EMBOLDEN HIS RESOLVE TO SET AN EXAMPLE FOR OTHERS. IN HIS MIND, HE PICTURES HIMSELF AS A LONE CRUSADER FOR RACIAL JUSTICE. LIKE MANY CRUSADERS, HE WILL NOT BE SATISFIED WITH JUST ONE VICTORIOUS BATTLE. LIKE THOMAS EDWARDS JR., PEACE OF MIND WILL ONLY COME WHEN THE "WAR" AGAINST THE STATUS QUO IS WON.

IT IS THIS FRAME OF MIND THAT CAUSES HIM TO GO ONE STEP FURTHER IN EXAMPLE SETTING. HE DECIDES TO INVITE THE EDWARDS FAMILY TO HIS HOME FOR DINNER. SOME MIGHT CALL THIS "GRANDSTANDING" OR "EGO EMBELLISHMENT."

BUT, MR. JOHNSON IS SINCERE. HE CAN THINK OF NO BETTER WAY TO ESTABLISH A GENUINE SENSE OF SOCIAL EQUALITY THAN FOR BLACKS AND WHITES TO INTERACT SOCIALLY IN THE INFORMAL ATMOSPHERE OF THEIR HOMES. WHAT BETTER WAY IS THERE FOR PEOPLE TO TEAR DOWN THE ARTIFICIAL BARRIERS OF THE STATUS QUO? IT PROVIDES ONE WITH AN OPPORTUNITY TO OVERCOME THE MOST SUBTLE OF PREJUDICES.

MR. JOHNSON: COME RIGHT IN THOMAS. I ASKED FOR YOU TO COME TO MY OFFICE THIS MORNING FOR A SPECIAL REASON. THIS HAS NOTHING TO DO WITH ANY PARTICULAR PROBLEM ON THE JOB. WELL, LET ME TAKE THAT BACK. IN A WAY IT DOES AFFECT THE JOB. THOMAS, I WANT TO INVITE YOU AND YOUR FAMILY TO MY HOME FOR DINNER THIS WEEKEND.

THOMAS SR.: DINNER AT YOUR HOME?

MR. JOHNSON: I KNOW. BLACKS AND WHITES SELDOM MIX SOCIALLY IN THIS TOWN. THAT'S PART OF THE PROBLEM. I BELIEVE THAT IF PEOPLE GET TO KNOW EACH OTHER SOCIALLY, IT WILL BREAK DOWN SOME OF THESE RACIAL BARRIERS. IT SETS A GOOD EXAMPLE.

THOMAS SR.: WELL, I WOULD HOPE THAT YOU ARE NOT JUST DOING THIS TO SET AN EXAMPLE.

MR. JOHNSON: WHAT DO YOU MEAN?

THOMAS SR.: LET ME EXPLAIN IT THE WAY THAT MY SON WOULD. I WOULD HOPE THAT YOU INVITED US BECAUSE WE'RE DECENT HUMAN BEINGS WHOM YOU LIKE AND RESPECT, AND NOT JUST BECAUSE WE HAPPEN TO BE WHITE.

MR. JOHNSON: THOMAS, I APOLOGIZE. I GUESS I DID COME ACROSS LIKE SOME "SELF RIGHTEOUS DO-GOODER" TRYING TO MAKE MYSELF FEEL GOOD. I'M NOT DENYING THAT RACE PLAYS A MAJOR ROLE IN THIS. IT CAN'T BE AVOIDED. BUT, DAMN-IT MAN, IF YOU WERE BLACK, I WOULD STILL INVITE YOU! YOU ARE A DECENT HUMAN BEING! IF YOU WERE NOT, I SURE AS HELL WOULD NOT INVITE YOU TO MY HOME. BLACK OR WHITE!

THOMAS SR.: I APPRECIATE WHAT YOU JUST SAID. IT'S A SHAME HOW THIS RACIAL STUFF KEEPS PEOPLE FROM

RELATING TO EACH OTHER AS HUMAN BEINGS.

MR. JOHNSON: YES, IT IS A SHAME. IT WILL CONTINUE TO BE THAT WAY UNTIL GOOD PEOPLE OF BOTH RACES DECIDE TO CHANGE THINGS. THAT'S ABOUT AS SINCERE AS I CAN BE. NOW, WILL YOU ACCEPT MY INVITATION?

THOMAS SR.: I WILL. BUT, LET ME CHECK WITH MY FAMILY TO SEE HOW THEY FEEL ABOUT IT.

MR. JOHNSON: GOOD. FAIR ENOUGH. I THINK OUR FAMILIES BOTH HAVE A LOT IN COMMON. MY DAUGHTER MARY IS ABOUT THE AGE OF YOUR SON AND MY WIFE WOULD LIKE TO MEET WITH YOU ALL.

MRS. EDWARDS: DINNER?!

THOMAS SR.: THAT'S RIGHT. THEY WANT US TO COME OVER FOR DINNER. I WANT TO GO. BUT, I WANT US ALL TO AGREE.

THOMAS JR.: YOU'VE WORKED FOR THAT GUY ALL THOSE YEARS, AND NOW HE INVITES YOU TO HIS HOME. THIS IS AFTER HE MAKES YOU THE FIRST WHITE FOREMAN.

THOMAS SR.: OKAY SON, I KNOW WHAT YOU'RE THINKING. I SAID THE SAME THING TO HIM. I'M SATISFIED THAT THE MAN IS

SINCERE AND THAT THERE IS MORE TO THIS THAN "TOKENISM."

MRS. EDWARDS: I'M NOT AFRAID TO RUN FOR THE SCHOOL BOARD. THE "HATE STARES" THAT I GOT WHEN I WENT TO REGISTER DIDN'T DETER ME. SITTING DOWN AT THE DINNER TABLE WITH BLACKS CAN'T BE ANY MORE STRESSFUL.

THOMAS SR.: WHAT ABOUT YOU SON?

THOMAS JR.: IF I CAN HOPE FOR THE BLUES AND REDS TO COME TOGETHER AND STOP KILLING EACH OTHER, THEN BLACKS AND WHITES SHOULD BE ABLE TO HAVE DINNER TOGETHER WITHOUT IT BEING A PROBLEM.

THOMAS SR.: APPARENTLY, NO ONE SEES ANY MAJOR OBSTACLE THAT WOULD PREVENT US FROM GOING. SO, "GUESS WHO'S COMING TO DINNER?"

PHASE 17

PECKERWOOD

"READING, WRITING, AND ARITHMETIC." THESE ARE THE TRADITIONAL AREAS THAT ARE THE FORMAL FOCUS OF SCHOOLS. SOME WOULD SAY THAT THE ESSENCE OF EDUCATION IS IN THESE THREE GENERAL CATEGORIES. BUT AS IN MOST ORGANIZATIONS, HUMAN INTERACTIONS OCCUR ON TWO LEVELS IN SCHOOLS.

ONE LEVEL IS THE FORMAL ONE THAT HAS PRESCRIBED ROLES FOR THE INDIVIDUALS WHICH ARE DESIGNED TO INSURE THE SMOOTH OPERATION OF THE SYSTEM AND THE ACCOMPLISHMENT OF ITS GOALS. INDIVIDUALS WHO DON'T CONFORM TO THEIR PRESCRIBED ROLES ARE USUALLY PENALIZED IN SOME WAY. TEACHERS AND PRINCIPALS WHO DON'T DO THEIR JOB SATISFACTORY CAN BE FIRED. STUDENTS WHO DON'T DO CLASS ASSIGNMENTS CAN FAIL. STUDENTS WHO DON'T CONFORM TO BEHAVIORAL EXPECTATIONS CAN BE SUSPENDED OR EXPELLED. INDIVIDUAL FREEDOM IS DEFINED BY ORGANIZATIONAL LIMITATIONS.

THE OTHER LEVEL OF HUMAN INTERACTION IS INFORMAL. THIS IS WHAT OCCURS BETWEEN THE UNIQUE PERSONALITIES OF INDIVIDUALS. IT MAY OR MAY NOT BE CONCERNED WITH THE FORMAL GOALS OF THE ORGANIZATION. QUITE OFTEN, IT IS FOCUSED ON GOALS THAT ARE NOT FORMALLY RECOGNIZED BY THE ORGANIZATION, LIKE THE COMPETITION TO BE THE MOST LIKED PERSON OR TO BE THE SOCIAL LEADER. INFORMAL BEHAVIOR CAN EVEN BE DIRECTED TOWARDS CHANGING THE FORMAL GOALS OF THE ORGANIZATION.

THE INFORMAL BEHAVIOR OF THOMAS EDWARDS JR. HAS BEEN BOTH PRAISED AND DENOUNCED BECAUSE OF IT'S DEFIANCE OF THE STATUS QUO. HIS CHALLENGING OF THE SCHOOL AUTHORITY ON THE ISSUE OF "WHITE HISTORY" INITIALLY PORTRAYED HIM AS A "RABBLE-ROUSER." BUT DURING THE COURSE OF TIME, HE HAS BECOME A HERO IN THE EYES OF MANY IN THE WHITE COMMUNITY. NOW, ONLY THE MOST SHORT SIGHTED AND CONSERVATIVE OF WHITES DISAGREE WITH HIS GOAL OF GETTING WHITE HISTORY TAUGHT IN THE SCHOOLS.

FOR MANY, PRINCIPAL JACKSON AND THOMAS JR. REPRESENT THE PAST AND THE FUTURE. PRINCIPAL JACKSON IS THE CLASSIC STEREOTYPE OF THE TRADITIONAL WHITE WHO, OUT OF FEAR, ACCEPTS THE SUBORDINATE SOCIAL STATUS OF WHITES. HE BELIEVES THAT WHITES SHOULD "LEAVE WELL ENOUGH ALONE," AND BE GRATEFUL THAT THEY LIVE WITHIN THE PROSPERITY OF THE UNITED STATES OF NEW AFRICA. THOMAS JR. SYMBOLIZES THE BEGINNING OF A NEW PHASE IN RACE RELATIONS IN THE COUNTRY. THIS NEW PHASE GOES BEYOND INDIVIDUAL FREEDOM IN THE PHYSICAL SENSE. IT REPRESENTS "FREEDOM OF THE MIND!" THIS IS FREEDOM FROM THE ATTITUDES AND MIND-SETS THAT CAUSE INDIVIDUALS TO BEHAVE IN WAYS THAT REVEAL A LACK OF SELF-ASSUREDNESS AND SELF-RESPECT.

WITHIN THIS SETTING, THE HIGH SCHOOL HAS BECOME AN IDEOLOGICAL BATTLEGROUND. THE WEAPONS ARE THE INTELLECTUAL AND EMOTIONAL ARGUMENTS USED BY THOMAS JR. ON THE ONE HAND, AND PRINCIPAL JACKSON'S APPEAL TO AUTHORITY AND TRADITION ON THE OTHER. THE PRIZE, WHICH BOTH SIDES REALIZE AS ESSENTIAL FOR EITHER'S VICTORY, IS THE HEARTS AND MINDS OF THE STUDENTS.

THOMAS JR.:	THAT'S RIGHT REGGIE, B.G.M. #1 AND THE BLUES MIGHT BE WILLING TO HAVE A TRUCE WITH YOU REDS AND PUT A STOP TO ALL OF THE FIGHTING AND KILLINGS.
REGGIE:	MIGHT BE WILLING! MAN, YOU CAN'T TRUST THOSE BLUES. THEY ARE DUMB HIGH SCHOOL DROP OUTS. AT LEAST WE REDS HAVE SENSE ENOUGH TO STAY IN SCHOOL AND GET AN EDUCATION. HAVE YOU FORGOTTEN?! THEY CAME TO SCHOOL AND SHOT JASON REEVES IN "COLD BLOOD."
THOMAS JR.:	YES, AND I ALSO REMEMBER A BLUE BEING GUNNED DOWN ON THE STREETS BY A CAR FULL OF REDS. IF IT DOESN'T STOP SOMETIME, THE KILLING WILL GO ON FOREVER. IT'S JUST WHITES KILLING WHITES. JUST THINK ABOUT ALL OF THE OTHER PROBLEMS THAT WE HAVE. KILLING EACH OTHER JUST DOESN'T MAKE SENSE. I'M WHITE, YOU'RE WHITE, B.G.M. #1 IS WHITE. WE'RE ALL WHITE, MAN! LET'S FORGET ABOUT THIS "GANG-BANGING" STUFF.
REGGIE:	WE'VE BEEN BANGING WITH THE BLUES FOR YEARS... SHH... HERE COMES PRINCIPAL JACKSON.

PRINCIPAL JACKSON: GOOD MORNING, THOMAS AND REGGIE. I'M JUST OBSERVING THE STUDENT BODY IN THE HALLS THIS MORNING AS I LOOK FOR ANY SIGNS OF GANG ACTIVITY. I APPRECIATE THE FACT THAT NEITHER OF YOU ARE WEARING ANYTHING THAT SYMBOLIZES GANG AFFILIATION. I AM TRULY SADDENED BY THE LACK OF SELF-RESPECT THAT IS BEING DISPLAYED AMONG SOME OF OUR YOUNG PEOPLE. KIDS KILLING EACH OTHER OVER COLORS! DISRESPECT FOR SCHOOL AUTHORITY! THIS SELF-DESTRUCTIVE BEHAVIOR IS GIVING OUR RACE A BAD NAME. THOMAS, I NEVER THOUGHT I WOULD SAY THIS. I NEED YOUR HELP. MANY OF THE STUDENTS LOOK UP TO YOU. WE NEED TO TALK. MAYBE WE CAN DEVELOP SOME IDEAS TO SOLVE THESE PROBLEMS.

THOMAS JR.: ARE YOU SERIOUS?!

PRINCIPAL JACKSON: YES, I AM.

THOMAS JR.: WILL YOU CONSIDER WHITE HISTORY?

PRINCIPAL JACKSON: WELL, WE CAN TALK ABOUT ALL OF THIS LATER. THE BELL WILL RING SOON AND I DON'T WANT THE TWO OF YOU TO BE LATE FOR CLASS.

REGGIE: WOULDN'T THAT OLD "UNCLE TOM" BE SURPRISED IF HE KNEW THAT I WAS THE LEADER OF THE REDS?

THOMAS JR.: YEAH. YOU'RE PRETTY SLICK. ALL OF THE TEACHERS THINK THAT YOU ARE THE PERFECT STUDENT. YOU MAKE GOOD GRADES. YOU DON'T GET INTO TROUBLE. NOBODY SUSPECTS THAT YOU ARE R.G.M #1.

REGGIE: THAT'S RIGHT. THERE IS A CODE AMONG STUDENTS. WE DON'T "SQUEAL" ON EACH OTHER. ARE YOU PLANNING ON GOING AGAINST THE CODE?

THOMAS JR.: I'M NO SQUEALER.

REGGIE: WELL, JUST REMEMBER <u>THAT</u> WHEN YOU HAVE YOUR TALK WITH JACKSON. IF THERE'S ANYTHING WORST THAN A BLUE, IT'S A SQUEALER.

THOMAS JR.: ARE YOU WILLING TO AT LEAST CONSIDER A TRUCE WITH THE BLUES?

REGGIE: THAT DEPENDS ON THE REST OF MY "HOME-BOYS." WHO KNOWS? THEY MIGHT BE WILLING. THEN AGAIN, THEY MIGHT NOT. NOW, DON'T BE LATE TO CLASS.

MS. MAYFIELD: CLASS, TODAY I WANT TO SPEND SOME CLASS TIME DISCUSSING SOMETHING OTHER THAN HISTORY. I AND THE OTHER STAFF MEMBERS ARE CONCERNED ABOUT THE BEHAVIOR AND ATTITUDES THAT WE SEE DEVELOPING AMONG THE STUDENTS. SINCE THE DEATH OF JASON REEVES, IT SEEMS AS THOUGH STUDENTS HAVE LESS SELF-RESPECT AND HAVE BECOME BENT ON SELF-DESTRUCTION. THE NUMBER OF FIGHTS HAVE DOUBLED AND THE FOUL LANGUAGE BETWEEN STUDENTS HAS INCREASED. I WANT YOUR IDEAS ON WHAT TO DO ABOUT THIS SITUATION.

BETTY: MS. MAYFIELD, I DON'T THINK ANYTHING CAN BE DONE. THESE PECKERWOODS ARE JUST GOING CRAZY.

THOMAS JR.: THAT'S ONE OF THE PROBLEMS. WE SHOULDN'T CALL EACH OTHER "PECKERWOODS." IF WE HAVE A NEGATIVE NAME FOR OURSELVES, THEN WE WILL PROBABLY ACT IN A NEGATIVE WAY.

MS. MAYFIELD: I LIKE THAT IDEA THOMAS. WHAT DO THE REST OF YOU THINK OF WHAT THOMAS JUST SAID?

BETTY: THAT'S JUST ONE OF THE PROBLEMS. THE GANG PROBLEM AND STUDENTS NOT CARING ABOUT LEARNING ARE PROBABLY MORE SERIOUS. BESIDES, HOW DO YOU STOP PEOPLE FROM

CALLING EACH OTHER "PECKERWOOD?"

MS. MAYFIELD: I'VE CAUTIONED STUDENTS MANY TIMES ABOUT USING THE "P" WORD IN CLASS. NOW, I'M GOING TO USE IT. THIS IS NOT INTENDED TO BE NEGATIVE ABOUT WHITE PEOPLE. I INTEND TO USE IT ONLY TO IDENTIFY THE WORD ITSELF. MY DESIRE IS TO PREVENT STUDENTS FROM APPLYING THE WORD TO EACH OTHER.

THOMAS JR.: I UNDERSTAND WHAT YOU'RE TRYING TO SAY MS. MAYFIELD. THE POINT IS THAT CALLING EACH OTHER PECKERWOOD IS A SIGN THAT WE DON'T RESPECT EACH OTHER. IF WE DON'T RESPECT EACH OTHER, THEN IT BECOMES EASY TO FIGHT AND KILL EACH OTHER OVER COLORS LIKE BLUE AND RED. WE CANNOT SOLVE ALL OF OUR PROBLEMS AT ONE TIME. WHY NOT START WITH WHAT WE CALL EACH OTHER?

MS. MAYFIELD: OKAY. DOES ANYONE ELSE AGREE WITH THOMAS?

BETTY: I AGREE WITH THOMAS, BUT AGAIN I ASK WHAT CAN WE DO ABOUT IT?

MS. MAYFIELD: LET'S FIRST TRY TO UNDERSTAND WHY WE CALL EACH OTHER PECKERWOOD. THE WORD WAS BEING USED EVEN WHEN I WAS YOUR AGE. I'M NOT TELLING YOU HOW LONG AGO THAT WAS.

BETTY: MS. MAYFIELD, MY GREAT GRANDMOTHER USES THE WORD AND SHE'S 95 YEARS OLD!

MS. MAYFIELD: WELL, I'M DEFINITELY NOT THAT OLD. THE POINT IS THAT THE WORD HAS BEEN IN USE FOR A LONG TIME. WHY? AFTER WE ANSWER THAT QUESTION, WHAT CAN WE DO ABOUT IT?

THOMAS JR.: THE ANSWER TO BOTH OF THOSE QUESTIONS IS "WHITE HISTORY!"

MS. MAYFIELD: WHITE HISTORY!?

THOMAS JR.: YES. I MEAN THE SAME WHITE HISTORY THAT YOU SENT ME TO THE OFFICE FOR CHALLENGING YOU ABOUT. THE SAME WHITE HISTORY THAT MR. JACKSON IS AFRAID TO HAVE TAUGHT IN THIS SCHOOL. THE SAME WHITE HISTORY THAT THE SCHOOL BOARD SEES AS A THREAT TO THEIR AUTHORITY. EVERYTHING THAT WE'RE TAUGHT IN CLASS ABOUT HISTORY IS ALWAYS NEGATIVE FOR WHITES AND POSITIVE FOR BLACKS. BLACKS TAUGHT US TO CALL EACH OTHER PECKERWOODS.

MS. MAYFIELD: I DON'T KNOW ABOUT THIS WHITE HISTORY. THAT'S SOMETHING WE WOULD NEED TO GO THROUGH MR. JACKSON ABOUT.

BETTY: WELL, WOULDN'T YOU KNOW IT. WE STUDENTS COME UP WITH AN IDEA TO MAKE THE SCHOOL BETTER, AND THE

ADULTS ARE AFRAID TO DO ANYTHING.

MS. MAYFIELD: NO. IT'S NOT THAT WAY. LET ME TALK TO MR. JACKSON ABOUT THIS. THERE ARE STILL OTHER THINGS THAT WE CAN DO TO DISCOURAGE THE USE OF THE WORD "PECKERWOOD."

THOMAS JR.: LIKE WHAT?

MS. MAYFIELD: LET'S TRY TO ENCOURAGE SELF-DISCIPLINE AMONG OURSELVES. I HAVE AN IDEA. I'LL CHALLENGE ALL OF YOU IN THE CLASS TO GO FOR ONE FULL WEEK WITHOUT CALLING SOMEONE A PECKERWOOD. I ALSO CHALLENGE YOU TO CORRECT ANY OF YOUR PEERS IN THIS SCHOOL WHO USE THE WORD IN A NEGATIVE WAY. ONE WEEK FROM TODAY, WE WILL SHARE OUR EXPERIENCES IN A CLASS DISCUSSION.

THOMAS JR.: WILL YOU TRY TO GET WHITE HISTORY TAUGHT?

MS. MAYFIELD: I'LL TRY.

THOMAS JR.: THEN WE CAN ACCEPT YOUR CHALLENGE.

PHASE 18

SELF-CONTEMPT

"IN THE BEGINNING WAS THE WORD." THE POWER OF THE WRITTEN AND SPOKEN WORD HAS LONG BEEN ACKNOWLEDGED. BIBLE SCRIPTURE IDENTIFIES AS ONE AND THE SAME, THE WRITTEN OR SPOKEN WORD OF GOD AND GOD THE ENTITY ITSELF ("...AND THE WORD WAS GOD."). ACCORDING TO THE SCRIPTURES, REALITY ITSELF WAS CALLED INTO EXISTENCE BY THE SPOKEN WORD OF GOD ("LET THERE BE LIGHT.").

USING THE ANALOGY OF MIND AND MATTER AS APPLIED IN QUANTUM THEORY "WORD" BECOMES SYNONYMOUS WITH MIND. BOTH REPRESENT THE IDEAS THAT GIVE RISE TO PHYSICAL REALITIES. THE INFINITESIMALLY SMALL STEP FROM THE MENTAL TO THE PHYSICAL BECOMES AN IMMEASURABLE "QUANTUM LEAP." IT IS WITHIN THIS FRAMEWORK THAT THE PHRASE "LET THERE BE..." TAKES ON THE FULL SIGNIFICANCE OF IT'S MEANING.

"MA'AT" WAS THE ANCIENT EGYPTIAN TERM THAT SYMBOLIZED THAT HIGHEST ETHICAL DEVELOPMENT. MA'AT MEANING TRUTH, JUSTICE, AND RIGHTEOUSNESS. THE EGYPTIANS BELIEVED THAT MORAL AND ETHICAL CHARACTER WOULD SURVIVE DEATH IN THE COLLECTIVE MEMORY AND CHARACTER OF MEN. TODAY, WORDS LIKE FREEDOM, LIBERTY, EQUALITY AND DEMOCRACY REPRESENT IDEAS WHICH MILLIONS OF HUMAN BEINGS HAVE BEEN WILLING TO FIGHT AND DIE FOR. WORDS HAVE DEFINITELY BEEN JUST AS LETHAL AS STICKS AND STONES AND EVEN ATOMIC WEAPONS DURING THE COURSE OF HUMAN HISTORY. THESE INTELLIGIBLE HUMAN UTTERANCES CARRY THE POTENTIAL FOR HUMAN DESTRUCTION. THEY ALSO CARRY THE POTENTIAL FOR HUMAN

SALVATION. THE WORD "PEACE" FALLS WITHIN THIS LATTER CATEGORY.

IT IS THE POTENTIAL FOR HUMAN DESTRUCTION THAT RAISES CONCERN ABOUT THE USE OF CERTAIN WORDS. IT IS IN THIS CONTEXT THAT THE HISTORY AND FUTURE OF THE WORD "PECKERWOOD" BECOMES A SERIOUS MATTER OF CONCERN. FOR THE SOCIALLY CONSCIOUS IN THE WHITE COMMUNITY, THE WORD HAS NO FUTURE. IN THE HISTORICAL PAST IT WAS SYNONYMOUS WITH SLAVE. LIKE WHITE SKIN, IN NEW AFRICA THE WORD BECAME A BADGE OF SHAME. LONG AFTER THE ABOLITION OF SLAVERY, THE WORD HAD A HIGH FREQUENCY OF USE AMONG WHITES THEMSELVES. IT HAD BECOME A VERBAL EXPRESSION OF WHITE SELF-CONTEMPT.

IT IS THIS SELF-CONTEMPT THAT IS PARTIALLY TO BLAME FOR THE SOCIAL ILLS THAT PLAGUE WHITE NEW AFRICANS TODAY. THE INFIGHTING REPRESENTED BY STREET GANG WARFARE IS ONE OF THE WORST MANIFESTATIONS OF WHITE SELF-CONTEMPT. EVEN INDIVIDUAL CONFRONTATIONS ARE FREQUENTLY PRECEDED BY EPITHETS THAT INCLUDE THE WORD "PECKERWOOD." SOME MIGHT ARGUE THAT THE WORD ITSELF AND THE SELF-CONTEMPT THAT IT EXPRESSES ARE TWO SEPARATE THINGS. BEHAVIOR THAT IS SELF-CONTEMPTUOUS IS NOT DEPENDENT ON THE UTTERANCE OF A SINGLE WORD. FROM A STATISTICAL STANDPOINT, ONE COULD PROBABLY SAFELY STATE THAT THERE IS NO ABSOLUTE CORRELATION BETWEEN USE OF THE WORD PECKERWOOD AND INDIVIDUAL WHITE ACTS OF SELF-CONTEMPT. HOWEVER, THERE CAN BE NO DENIAL THAT A HIGH FREQUENCY OF USE OF THE TERM OCCURS IN SITUATIONS WHERE WHITE SELF-CONTEMPT IS OBVIOUS. AT THE LEAST, USE OF THE WORD CAN BE SAID TO BE AN EXAMPLE OF WHITE SELF-CONTEMPT. WITHOUT THE EXAMPLES, THE SELF-CONTEMPT HAS NO MEANINGFUL EXISTENCE.

USE OF THE WORD PECKERWOOD CAN BE PLACED IN THE SAME CATEGORY AS ATTEMPTS TO CHANGE

PHYSICAL APPEARANCE TO BE MORE BLACK-LIKE. PHYSICAL APPEARANCE, PARTICULARLY AS IT APPLIES TO HAIR STYLES WOULD BE AN AREA THAT MS. MAYFIELD AND THOMAS JR. WOULD DISAGREE ON AS FAR AS WHITE SELF-CONTEMPT IS CONCERNED. TRADITIONALLY, WHITE WOMEN HAVE CURLED THEIR HAIR. BUT, BOTH THE TEACHER AND THE STUDENT AGREE THAT ELIMINATING THE SELF-CONTEMPTUOUS USE OF THE WORD "PECKERWOOD" AMONG THE STUDENT BODY IS A WORTHWHILE GOAL THAT WOULD BE AN IMPROVEMENT FOR WHITE STUDENT SELF-RESPECT AND THE WHITE COMMUNITY IN GENERAL. THOMAS JR. IS QUICK TO SEE THIS AGREEMENT AS A FIRST STEP TOWARD WHITE COOPERATION ON ELIMINATING OTHER EXAMPLES OF WHITE SELF-CONTEMPT. IF THE EXAMPLES ARE ELIMINATED, THE SELF-CONTEMPT HAS NO MEANINGFUL EXISTENCE.

PRINCIPAL JACKSON: "PECKERWOOD?"

MS. MAYFIELD: YES. I WOULD LIKE TO HAVE AN ALL SCHOOL CHALLENGE FOR STUDENTS TO GO ONE WEEK WITHOUT USING THE WORD "PECKERWOOD." ALL CLASSES WOULD BE INVOLVED IN THIS PROJECT. TEACHERS COULD HAVE CLASSROOM DISCUSSIONS AND EVEN ASSIGNMENTS HAVING TO DO WITH SELF-RESPECT AND THE WORD PECKERWOOD.

PRINCIPAL JACKSON: AND, YOU THINK THAT WILL HELP MATTERS HERE AT THE SCHOOL?

MS. MAYFIELD: YES. I HAVE ALWAYS DISCOURAGED THE USE OF STREET LANGUAGE AND

PROFANITY IN MY CLASSROOM. I HAVE LONG OBSERVED THAT THE USE OF THE WORD PECKERWOOD HELPS TO CREATE AN ENVIRONMENT THAT IS NEGATIVE. I THINK THAT BY FOCUSING ON THIS TERM, STUDENTS WILL RAISE THEIR LEVEL OF CONCERN ABOUT SELF-RESPECT IN GENERAL. I'M SURE THAT YOU WOULD AGREE THAT DISRESPECTFUL BEHAVIOR IS A PROBLEM AT THIS SCHOOL.

PRINCIPAL JACKSON: THAT'S FOR SURE! BUT, THEY ALSO SEEM TO DISRESPECT THE SCHOOLS AUTHORITY AS WELL AS THEMSELVES. THEY MIGHT SEE THIS AS JUST ANOTHER EXAMPLE OF ADULTS TRYING TO TELL THEM WHAT TO DO. THAT WOULD LEAD TO MORE REBELLION AND DISRESPECT.

MS. MAYFIELD: NO, I THINK THIS TYPE OF SELF EXAMINATION HAS TOUCHED A BASIC CORD WITHIN THE STUDENTS. MOST OF THEM KNOW THAT WHITES IN GENERAL DO NOT HAVE THE LEVEL OF SOCIAL STATUS AS BLACKS. I THINK THEY REALIZE THAT LACK OF SELF-RESPECT DOES NOTHING TO IMPROVE THE PLIGHT OF US ALL. THOMAS EDWARDS SEEMS TO HAVE A BETTER UNDERSTANDING OF THIS THAN ANY OF THEM.

PRINCIPAL JACKSON: THOMAS JR.! OKAY. OKAY. NOW, I'M BEGINNING TO SEE THE PICTURE. IS THIS ANOTHER ONE OF HIS WHITE MILITANT IDEAS? WHITE HISTORY WILL BE NEXT, RIGHT?!

MS. MAYFIELD: IT WAS MY IDEA! DON'T TRY TO BLAME THIS ON THOMAS. BESIDES, YOU AND I BOTH KNOW THAT HE IS RIGHT. WHITE KIDS NEED SELF-RESPECT. THEY CAN'T HAVE SELF-RESPECT IF THEY DON'T RESPECT WHITES IN GENERAL. AND, THEY WON'T RESPECT WHITES IN GENERAL UNLESS....

PRINCIPAL JACKSON: ...UNLESS THEY KNOW THEIR HISTORY.

WELL, I KNEW THIS DAY WOULD COME. THIRTY YEARS AGO I WAS A HIGH SCHOOL STUDENT. I WAS A YOUNG, INQUISITIVE WHITE STUDENT WHO LOVED TO READ. I ESPECIALLY LOVED READING ABOUT HISTORY. THE MORE I READ, THE MORE I WANTED TO KNOW. I FELT THAT KNOWING HISTORY WAS LIKE KNOWING MYSELF. I BECAME QUITE KNOWLEDGEABLE ABOUT THE HISTORY OF AFRICA AND NEW AFRICA. BUT, SOMETHING WAS MISSING. I WAS MISSING! NOT ME IN THE LITERAL SENSE, BUT MY SENSE OF WHERE I AND WHITES CAME FROM. YES, THEY TAUGHT

US ABOUT SLAVERY. BUT, SLAVERY WASN'T SOMETHING TO BE PROUD OF. I KNEW THERE HAD TO BE MORE. THERE WAS!

I BEGAN TO DO MY OWN RESEARCH. IN THOSE DAYS IT WASN'T EASY. WE DIDN'T HAVE TODAY'S EURO-CENTRICS AND WHITE MILITANTS WRITING BOOKS ABOUT WHITE HISTORY. WHAT LITTLE I LEARNED, I HAD TO LEARN INDIRECTLY. I HAD TO ANALYZE THE CONTRADICTIONS AND UNEXPLAINED FACTS FROM BLACK HISTORY BOOKS. I HAD TO PAINSTAKINGLY SEARCH OUT THOSE DUSTY OLD DOCUMENTS HIDDEN AWAY IN THE ATTICS AND BASEMENTS OF LIBRARIES.

LITTLE BY LITTLE, I BEGAN TO PUT THE MISSING PIECES TOGETHER. LONG BEFORE THE ANCIENT BLACK EGYPTIANS, CIVILIZED NATIONS EXISTED IN NORTHERN EUROPE. YES, I MEAN BLUE-EYED, BLOND, FAIR-SKINNED PEOPLE WERE ACTUALLY CIVILIZED! WHAT WAS EVEN MORE AMAZING WAS THAT THE HISTORICAL EVIDENCE SUGGESTS THAT MAN MAY HAVE ORIGINATED IN EUROPE AND WAS PROBABLY WHITE!

HOWEVER, NOTHING LASTS FOREVER. IN PHYSICS THEY CALL IT THE "SECOND LAW OF

THERMODYNAMICS." YOU KNOW. SYSTEMS NATURALLY TEND TO WIND DOWN. THE WHITE SYSTEM DID WIND DOWN. WHITE CIVILIZATION DECLINED INTO BARBARISM JUST AS THE BLACKS WERE ON THE INCLINE TOWARD CIVILIZATION AND WORLD DOMINATION.

THERE IS AN OLD ADAGE THAT SAYS "WHAT GOES AROUND, COMES AROUND." NOW, I KNOW THE TRUTH. WHITES AND BLACKS HAVE JUST SIMPLY CHANGED POSITIONS ON THE CIRCLE.

MS. MAYFIELD: MR. JACKSON, HOW COULD YOU HAVE EXPERIENCED ALL OF THAT AND YET BE SO INSENSITIVE ABOUT THE NEEDS OF OUR STUDENTS?

PRINCIPAL JACKSON: IT'S CALLED CONFORMITY, MS. MAYFIELD. I WAS ONCE YOUNG AND FULL OF IDEAS ABOUT CHANGING THE WORLD. THOMAS JR. REMINDS ME A LOT OF MY YOUNGER SELF. LATER, I BECAME A 21 YEAR OLD FIREBRAND OF A TEACHER, WHO WAS GOING TO "TRULY EDUCATE" WHITE STUDENTS.

MS. MAYFIELD: WHAT HAPPENED?

PRINCIPAL JACKSON: I WAS JUST ONE LONE ZEALOT IN A COMMUNITY OF WHITE CONSERVATIVES, WHO DID NOT

BELIEVE IN "ROCKING THE BOAT." I SOON FOUND MYSELF SOCIALLY OSTRACIZED BY MY FELLOW TEACHERS AND THE PRINCIPAL. THEY SUCCEEDED IN EVEN TURNING MY STUDENTS AGAINST ME. NEEDLESS TO SAY, FOR A YOUNG 21 YEAR OLD, THE PRESSURE WAS TOO MUCH TO BEAR. I GAVE UP MY IDEALISM AND TAUGHT THE STANDARD CURRICULUM. I BECAME A MEMBER OF THE STATUS QUO!

MS. MAYFIELD: THIS IS TRULY A REVELATION! YOU PROBABLY LOOK AT YOUNG THOMAS AND SEE YOUR TRUE LOST SELF.

PRINCIPAL JACKSON: YES I DO. THAT'S WHY I HAVE BEEN SO HARD ON HIM. I HATE BEING REMINDED OF THE FACT THAT I GAVE UP MY IDEALS IN EXCHANGE FOR JOB SECURITY. BUT, ON THE OTHER HAND, I ENVY HIM. HE IS STANDING UP FOR WHAT HE BELIEVES IN. I DIDN'T HAVE THE COURAGE TO DO SO.

MS. MAYFIELD: MR. JACKSON, DO YOU HAVE THE COURAGE TO LET US HAVE THAT ALL SCHOOL CHALLENGE TO STOP USING THE WORD "PECKERWOOD."

PRINCIPAL JACKSON: YES, I DO.

PHASE 19

THE FIRST DINNER

ONE FAMILY IS BLACK. THE OTHER FAMILY IS WHITE. AT FIRST GLANCE, THAT SEEMS TO BE THE ONLY SIGNIFICANT DIFFERENCE BETWEEN THE TWO. SITTING AT THE CIRCULAR TABLE TOGETHER, THIS OBVIOUS PHYSICAL DIFFERENCE MAKES FOR A VIVID CONTRAST. THE EDWARDS ON ONE HALF OF THE TABLE ARE REPRESENTED BY THOMAS SR., MRS. EDWARDS, AND THOMAS JR. ON THE OTHER HALF OF THE TABLE TO THOMAS JR.'S LEFT ARE MARY, MR. JOHNSON, AND MRS. JOHNSON.

MARY IS AN ATTRACTIVE BLACK GIRL WHO IS A YEAR YOUNGER THAN THOMAS JR. SHE REMINDS HIM OF THE DAILY IMAGES ON TELEVISION AND IN MAGAZINES OF THE POPULAR ALL-NEW AFRICAN GIRL WHOM ALL THE BOYS WANT TO DATE. EVEN WHITE BOYS LOOKED UPON THIS PROTOTYPE AS THE IDEAL FOR FEMALE SEXUALITY. AS MUCH WHITE PRIDE AS HE FANCIES HIMSELF TO HAVE, THOMAS JR. FINDS HIMSELF BLUSHING AS HE SITS NEXT TO THIS BLACK BEAUTY.

THOMAS JR. WHO HAS BECOME A LEADER AMONG HIS PEERS AS AN ADVOCATE FOR WHITE PRIDE AND WHITE HISTORY, IS NOW ENGAGED IN A STRUGGLE WITH SOME OF THE SUBCONSCIOUS EMOTIONS OF HIS OWN PERSONALITY. SITTING NEXT TO HIM IS DARK SKIN, TIGHTLY-CURLED HAIR, AND FULL LIPS REPRESENTING THE SO-CALLED ULTIMATE STANDARD OF FEMALE BEAUTY. BUT, INSTEAD OF THE OBJECTIVE ANALYSIS OF AN ASPIRING INTELLECTUAL, HE FINDS HIMSELF BEING INTRIGUED BY A BLACK GIRL.

FOR WHAT SEEMS LIKE AN ETERNITY, THERE IS SILENCE AT THE TABLE EXCEPT FOR THE MOVEMENT

OF TABLE WARE AS THE TWO FAMILIES METHODICALLY EAT DINNER. SUDDENLY, MARY SPEAKS!

MARY: THOMAS, WHAT SCHOOL DO YOU GO TO?

IT IS A SIMPLE QUESTION. INDEED, IT IS A VERY SIMPLE QUESTION FOR SOMEONE WHO HAS EXPLAINED THE BASIC PRINCIPLES OF QUANTUM THEORY TO HIS OWN FATHER. BUT, COMING FROM THE LIPS OF THIS BLACK BEAUTY, THE QUESTION SEEMS TO DUMBFOUND THOMAS JR. HE SLOWLY SWALLOWS THE FOOD IN HIS MOUTH AND TAKES A DEEP BREATH.

THOMAS JR.: I'M A SENIOR AT GEORGE WASHINGTON HIGH SCHOOL.

MARY: I'M A JUNIOR AT WEST EGYPTIAN HIGH SCHOOL. IT'S QUITE A WAYS FROM GEORGE WASHINGTON.

THOMAS JR.: I KNOW. I SEE A SCHOOL BUS TAKING KIDS THERE EVERY DAY. IT PASSES RIGHT BY GEORGE WASHINGTON.

MR. JOHNSON: MARY, THOMAS IS INTERESTED IN PHYSICS. HE PLANS TO MAJOR IN IT IN COLLEGE.

MARY: PHYSICS! THAT'S A DIFFICULT SUBJECT. I ALWAYS DO POORLY IN SCIENCE. HOW DID YOU BECOME INTERESTED IN PHYSICS?

THOMAS JR.: I GUESS I'VE ALWAYS BEEN CURIOUS ABOUT WHY THINGS ARE THE WAY THEY ARE. I LIKE TO THINK ABOUT HOW THINGS COULD BE DIFFERENT AND HOW TO MAKE THEM DIFFERENT.

ESPECIALLY THINGS THAT I THINK ARE WRONG. LIKE AT MY SCHOOL FOR EXAMPLE. MANY OF THE STUDENTS HAVE NEGATIVE ATTITUDES ABOUT THEMSELVES, OUR NEIGHBORHOOD, AND EDUCATION.

THOMAS SR.: DON'T GET HIM STARTED. HE CAN TALK ALL DAY ABOUT QUANTUM THEORY AND STUFF LIKE THAT.

MRS. JOHNSON: THAT'S INTERESTING. YOU SEEM TO HAVE MADE A CONNECTION BETWEEN PHYSICAL SCIENCE AND SOCIOLOGY.

MRS. EDWARDS: HE'S A VERY SMART BOY. WE'RE VERY PROUD OF HIM.

MARY: I WISH I WAS THAT SMART. MAYBE MY GRADES IN SCHOOL WOULD BE BETTER.

MR. JOHNSON: YOUNG LADY, YOUR PROBLEM IS TALKING TOO MUCH TO YOUR FRIENDS ON THE PHONE EVERY NIGHT. IF YOU USED THAT TIME TO STUDY, YOUR GRADES WOULD IMPROVE.

MRS. JOHNSON: HONEY, DON'T EMBARRASS HER IN FRONT OF COMPANY.

MARY: DAD, YOU JUST DON'T LIKE MY FRIENDS. YOU NEVER HAVE.

MRS. JOHNSON: PLEASE, YOU TWO, NOT IN FRONT OF OUR GUESTS.

MR. JOHNSON: YOU'RE RIGHT. FORGIVE ME. I HOPE THIS HASN'T RUINED DINNER FOR YOU FOLKS.

THOMAS SR.: OH NO. I UNDERSTAND. WE'VE HAD OUR DIFFERENCES WITH THOMAS JR. ALSO. IT COMES WITH HAVING TEENAGERS.

MRS. JOHNSON: LET'S CHANGE THE SUBJECT. MRS. EDWARDS, ARE YOU INVOLVED WITH ACTIVITIES OUTSIDE OF YOUR HOME? I FIND MY TIME PREOCCUPIED WITH JUST BEING A HOUSEWIFE.

MRS. EDWARDS: UNTIL RECENTLY, I WAS JUST AS PREOCCUPIED WITH BEING A HOUSEWIFE AS YOU ARE. THAT ALL CHANGED WHEN MY TWO THOMAS' CONVINCED ME TO RUN FOR THE SCHOOL BOARD.

MRS. JOHNSON: YOU'RE RUNNING FOR THE SCHOOL BOARD?! NO WOMAN HAS EVER BEEN A CANDIDATE FOR SCHOOL BOARD IN THIS TOWN.

THOMAS JR.: AND NO WHITE PERSON EITHER!

MRS. EDWARDS: NOW SON, LET'S NOT…

MR. JOHNSON: THAT'S QUITE ALRIGHT MRS. EDWARDS. HE'S RIGHT. NO WHITE PERSON HAS EVER RUN FOR SCHOOL BOARD. IT'S ABOUT TIME THAT ONE DID. AT LEAST A FOURTH OF OUR STUDENTS ARE WHITE. THEY NEED TO BE REPRESENTED.

MRS. JOHNSON: MRS. EDWARDS, YOU MUST INDEED BE A BRAVE PERSON. MOST WOMEN, BLACK OR WHITE, WOULD NOT EVEN THINK ABOUT BEING A CANDIDATE IN A SCHOOL BOARD ELECTION.

MRS. EDWARDS: WELL, I'VE GOT THE SUPPORT OF MY FAMILY. THAT MEANS A LOT TO ME.

MR. JOHNSON: YOU'VE GOT OUR SUPPORT TOO. THIS IS GREAT. IT'S THE TYPE OF CHANGE THAT WE NEED TO MAKE IN OUR SOCIETY. THIS COUNTRY ISN'T JUST HOME FOR ONE RACE OF PEOPLE.

MARY: OH, OH! DON'T GET MY DAD STARTED. HE'LL PREACH ALL EVENING.

THOMAS JR.: IF HE IS SERIOUS, I LIKE THAT KIND OF PREACHING.

MR. JOHNSON: I AM SERIOUS, SON.

THOMAS SR.: NOW, BEFORE WE ALL GET TOO SERIOUS, WHAT'S FOR DESSERT?

AS THE EDWARDS FAMILY DRIVES BACK TO THEIR HOME, THOUGHTS OF THEIR DINNER WITH THE JOHNSON'S PREOCCUPY EACH OF THEIR MINDS. THOMAS SR. IS AGAIN THANKFUL FOR HAVING A BOSS LIKE MR. JOHNSON. HE THINKS TO HIMSELF THAT IF WHITE PEOPLE ARE GOING TO MAKE ANY GAINS IN THIS SOCIETY, THEY MUST HAVE LIBERAL MINDED BLACKS ON THEIR SIDE. MR. JOHNSON'S OFFER TO HELP MRS. EDWARDS IN HER BID FOR SCHOOL BOARD IS JUST MORE EVIDENCE THAT MR. JOHNSON IS A "GOOD" MAN.

MRS. EDWARDS IS AMAZED AT HOW SIMILAR THE TWO FAMILIES ARE. SHE AND MRS. JOHNSON ARE BOTH BASICALLY HOUSEWIVES WHO VALUE THEIR FAMILIES AND THEIR ROLES WITHIN THE FAMILY STRUCTURE. THE FACT THAT SHE IS VENTURING OUT FROM THE HOUSEWIFE ROLE AND SEEKING A SEAT ON THE SCHOOL BOARD, HAS EVEN CAUSED HER TO BECOME SORT OF A ROLE MODEL FOR MRS. JOHNSON. THE FACT THAT BOTH MR. AND MRS. JOHNSON ARE SUPPORTIVE OF HER BID FOR THE SCHOOL BOARD IS A PLUS IN HER EVALUATION OF THE JOHNSON FAMILY.

AS FOR THOMAS JR., TRY AS HE MAY, HE CANNOT ERASE THE IMAGE OF MARY FROM HIS THOUGHTS. EVEN AS HE LIES IN BED THAT NIGHT, HE IS BAFFLED BY HIS OWN INFATUATION. AFTER ALL OF HIS AGITATION FOR WHITE PRIDE AND WHITE HISTORY, HOW CAN HE HAVE A "CRUSH" ON A BLACK GIRL? WHAT WOULD THE BLUES AND REDS THINK? WOULD EVERYBODY CONSIDER HIM TO BE A HYPOCRITE? AS THE REST OF THE FAMILY FALLS SOUND ASLEEP, THOMAS JR. IS STILL DEBATING THESE QUESTIONS IN HIS MIND. THE DEBATE IS ABRUPTLY INTERRUPTED BY THE RINGING OF THE PHONE.

THE QUESTION OF WHO COULD BE CALLING THIS LATE AT NIGHT IS NOT DEBATABLE. ALMOST INTUITIVELY, THOMAS JR. KNOWS THE ANSWER.

MARY: HI, THOMAS. THIS IS MARY. DID I WAKE YOU?

THOMAS JR.:   NO. I WAS JUST LYING IN BED THINKING.

MARY: YOU MUST REALLY BE SMART IF YOU'RE THINKING THIS LATE AT NIGHT. WHAT WERE YOU THINKING ABOUT?

THOMAS JR.: UH...UH...NOTHING IN PARTICULAR. I WAS JUST KIND OF DAYDREAMING IN BED LATE AT NIGHT.

MARY: I BET RIGHT NOW YOU'RE WONDERING WHY I CALLED.

THOMAS JR.: WELL, YES I AM.

MARY: THOMAS, YOU'RE GOOD AT SCIENCE AND MATH. I WAS JUST WONDERING IF WE COULD GET TOGETHER SOMETIME AND YOU HELP ME WITH THOSE SUBJECTS. IF MY GRADES DON'T IMPROVE, I JUST KNOW MY DAD WILL GROUND ME AND MAYBE TAKE AWAY MY CAR.

THOMAS JR.: WELL, MARY I DON'T KNOW. YOU LIVE WAY ACROSS TOWN.

MARY: I'VE GOT A CAR. I COULD PICK YOU UP OR MEET YOU SOMEWHERE TO STUDY.

THOMAS JR.: WELL, MARY, I...I DON'T KNOW.

MARY: WHAT'S THE MATTER? ARE YOU AFRAID OF BLACK GIRLS?

THOMAS JR.: NO, I AM NOT!

MARY: THEN WILL YOU MEET ME AT THE CITY LIBRARY FRIDAY NIGHT?

THOMAS JR.: THE LIBRARY?

MARY: YES. HARDLY ANYONE IS THERE ON FRIDAY NIGHTS. WE COULD MEET ON

THE SECOND FLOOR AND USE ONE OF THE CONFERENCE ROOMS. WE WOULD PRACTICALLY BE BY OURSELVES. WELL?

THOMAS JR.:   OKAY. I'LL BE THERE.

MARY: 7 P.M.?

THOMAS JR.:   OKAY. 7 P.M.

PHASE 20

REDEMPTION

IT IS OFFICIAL. WASHINGTON HIGH SCHOOL WILL HAVE AN ALL SCHOOL CHALLENGE FOR STUDENTS TO NOT USE THE WORD "PECKERWOOD". PRINCIPAL JACKSON HAS GIVEN HIS SUPPORT FOR THE ACTIVITY. HE HAS EVEN CALLED FOR AN ALL SCHOOL ASSEMBLY IN WHICH HE WILL STRESS THE IMPORTANCE OF INDIVIDUAL SELF- RESPECT AND SCHOOL PRIDE. FOR THE FIRST TIME, HE EVEN ENCOURAGES RACIAL PRIDE.

LETTERS ARE SENT TO HOMES EXPLAINING THE NATURE AND PURPOSE OF THE CHALLENGE. THESE LETTERS ALSO ASK PARENTS TO AID IN THE SCHOOL'S ENDEAVOR BY DISCOURAGING THE USE OF "PECKERWOOD" IN THE HOME. THIS HAD THE EFFECT OF DEVELOPING A NEW DIALOGUE WITHIN FAMILIES. PARENTS, WHO OUT OF CUSTOM, HAD USED THE WORD AS PART OF THEIR DAILY VOCABULARY, FOUND THEMSELVES BEING QUESTIONED BY THEIR OWN CHILDREN. PROVIDING THEIR CHILDREN WITH A SUITABLE ANSWER PROVED TO BE JUST AS CHALLENGING AS BREAKING THE HABIT OF USING THE WORD. FOR THE FIRST TIME, MANY PARENTS WERE BECOMING ACTIVELY INVOLVED IN THEIR CHILD'S SCHOOL ACTIVITIES.

TEACHERS FOUND THEMSELVES UNITED BY A COMMON GOAL THAT TRANSCENDED THEIR VARIOUS SUBJECTS. THE SCHOOL CHALLENGE BECAME AN INTERDISCIPLINARY ADDITION TO THE SCHOOL'S CURRICULUM. MATH TEACHERS AS WELL AS SOCIAL STUDIES TEACHERS EXCHANGED IDEAS ABOUT TECHNIQUES TO USE IN THE CLASSROOM FOR DISCOURAGING THE USE OF THE WORD AND TO ENCOURAGE PRIDE AND SELF-RESPECT. STUDENTS

CORRECTED EACH OTHER IN AND OUT OF SCHOOL WHEN ONE OF THEM UTTERED THE FORBIDDEN WORD. THE CLIMATE OF THE SCHOOL BEGAN TO CHANGE. THE NEGATIVISM THAT HAD LOOMED OVER THE SCHOOL WAS GRADUALLY BEING REPLACED BY AN UPBEAT MOOD AMONG STAFF AND STUDENTS. PRINCIPAL JACKSON BEGIN TO NOTICE LESS TENSION IN THE HALLWAYS BETWEEN STUDENTS. CONFRONTATIONS AND FIGHTS WERE BECOMING VERY INFREQUENT.

HOWEVER, THESE WELCOME SIGNS OF POSITIVE CHANGE DID NOT CALM THE UNEASY FEELING THAT PRINCIPAL JACKSON NOW HAD. THIS FEELING WAS A RESULT OF MEMORIES OF HIS OWN PAST. THAT PAST WAS AN UNFULFILLED DESIRE TO KNOW HIS RACIAL HERITAGE AND MAKE IT KNOWN TO OTHERS. PRINCIPAL JACKSON NOW KNOWS THAT THE STUDENTS MUST BE EXPOSED TO THEIR HISTORY IN ORDER FOR THEM TO HAVE A LASTING FOUNDATION FOR RESPECTING THEMSELVES AS WHITE PEOPLE. PRINCIPAL JACKSON ALSO KNOWS THAT THIS IS HIS LAST CHANCE TO REDEEM HIMSELF. THIS IS HIS LAST CHANCE TO RECLAIM THE MANHOOD THAT YEARS AGO HE EXCHANGED FOR SOCIAL ACCEPTANCE AND SECURITY. HE KNOWS WHAT HE SHOULD DO. HE ALSO KNOWS THAT THERE IS A FORMIDABLE OBSTACLE IN HIS WAY. HE KNOWS THE AUTHORITY OF THE SCHOOL BOARD.

THOMAS SR.:   OLD HABITS ARE HARD TO BREAK. MANY OF US SAY "PECKERWOOD" WITHOUT EVEN THINKING ABOUT IT. I WONDER IF USING THE WORD REALLY MATTERS THAT MUCH.

THOMAS JR.:   IT DOES MATTER. WHEN YOU THINK ABOUT NOT USING THE WORD IT FORCES YOU TO THINK ABOUT WHAT IT MEANS. TO UNDERSTAND WHAT IT MEANS, YOU HAVE TO KNOW ABOUT

OUR HISTORY. KNOWING OUR HISTORY HELPS US TO VALUE WHO AND WHAT WE ARE.

THOMAS SR.: THANKS FOR THE LECTURE, "PROFESSOR." BUT, WHITE HISTORY ISN'T TAUGHT AT THE SCHOOLS. IS JACKSON PREPARED TO GO THAT FAR?

MRS. EDWARDS: THE QUESTION IS WHETHER OR NOT THE SCHOOL BOARD IS PREPARED TO GO THAT FAR. I GUESS THAT'S ONE REASON WHY I'M RUNNING FOR THE BOARD. IT'S TIME FOR THEM TO START MEETING THE NEEDS OF OUR CHILDREN.

THOMAS JR.: THAT'S TRUE MOM, BUT DAD'S RIGHT. PRINCIPAL JACKSON SHOULD TELL EVERYONE THAT HE SUPPORTS THE TEACHING OF WHITE HISTORY.

THOMAS SR.: BUT, DOES HE <u>REALLY</u> SUPPORT IT?

THOMAS JR.: TOMORROW AT SCHOOL, I'LL ASK HIM.

MRS. EDWARDS: THAT REMINDS ME. TOMORROW IS FRIDAY AND FAMILY DISCOUNT NIGHT AT THE FAMILY RESTAURANT. LET'S HAVE DINNER THERE.

THOMAS JR.: ER...HUH...FRIDAY NIGHT? I JUST REMEMBERED. I'M SUPPOSED TO DO SOMETHING FRIDAY NIGHT.

THOMAS SR.: DO SOMETHING? SON, ARE YOU TRYING TO TELL US THAT YOU HAVE A DATE?

THOMAS JR.: WELL, SORT OF. I'M JUST GOING TO THE LIBRARY.

THOMAS SR.: THE LIBRARY?! SOME DATE. WHAT ARE THE TWO OF YOU GOING TO DO? READ ABOUT QUANTUM THEORY?

MRS. EDWARDS: NOW, THOMAS, THAT'S ENOUGH. WHO EVER HE IS TAKING TO THE LIBRARY AND WHATEVER THEY DO IS THEIR BUSINESS. THERE ARE A LOT WORST PLACES THAT YOUNG PEOPLE COULD GO TO.

PRINCIPAL JACKSON: DO I SUPPORT THE TEACHING OF WHITE HISTORY? THOMAS, YOU REMIND ME OF MY FORMER, YOUNGER SELF. BELIEVE IT OR NOT, I WAS A BIT OF A REBEL. OF COURSE I SUPPORT THE TEACHING OF WHITE HISTORY. IF IT WAS STRICTLY MY DECISION, **ALL OF THE HISTORY TEACHERS WOULD INCLUDE THAT SUBJECT MATTER IN THEIR INSTRUCTION.**

THOMAS JR.: I AM GLAD TO HEAR THAT.

PRINCIPAL JACKSON: BUT, THOMAS, DON'T FORGET. THE SCHOOL BOARD HAS TO GIVE IT'S APPROVAL. THERE ARE NO WHITE PEOPLE ON THE SCHOOL BOARD.

THOMAS JR.:	NOT YET. MY MOM HAS FILED TO BE A CANDIDATE IN THE UPCOMING ELECTION.
PRINCIPAL JACKSON:	SHE DID WHAT?!
THOMAS JR.:	SHE IS RUNNING FOR THE SCHOOL BOARD.
PRINCIPAL JACKSON:	WELL I'LL BE. I GUESS YOU'RE NOT THE ONLY REBEL IN YOUR FAMILY.
THOMAS JR.:	IF SHE GETS ELECTED, THEN SOMEONE WOULD REPRESENT US. SHE COULD RAISE THE ISSUE OF WHITE HISTORY. AS IT IS NOW, WE DON'T HAVE A VOICE ON THE SCHOOL BOARD.
PRINCIPAL JACKSON:	BUT, EVEN IF SHE GETS ELECTED, SHE'LL STILL ONLY BE ONE WHITE PERSON ON A SEVEN MEMBER BOARD. WE HAVE TO GET SUPPORT FROM THE BLACK BOARD MEMBERS. WE'LL HAVE TO GO FURTHER THAN THAT. WE NEED SUPPORT FROM THE BLACK COMMUNITY. IF THE BOARD KNOWS THAT OTHER BLACKS SUPPORT US, THEN THEY ARE MORE LIKELY TO GIVE US WHAT WE WANT.
THOMAS JR.:	MR. JOHNSON, MY DAD'S BOSS, SAYS THAT HE WILL HELP MY MOM IN RUNNING FOR THE SCHOOL BOARD.

Eddie J. Thomas

PRINCIPAL JACKSON: HE DID? WELL NOW, THAT MAKES A DIFFERENCE. MR. JOHNSON IS A RESPECTED AND VERY INFLUENTIAL MEMBER OF THIS TOWN'S BUSINESS COMMUNITY. HE HAS PROBABLY DONATED MORE MONEY TO HELP THE SCHOOLS THAN ALL THE OTHER TOWN CONTRIBUTORS COMBINED. IF HE WILL SUPPORT CURRICULUM CHANGES TO INSURE THE TEACHING OF WHITE HISTORY, THEN I'M SURE THAT THE BOARD WILL BE MORE INCLINED TO GIVE IT SERIOUS CONSIDERATION.

THOMAS JR.: BUT, NO ONE HAS ASKED HIM ABOUT WHITE HISTORY. HE HAS ONLY SAID THAT HE WILL HELP MY MOTHER IN RUNNING FOR THE SCHOOL BOARD.

PRINCIPAL JACKSON: IF YOU REALLY WANT WHITE HISTORY INCLUDED IN THE TEACHING OF HISTORY, WE NEED TO GET HIS SUPPORT. SOMEONE NEEDS TO DISCUSS THE MATTER WITH HIM. EITHER YOU OR YOUR MOTHER NEEDS TO CONVINCE HIM. DO YOU KNOW THE MAN WELL ENOUGH TO TALK WITH HIM ABOUT IT?

THOMAS JR.: WELL, I'VE MET HIM BEFORE. I'VE BEEN TO HIS HOUSE. WE HAD DINNER WITH HIS FAMILY.

PRINCIPAL JACKSON: DINNER?! WELL I GUESS THE NEXT THING YOU'LL TELL ME IS THAT YOU'RE ENGAGED TO MARRY HIS DAUGHTER. THOMAS. IF YOU WANT WHITE HISTORY, YOU KNOW WHAT YOU HAVE TO DO.

PHASE 21

RENDEZVOUS

AS HE WALKS UP THE STEPS TO THE LIBRARY, THOMAS JR. THINKS ABOUT THE LAST REMARKS OF PRINCIPAL JACKSON. BEING MARRIED TO MARY JOHNSON IS SO FARFETCHED THAT IT CAN ONLY BE VIEWED IN THE MANNER THAT PRINCIPAL JACKSON PRESENTED IT. IT IS A LAUGHABLE JOKE. BUT, IF ANYONE HAD SUGGESTED SEVERAL WEEKS AGO THAT HE WOULD BE MEETING THE DAUGHTER OF A PROMINENT BLACK BUSINESSMAN AT THE LIBRARY ON A FRIDAY NIGHT, HE WOULD HAVE LAUGHED AT THE IDEA.

SURELY, WHEN PRINCIPAL JACKSON SAID "...YOU KNOW WHAT YOU HAVE TO DO", HE WAS NOT REFERRING TO A RELATIONSHIP WITH MARY JOHNSON. BUT, THAT NOTION LINGERS IN THOMAS' MIND AND HE CANNOT IGNORE IT. HE CAN NOT EVEN ADEQUATELY JUSTIFY TO HIMSELF WHY HE AGREED TO MEET HER. THESE THOUGHTS GIVE HIM, FOR THE FIRST TIME, AN UNCOMFORTABLE FEELING OF LOSING SELF-CONTROL.

FOR ONE WHO HAS DISCIPLINED HIS REASONING SKILLS TO PURSUE THE STUDY OF QUANTUM THEORY, THE POWER OF IRRATIONAL EMOTION IS INDEED BEWILDERING. HE TRIES TO RATIONALIZE THE MEETING AS SIMPLY FOR HELPING ANOTHER STUDENT WITH SCHOOL WORK. BOTH HE AND THE OTHER STUDENT KNOW THAT THIS IS ABOUT MORE THAN ACADEMICS. BUT, JUST HOW MUCH MORE? IT IS THE ANSWER TO THAT QUESTION THAT INTRIGUES ONE JUST AS MUCH AS THE OTHER.

MARY: THOMAS! I WAS AFRAID THAT YOU WOULD NOT COME. IT'S KIND OF

SPOOKY HERE ON FRIDAY NIGHTS. I HAVE NOT SEEN ANOTHER PERSON ON THIS FLOOR SINCE I ARRIVED.

THOMAS JR.: I'M SORRY IF I AM A LITTLE LATE. I WALKED HERE.

MARY: WERE YOU AFRAID?

THOMAS JR.: AFRAID OF WHAT?

MARY: YOU KNOW. AFRAID THAT SOMEONE MIGHT SEE YOU WITH ME. LIKE YOUR FRIENDS OR....

THOMAS JR.: LOOK, I'VE GOT NOTHING TO BE AFRAID OF. WHAT ABOUT YOU?

MARY: OH, DO NOT TRY TO PRETEND TO BE SO COOL ABOUT EVERYTHING. YOU HAVE NEVER BEEN OUT WITH A BLACK GIRL AND I HAVE NEVER BEEN OUT WITH A WHITE GUY.

THOMAS JR.: WAIT A MINUTE! IS THIS JUST A CURIOSITY THING WITH YOU? I THOUGHT YOU WANTED HELP WITH YOUR MATH.

MARY: I DO. BUT, NOT TONIGHT. HEY! LET'S GO FOR A DRIVE AROUND TOWN. MY CAR IS PARKED OUTSIDE.

THOMAS JR.: YOU'RE KIND OF PUSHY. I BET YOU GET YOUR WAY AT HOME MOST OF THE TIME.

MARY: YEAH, MY MOM COMPLAINS THAT DADDY HAS SPOILED ME AND TURNED ME INTO A "DADDY'S GIRL."

THOMAS JR.:   WELL, "DADDY'S GIRL," WHAT MAKES YOU THINK THAT I WILL GO RIDING AROUND TOWN WITH YOU?

MARY: THE SAME THING THAT MADE ME THINK THAT YOU WOULD SHOW UP TONIGHT.

THOMAS JR.:   MAN! YOU ARE PUSHY!

MARY: I KNOW. HERE ARE MY KEYS. YOU DRIVE.

WHITE MEN AND BLACK WOMEN. THE COMBINATION HAS TRADITIONALLY BEEN A SOURCE FOR CONTROVERSY THOUGH OUT THE HISTORY OF NEW AFRICA. DURING THE ERA OF WHITE SLAVERY IN THE NATION, IT WAS COMMON PRACTICE FOR BLACK MEN TO ENGAGE IN SEXUAL RELATIONSHIPS WITH THEIR FEMALE WHITE SLAVES. EVEN IN THE PRESENT SOCIETY, BLACK MEN AND WHITE WOMEN OFTEN ENGAGE IN SECRETIVE RELATIONSHIPS. THESE RELATIONSHIPS, LIKE THOSE OF THE SLAVE ERA, ARE ONE SIDED AFFAIRS CHARACTERIZED BY ONE PARTY BEING A MEMBER OF THE DOMINANT GROUP AND THE OTHER A MEMBER OF THE SUBORDINATE GROUP. (HOWEVER, IN A FEW INSTANCES, MARRIAGES HAVE RESULTED).

ALTHOUGH, RELATIONSHIPS BETWEEN BLACK MEN AND WHITE WOMEN HAD THE SUBTLE CONSENT OF THE DOMINANT BLACK MALE GROUP, THE REVERSE (WHITE MEN AND BLACK WOMEN) WAS HISTORICALLY MET WITH CLEAR-CUT DISAPPROVAL. MANY WHITE MEN HAVE

BEEN THE VICTIMS OF BLACK AGGRESSION DUE TO REAL OR IMAGINED TRYST WITH BLACK WOMEN. THE SOCIAL TABOO HAS GRADUALLY LOST IT'S POWER TO CONTROL BEHAVIOR. INDEED, AMONG SOME WHITE MEN, HAVING A RELATIONSHIP WITH A BLACK WOMAN IS EITHER VIEWED AS OBTAINING A VALUED SOCIAL PRIZE OR AS AN OPPORTUNITY TO "THUMB ONE'S NOSE" AT THE STATUS QUO. AMONG THE MORE MILITANT OR EXTREMELY EURO-CENTRIC WHITES, INTERRACIAL COUPLING IS VIEWED AS SELLING-OUT OR BETRAYAL OF WHITE PRIDE.

THOMAS JR.: I CAN NOT BELIEVE IT. YOU'VE GOT ME DRIVING AROUND, AND THE FIRST PLACE YOU WANT TO GO IS THE WHITE PART OF TOWN.

MARY: OH, STOP COMPLAINING. DON'T YOU EVER WANT TO DO SOMETHING EXCITING. HEY! SEE THAT BLACK AND WHITE CONVERTIBLE PARKED DOWN THE STREET.

THOMAS JR: YEAH.

MARY: PULL UP AND PARK BEHIND IT.

THOMAS JR.: HEY! THAT GUY GETTING OUT OF THE CONVERTIBLE....I KNOW HIM. THAT'S...

PRETTY BOY: WELL, I'LL BE DAMNED. IF IT ISN'T THE SMART MAN HIMSELF.

THOMAS JR.: PRETTY BOY, WHAT ARE YOU DOING HERE?

PRETTY BOY: PECKERWOOD, PLEASE! I SHOULD BE ASKING YOU THAT QUESTION. THIS IS WHERE I HANG OUT EVERY FRIDAY NIGHT. ME AND MY DATE WERE JUST SITTING HERE LISTENING TO THE RADIO. I WANT YOU TO MEET JOYCE.

THOMAS JR: HELLO, JOYCE.

PRETTY BOY: YOU DON'T HAVE TO STARE. YEAH, SHE'S BLACK.

JOYCE: HI.

THOMAS JR.:   LET ME INTRODUCE YOU TO…

PRETTY BOY: MARY JOHNSON.

MARY: HEY, WHAT'S UP PRETTY? JOYCE, WHAT TIME DID YOU GET HERE? I CALLED YOUR HOME BEFORE I LEFT AND NO ONE ANSWERED THE PHONE.

THOMAS JR.:   YOU ALL KNOW EACH OTHER?

MARY: OH, THOMAS. YOU'RE SO NAÏVE.

PRETTY BOY: PECKERWOOD, I THOUGHT YOU WERE TOO WHITE TO DATE SOMEONE LIKE MARY.

JOYCE: NOW PRETTY, THAT'S ENOUGH. WHY DON'T ALL FOUR OF US GET IN YOUR CAR AND JUST CRUISE AROUND FOR A WHILE.

MARY: YEAH, THAT'S A GOOD IDEA. DO YOU FEEL LIKE CRUISING THOMAS?

THOMAS JR.:   YOU MEAN YOU'RE ASKING ME TO DO SOMETHING FOR A CHANGE?

MARY: OKAY! OKAY! DO YOU WANT TO GO?

THOMAS JR.:   LET'S GO.

PHASE 22

LOVE OR LUST

FRIDAY NIGHT FOR MOST TEENS IS A SPECIAL NIGHT. WHILE MOST ADULTS IDENTIFY THE DAY ITSELF WITH THE PHASE "THANK GOD IT'S FRIDAY", TEENAGERS RESERVE THE NIGHT HOURS AS THEIR TIME FOR RELAXATION AND SOCIAL RECREATION. WITH NO SCHOOL OR CHURCH TO BE LATE TO ON SATURDAY MORNING, FRIDAY NIGHT IS THE IDEAL TIME FOR ONE POPULAR LATE NIGHT ACTIVITY. "CRUISING" IS THE NAME FOR THESE SEEMINGLY PURPOSELESS DRIVES THROUGHOUT THE CITY. THEY MAY SEEM PURPOSELESS TO ADULT EVALUATORS. HOWEVER, FOR TEENAGERS IT IS THE IDEAL WAY TO MAXIMIZE ONE'S SOCIAL INTERACTIONS AMONG PEERS. IN OTHER WORDS, CRUISING IS HOW ONE FINDS OUT "WHERE THE ACTION IS".

ACTION DEFINITELY AWAITS THE BLACK AND WHITE PASSENGERS IN THIS BLACK AND WHITE CONVERTIBLE AS THEY CRUISE THE MAIN STREETS OF THE TOWN. BLACK GIRLS SITTING CLOSE TO WHITE GUYS IS AN ATTENTION GETTER, EVEN IN THE DARK OF THE NIGHT. EACH STOP LIGHT THE CONVERTIBLE COMES TO A HALT AT HAS IT'S SHARE OF STARING OCCUPANTS OF OTHER VEHICLES. MOST OF THE STARES ARE SIMPLY EXPRESSIONS OF CURIOSITY. BUT, MANY OF THE STARING BLACK FACES ARE DISAPPROVING EXPRESSIONS OF CONTEMPT AND OUTRIGHT HATRED. AT A FEW STOP LIGHTS THE CONTEMPT AND OUTRIGHT HATRED RESULTS IN A VERBAL EXCHANGE OF RACIAL EPITHETS.

BLACK DRIVER: HEY, YOU BLACK BITCHES. WHAT ARE YOU DOING WITH THOSE PECKERWOODS?

PRETTY BOY: THEY ARE DOING THE SAME THING THAT YOU AND YOUR MAMA DO TO EACH OTHER.

BLACK DRIVER: FUCK YOU, PECKERWOOD.

MARY: FUCK YOURSELF. NO ONE ELSE WANTS TO.

THOMAS JR.:   SHHH....WE DON'T NEED ANY TROUBLE.

MARY: HE DESERVES IT. HE SHOULD MIND HIS OWN BUSINESS.

JOYCE: THE LIGHT JUST CHANGED. LET'S GO.

PRETTY BOY: WHAT IS THE MATTER PECKERWOOD? ARE YOU AFRAID OF A GOOD FIGHT?

THOMAS JR.:   I AM NOT AFRAID. I JUST DO NOT BELIEVE IN FIGHTING, UNLESS IT IS IN SELF-DEFENSE. AND, DON'T CALL ME PECKERWOOD AGAIN.

PRETTY BOY: IF I DO, ARE YOU GOING TO FIGHT ME?

MARY: THOMAS, YOU WOULD FIGHT TO DEFEND ME, WOULDN'T YOU?

THOMAS: MAYBE.

PRETTY BOY: I WOULD FIGHT FOR JOYCE.

JOYCE: HEY PEOPLE, LET'S STOP TALKING ABOUT FIGHTING. WE ARE SUPPOSE TO BE HAVING FUN.

PRETTY BOY: I HAVE AN IDEA. LET'S GO TO LOVER'S LANE IN THE PARK.

THOMAS JR.:   LOVER'S LANE?!

PRETTY BOY: YEAH. OR, DOES THAT FRIGHTEN YOU TOO?

MARY: AHH...COME ON THOMAS. I WILL NOT BITE YOU.

FOR MANY YEARS LOVER'S LANE HAS BEEN AN AREA OF THE PARK FREQUENTLY USED BY TEENAGER COUPLES FOR EITHER KINDLING A TRUE ROMANCE OR PURELY FOR SEXUAL ENCOUNTERS. ALTHOUGH LOCATED WITHIN THE PREDOMINATELY WHITE PART OF TOWN, IT WASN'T UNUSUAL FOR BLACKS TO MAKE USE OF IT'S PRIVACY. BLACK GIRLS SEEKING THE EXCITEMENT OF VIOLATING THE SOCIAL TABOO OF "BLACK WOMEN-WHITE MEN" LOVE AFFAIRS, WERE FREQUENT VISITORS. BLACK MEN USUALLY PREFERRED TO CARRY ON THEIR INTERRACIAL TRYST CLOSER TO HOME.

IT IS THIS SETTING THAT PROVIDES THOMAS JR. HIS FIRST ROMANTIC ENCOUNTER. A WHITE BOY WITH HIS ARMS AROUND THE DAUGHTER OF HIS FATHER'S BLACK BOSS IS INDEED IRONIC. AND, TO BE ACCOMPANIED BY THE PROTOTYPE OF A WHITE PIMP AND ONE OF HIS WOMEN, GOES BEYOND IRONIC. THE WHOLE SCENE IS CLOSER TO BEING BIZARRE. IS THIS WHAT IT MEANS FOR BLACKS AND WHITES TO BE ROMANTICALLY INVOLVED? DOES IT ALL BOIL DOWN TO JUST BEING A MATTER OF LUST AND CURIOSITY WITH THE INITIATIVE MAINLY BEING TAKEN BY THE MEMBERS OF THE

SOCIALLY DOMINATE GROUP? THESE ARE THOUGHTS THAT DWELL UPON THE MIND OF THOMAS JR. AS PRETTY BOY AND JOYCE LEAVE THE PARKED CAR TO BE ALONE AT A FAMILIAR BENCH IN THE DARKNESS OF THE PARK.

PRETTY BOY: JOYCE AND I WILL BE BACK IN A FEW MINUTES. YOU TWO BEHAVE YOURSELVES. DON'T DO ANYTHING WE WOULD NOT DO.

THOMAS JR.: I GET THE FEELING THAT PRETTY AND JOYCE HAVE BEEN HERE SEVERAL TIMES BEFORE.

MARY: JOYCE HAS BEEN GOING OUT WITH HIM FOR ABOUT TWO MONTHS NOW.

THOMAS JR.: HOW DO HER PARENTS FEEL ABOUT IT?

MARY: THEY DON'T KNOW ABOUT IT. IF THEY DID, THEY WOULD PROBABLY GROUND HER.

THOMAS JR.: WHAT DOES SHE SEE IN PRETTY BOY ANYWAY? HE IS A HIGH SCHOOL DROP-OUT. HE HAS LOTS OF GIRL FRIENDS.

MARY: HE IS FUN AND HE IS EXCITING.

THOMAS JR.: YOU MEAN HE IS AN EXCITING <u>WHITE</u> GUY. IS THAT WHY YOU ARE SITTING SO CLOSE TO ME RIGHT NOW? IS THIS JUST A BLACK AND WHITE THING?

MARY: THOMAS ARE YOU PREJUDICE?

THOMAS JR.: NO, I AM NOT. I JUST BELIEVE THAT PEOPLE SHOULD BE HONEST WITH EACH OTHER.

MARY: YOU SURE KNOW HOW TO TAKE THE FUN OUT OF EVERYTHING.

THOMAS JR.: I AM JUST REALISTIC. I'VE ALWAYS BEEN THAT WAY. COME ON MARY, YOU KNOW WHAT THE REAL WORLD IS LIKE FOR BLACKS AND WHITES. WE WHITES ARE ALWAYS REMINDED THAT BLACKS ARE SUPPOSE TO BE BETTER THAN WHITES. WE SEE IT ON TELEVISION, IN THE MOVIES, AND WE EVEN HAVE IT TAUGHT US IN SCHOOL. I FOR ONE, WANT TO CHANGE ALL OF THAT. ESPECIALLY, WHAT WE ARE TAUGHT IN SCHOOL. MARY, WHAT DO YOU KNOW ABOUT WHITE HISTORY?

MARY: YOU MEAN ABOUT THE SLAVES?

THOMAS JR.: SEE, THAT IS THE PROBLEM. ALL WE LEARN IN SCHOOL IS ABOUT BLACKS AND THEIR HISTORY. THE ONLY THING WE STUDY CONCERNING WHITES IS SLAVERY. THIS BELIEF THAT BLACK IS RIGHT AND WHITE IS WRONG AFFECTS ALL OF US.

MARY: THOMAS, IF I FELT THAT WAY WOULD I BE SITTING HERE NOW WITH YOUR ARM AROUND ME?

THOMAS JR.: I WONDER IF YOU ARE ONLY SITTING HERE BECAUSE I AM WHITE.

MARY: WHAT DOES THAT MEAN?

THOMAS JR.: LIKE I HAVE SAID BEFORE, MAYBE THIS IS JUST A CURIOSITY THING WITH YOU. MAYBE YOU JUST WANT TO SEE WHAT IT IS LIKE TO BE WITH A WHITE GUY. IS THAT WHY YOU ARE HERE?

MARY: WELL, THERE IS NO DENYING THE FACT THAT YOU ARE WHITE. SO, I AM SURE THAT IT HAD SOMETHING TO DO WITH IT. BUT, AFTER BEING WITH YOU TONIGHT, I HAVE LEARNED A LOT MORE ABOUT YOU THAT I LIKE.

THOMAS JR.: SUCH AS WHAT?

MARY: YOU ARE INTELLIGENT AND YOU ARE HONEST.

THOMAS JR.: SO ARE MANY OTHER BLACK GUYS.

MARY: YOU ARE PERSISTENT TOO. I AM THE SAME. I GUESS WE HAVE SOMETHING IN COMMON.

THOMAS JR.: YEAH, I GUESS WE DO.

MARY: WELL, I GUESS NOW IS AN APPROPRIATE TIME TO KISS. WHAT DO YOU THINK?

THOMAS JR.: I THINK YOU ARE RIGHT.

MARY: I AM SURE THAT KISS WAS A FIRST FOR BOTH OF US.

THOMAS JR.: DO YOU MEAN BLACK AND WHITE?

MARY: THERE YOU GO, JUMPING TO CONCLUSIONS AGAIN. I MEANT THE FIRST KISS BETWEEN THE TWO OF <u>US</u>. I WONDER WHAT IS TAKING PRETTY BOY AND JOYCE SO LONG.

THOMAS JR.:   IF I KNOW PRETTY, THEY ARE PROBABLY DOING MORE THAN KISSING.

MARY: WELL, DO NOT GET ANY IDEAS.

THOMAS JR.:   NOW, WHO IS JUMPING TO CONCLUSIONS?

MARY: THAT MAKES <u>TWO</u> THINGS THAT WE HAVE IN COMMON NOW.

PHASE 23

COMMON GROUND OR BATTLEGROUND

COMMON GROUND. THAT IS THE CONCEPT THAT OFTEN BRIDGES THE GAP BETWEEN OPPOSITES. IT IS THE INGREDIENT THAT CAN BRING UNITY WHERE THERE IS DIVERSITY. TOO OFTEN, IT IS THE INABILITY TO FIND COMMON GROUND OR A BASIS FOR AGREEMENT THAT BECOMES THE SOURCE OF CONTINUED CONFLICT, EVEN WHEN THERE IS A DESIRE FOR PEACE.

AS OUR INTERRACIAL COUPLES CRUISE INTO THE HEART OF THE WHITE NEIGHBORHOOD, EACH GIVES THOUGHT TO THE QUALITY OF COMMONALITY THAT PROVIDES A BASIS FOR THEIR UNIONS. FOR ONE COUPLE, THE THOUGHT IS AS FLEETING AND INSINCERE AS THE LUST THAT CEMENTS THEIR RELATIONSHIP. FULFILLMENT OF SELFISH DESIRE AND THE NOVELTY OF SOMETHING DIFFERENT IS THE GLUE THAT BINDS THIS PAIR TOGETHER.

PRETTY BOY FANCIES HIMSELF AS THE **LADY'S MAN**. HE IS THE CASANOVA WHO TAKES PRIDE IN HIS MANY CONQUESTS OF THE OPPOSITE SEX. IN A SOCIETY IN WHICH THE PHYSICAL ATTRIBUTES OF THE BLACK RACE ARE THE STANDARD FOR BEAUTY, PRETTY BOY CONSIDERS JOYCE TO INDEED BE A PRIZE. SHE WOULD CERTAINLY AROUSE THE ENVY OF THE BARBER SHOP CROWD AS THEY BRAG ABOUT THEIR SEXUAL EXPLOITS. FOR JOYCE ALSO, THIS UNION REPRESENTS SOMETHING OF A CONQUEST. THERE IS NO POSSIBILITY THAT SHE COULD EVER HAVE A TRUE LOVE RELATIONSHIP WITH PRETTY BOY. SHE WOULD EVEN BE EMBARRASSED TO BE SEEN IN THE BLACK PART OF TOWN WITH HIM. BUT, SHE HAS BEEN CAPTIVATED BY THE **GIRLS LOCKER ROOM TALK** OF WHITE SEXUAL PROWESS AND THE INTRIGUE OF CLANDESTINE DATING

ACROSS THE COLOR LINE. THUS, WE HAVE ONE MATCH THAT IS DERIVED FROM THE COMMONALITY OF OPPOSING LIFE STYLES AND VALUES AS THEY BECOME IRRESISTIBLE FORCES OF ATTRACTION. LIKE THE NORTH AND SOUTH POLES OF TWO MAGNETS, BLACK FEMALE AND WHITE MALE MAKE CONTACT.

IF THE FIRST COUPLE'S RELATIONSHIP IS ANALOGOUS TO THE OPPOSITE POLES OF TWO MAGNETS, THEN THE SECOND COUPLE'S WOULD BE COMPARABLE TO LIKE-POLES THAT ARE PARALLEL, YET KEEPING A RESPECTFUL DISTANCE FROM EACH OTHER. THOMAS JR. WOULD HAVE TO ADMIT THAT THE VALUES OF THE DOMINATE BLACK CULTURE HAVE AT LEAST A SUB-CONSCIOUS EFFECT ON HIS DECISIONS AND ACTIONS. NO ONE FORCED HIM TO GO OUT WITH MARY JOHNSON. THE CHOICE WAS HIS. HE CAN HONESTLY CONFESS THAT HE WAS ATTRACTED TO HER. BUT, WHEREAS PRETTY BOY'S ACTIONS SEEM TO BE ALMOST TOTALLY GUIDED BY EMOTION, THOMAS' ARE TEMPERED BY AN INTELLECTUAL ANALYSIS OF THE FORCES AFFECTING HIS BEHAVIOR.

THOMAS JR. UNDERSTANDS THAT THE CONSTANT MESSAGE THAT THE AVERAGE **NEW AFRICAN** GETS FROM THE FORMAL AND INFORMAL MEDIA IS THE MESSAGE THAT **BLACK IS BEAUTIFUL**. THE COUNTLESS TELEVISION SHOWS, COMMERCIALS, MOVIES AND PRINTED MEDIA HAS DRIVEN THAT MESSAGE INTO THE SUB-CONSCIOUS OF WHITES AND BLACKS. HE KNOWS THAT FORMAL EDUCATION IS CENTERED AROUND BLACK CULTURE, BLACK SOCIETY, AND BLACK HISTORY. HE KNOWS THAT THE WHITE COUNTERPART OF ALMOST EVERYTHING BLACK HAS BEEN UNFAIRLY MALIGNED. HE KNOWS THAT HE HAS TAKEN IT UPON HIMSELF TO BE AN ACTIVIST IN MAKING WHITE HISTORY AN **INTEGRAL PART** OF SCHOOL HISTORY CLASSES. HE KNOWS THAT THERE ARE THOSE WHO WOULD CRITICIZE HIS AFFAIR WITH MARY JOHNSON AS AN EXAMPLE OF HYPOCRISY. HE IS VERY MUCH AWARE OF ALL OF THIS. HE ALSO

KNOWS THAT HE LIKES A BLACK GIRL, AND HE BELIEVES THAT SHE LIKES HIM.

IT APPEARS THAT COMMON GROUND HAS BEEN DISCOVERED BY EACH OF OUR DATING PAIRS. EACH PAIR OF CONTRASTING INDIVIDUALS HAS AT LEAST A TENTATIVE BOND. ON THE SURFACE ALL SEEMS TRANQUIL AND EVEN A BIT ROMANTIC. BUT, **FURTHER ON UP THE ROAD** THERE IS NO PRETENSE OF TRANQUILITY AND DEFINITELY NO ROMANCE.

PRETTY BOY BRINGS HIS CAR TO A SCREECHING STOP. A LEAST A HUNDRED YARDS AHEAD, TWO OPPOSING FORCES ARE CONFRONTING EACH OTHER IN ANTICIPATION OF A VIOLENT DISPLAY OF THE INABILITY TO FIND COMMON GROUND. UNLIKE THE COUPLES IN THE CAR, THE INDIVIDUAL MEMBERS OF THESE OPPOSING FORCES SHARE A COMMON RACIAL IDENTITY AND GENDER. THE OBVIOUS AND APPARENT DIFFERENCE IS THE FACT THAT ONE SIDE IS WEARING RED AND THE OTHER SIDE IS WEARING BLUE. THE GIRLS IN THE CAR LOOK TO THEIR MALE DATES FOR AN EXPLANATION OF WHAT IS HAPPENING. THOMAS JR. AND PRETTY BOY HAVE SEEN ENOUGH OF THIS IN THEIR NEIGHBORHOOD TO EASILY RECOGNIZE THE BEGINNING OF **A GANG FIGHT BETWEEN THE REDS AND THE BLUES.**

PRETTY BOY: HOLD ON EVERYBODY! I AM GOING TO MAKE A QUICK TURN AND GET THE HELL OUT OF HERE!

THOMAS JR.: WAIT! I WANT TO TALK TO THOSE GUYS. THIS DOES NOT HAVE TO HAPPEN.

PRETTY BOY: PECKERWOOD, PLEASE! THIS IS NOT ANY OF OUR BUSINESS.

Eddie J. Thomas

THOMAS JR.: YOU DO NOT HAVE TO STAY. JUST LET ME OUT.

MARY: NO, THOMAS! PLEASE! YOU COULD GET HURT.

THOMAS JR.: MARY, YOU SOUND AS THOUGH YOU REALLY CARE.

MARY: WILL YOU STOP THE **MR. TOUGH-GUY ACT**? I DO CARE.

PRETTY BOY: YOU TWO ARE GOING TO MAKE ME CRY. PECKERWOOD, YOU WANT TO GET OUT? GO AHEAD!

THOMAS JR.: JUST GIVE ME ABOUT FIFTEEN MINUTES. IF THINGS GET OF HAND, GET MARY AND JOYCE OUT OF HERE.

PRETTY BOY: OKAY, IT'S YOUR ASS, PECKERWOOD. YOU GOT ANY OTHER LAST REQUESTS.

THOMAS JR.: YEAH. DON'T CALL ME PECKERWOOD!

THOMAS JR.: I GUESS ALL OF THOSE BLACK RACIST STATEMENTS ABOUT US WHITE FOLKS ARE TRUE. ESPECIALLY, THE ONE THAT SAYS WE HAVE NO RESPECT FOR OURSELVES. WELL? ARE THEY RIGHT? ARE WE INTELLIGENT, SELF-RESPECTING HUMAN BEING OR ARE WE JUST A BUNCH OF IGNORANT, SAVAGE PECKER...I ALMOST SAID THE WORD...THAT DAMN **P**-WORD. THE WAY YOU GUYS ARE ACTING MAKES IT

DIFFICULT FOR ME TO RESIST SAYING IT.

B.G.M. #1: PECKERWOOD, PLEASE! YOU AND YOUR **HIGH AND MIGHTY** PREACHING ABOUT THIS AND THAT. I TOLD YOU THAT WE CAN NOT TRUST THE REDS. YOU WERE SUPPOSE TO TALK TO THEM JUST LIKE YOU TALKED TO US. WHAT GOOD DID IT DO? WHITE PRIDE MY ASS. BLUE PRIDE, BLUE POWER!

REGGIE (B.G.M. #1) YOU SEE THOMAS, THESE STUPID BLUES CAN NOT BE TRUSTED. THEY ARE NOTHING BUT DROP-OUTS. THEY DO NOT KNOW WHAT THE WORD TRUST MEANS. WHAT THEY NEED IS A LITTLE RED...BLOOD RED.

B.G.M. #1 IF THERE IS GOING TO BE ANY BLEEDING, YOU REDS ARE THE ONES WHO...

THOMAS JR.: DAMN IT! LISTEN TO YOURSELVES. RED! BLUE! YOU ARE READY TO KILL EACH OTHER OVER A COUPLE OF COLORS. IF COLOR IS THAT IMPORTANT, WHY CAN'T YOU SEE YOUR COMMON COLOR, WHITE? ALL OF US ARE WHITE. WHY CAN'T WE VALUE THAT?

B.G.M. #1: PECKERWOOD, IF WHITE IS SO IMPORTANT, WHY ARE YOU AND PRETTY BOY SNEAKING AROUND AT NIGHT WITH THOSE BLACK CHICKS? ISN'T WHITE BEAUTIFUL?

REGGIE: THOMAS, THE WHITE SISTERS AT SCHOOL MIGHT BE DISAPPOINTED. A LOT OF THEM HAD THEIR EYES ON YOU.

THOMAS JR.: SEE THERE. YOU TWO JUST DID IT!

B.G.M. # 1: WHAT IN THE HELL ARE YOU TALKING ABOUT?

REGGIE: DON'T TRY TO AVOID EXPLAINING ABOUT THE BLACK CHICKS.

THOMAS JR.: I AM NOT TRYING TO AVOID ANYTHING. DON'T YOU SEE? YOU GUYS STOPPED ARGUING ABOUT BLUE AND RED. YOU BOTH WERE CRITICIZING MY DATING OF A BLACK GIRL. AS CRAZY AS IT SOUNDS, THE TWO OF YOU AGREED ON SOMETHING. FOR THE MOMENT, KILLING EACH OTHER WAS NOT YOUR NUMBER ONE PRIORITY. YOU HAD A COMMON GROUND. YOU BOTH BELIEVE THAT I AM HYPOCRITICAL. YOU BOTH BASE YOUR BELIEF ON YOUR DOUBTS ABOUT MY COMMITMENT TO WHITE PRIDE. WHITE IS THE COMMON GROUND. RED AND BLUE ARE NOT IMPORTANT. IT MAY NOT SEEM LIKE MUCH. BUT THAT IS WHERE WE HAVE TO START. WE ARE WHITE, NOT BLUE NOR RED!

REGGIE: THAT IS PRETTY SLICK TALK. BUT, WHAT ABOUT THE BLACK CHICKS?

THOMAS JR.: REGGIE, I'M GOING TO BE HONEST WITH YOU. THAT OLD RHYME HAS IT'S

EFFECT ON ALL OF US, INCLUDING ME. YOU KNOW. "IF YOU'RE BLACK, YOU'RE ON THE RIGHT TRACK..." WHEN I FIRST MET MARY, I SAW HER THROUGH BLACK BEAUTY STANDARDS. YOU KNOW. ALL OF THOSE TELEVISION SHOWS! BUT, NOW THAT I KNOW HER, I LIKE HER. I WOULD LIKE HER REGARDLESS OF HER COLOR. THE WHITE AND BLACK PROBLEM IS LIKE THE BLUE AND RED PROBLEM. THERE HAS TO BE SOME KIND OF COMMON GROUND. WE ARE ALL HUMAN BEINGS. MARY AND I, YOU AND B.G.M. #1. WE ARE ALL HUMAN BEINGS. NOW, THAT IS ALL THAT I HAVE TO SAY. IF YOU WANT TO KILL EACH OTHER, GO AHEAD! I'M TIRED. IT IS GETTING LATE. I'M HEADING BACK TO PRETTY BOY'S CAR AND GOING HOME.

AS THOMAS JR. WALKS DOWN THE ROAD TOWARDS PRETTY BOY'S CAR, THE BLUES AND REDS STAND STARING AT EACH OTHER IN ALMOST TOTAL SILENCE. THESE FEW MOMENTS SEEM LIKE AN ETERNITY. FINALLY, THE SILENCE IS BROKEN. THIS IS NOT CAUSED BY JUBILANT WORDS OF FORGIVENESS AND RECONCILIATION. THE SILENCE IS BROKEN BY THE SHUFFLE OF FEET AS REGGIE AND B.G.M. # 1 SLOWLY TURN AND WALK AWAY FROM EACH OTHER. THE NOISE OF THE SHUFFLE STEADILY INCREASES AS THE OTHER GANG MEMBERS ALSO TURN, WALK AWAY, AND FINALLY FADE INTO THE DARKNESS OF THE NIGHT.

AN EERIE SILENCE IS ALL THAT IS LEFT ON THE STRETCH OF ROAD WHERE ONCE PEACE AND WAR, AND POSSIBLY LIFE AND DEATH STOOD EYEBALL TO EYEBALL WAITING TO SEE WHICH WOULD BE THE FIRST TO BLINK. FURTHER DOWN THE ROAD, THE OCCUPANTS

OF THE BLACK AND WHITE CONVERTIBLE BREATHE A SIGH OF RELIEF.

MARY: THOMAS, WHAT DID YOU SAY TO THEM?

JOYCE: I JUST KNEW THAT SOMEONE WAS GOING TO GET HURT AND EVEN KILLED. YOU MUST HAVE NERVES OF STEEL.

THOMAS JR.: I WAS SCARED AS HELL. YOU WANT TO KNOW WHAT I SAID TO THEM? IT WAS THE SAME THING THAT I'M GOING TO SAY TO PRETTY. LET'S GET THE HELL OUT OF HERE! IT'S TIME TO GO HOME!

PRETTY BOY: DO YOU EXPECT US TO BELIEVE THAT IT WAS THAT SIMPLE. PECKERWOOD, PLEASE!

THOMAS JR.: IS PRETTY TAKING JOYCE TO HER HOME?

MARY: ARE YOU KIDDING? JOYCE'S PARENTS WOULD HAVE A FIT IF PRETTY PULLED UP IN THEIR DRIVEWAY WITH JOYCE. HER CAR IS NEAR BY. PRETTY WILL JUST TAKE HER TO IT AND SHE WILL DRIVE HOME. DO YOU WANT ME TO DRIVE YOU HOME?

THOMAS JR.: HOW DO YOU KNOW THAT MY PARENTS WON'T HAVE A FIT IF YOU PULLED UP IN THEIR DRIVEWAY WITH ME?

MARY: WELL SMARTY, I GUESS YOU CAN WALK HOME.

THOMAS JR.: HEY, WHERE'S YOUR SENSE OF HUMOR? LET'S GO. BESIDES, MY PARENTS ARE PROBABLY ASLEEP BY NOW. MARY, I NEED TO TALK TO YOUR DAD.

MARY: MY DAD! ABOUT WHAT?

THOMAS JR.: DO YOU REMEMBER ME MENTIONING TO YOU ONCE ABOUT WHITE HISTORY? NONE OF US KNOW THE TRUE STORY OF THE HISTORY OF EUROPE.

MARY: I REMEMBER. SOMETHING ABOUT SLAVERY.

THOMAS JR.: YOU SEE. THAT IS THE PROBLEM. SLAVERY IS ONLY PART OF THE STORY. THEY NEVER TEACH US IN SCHOOL ABOUT THE FACT THAT WHITES HAVE A HISTORY BEFORE SLAVERY. WE ARE LED TO BELIEVE THAT BLACKS ARE JUST NATURALLY BETTER THAN WHITES. WE ARE TAUGHT THAT THERE IS SOMETHING WRONG WITH OR LACKING IN BEING WHITE. ALL OF THAT NEEDS TO CHANGE. YOUR DAD IS A RESPECTED MAN IN THIS TOWN. EVEN THE BOARD MEMBERS RESPECT HIM. THEY MIGHT BE MOVED TO CORRECT WHAT WE ARE TAUGHT IN SCHOOL, IF HE SUPPORTS THE CHANGE.

135

MARY: NOW, WAIT A MINUTE. YOU DON'T EXPECT ME TO TRY TO CONVINCE MY DAD TO DO SOMETHING ABOUT IT.

THOMAS JR.: NO. LIKE I SAID, I NEED TO TALK TO HIM.

MARY: WELL, IF I GOT INVOLVED, HE WOULD KNOW THAT SOMETHING WAS GOING ON BETWEEN THE TWO OF US. WHY DON'T YOU JUST CALL HIM? HE LIKES YOUR FAMILY. HE'S DEFINITELY NOT A RACIST. JUST DON'T MENTION MY NAME!

THOMAS JR.: OKAY! OKAY! I'LL JUST CALL HIM.

PHASE 24

FREEDOM

MRS. EDWARDS: TELL THOMAS TO COME DOWN FOR BREAKFAST.

THOMAS SR.: ARE YOU KIDDING? THAT BOY CAME IN PRETTY LATE LAST NIGHT. HE WILL PROBABLY SLEEP UNTIL NOON.

MRS. EDWARDS: I THOUGHT HE WENT TO THE LIBRARY. IT CLOSES AT NINE.

THOMAS SR.: WELL, I GUESS HE AND WHOEVER HE WAS WITH DECIDED TO GO SOME WHERE ELSE. I WONDER WHO SHE IS. I HAVE NOT HEARD HIM SPEAK OF ANY OF THE GIRLS FROM THE HIGH SCHOOL.

MRS. EDWARDS: WHOEVER SHE IS, I'M SURE SHE IS A NIECE GIRL.

THOMAS SR.: I'M GLAD TO KNOW THAT HE HAS OTHER THINGS ON HIS MIND BESIDES QUANTUM THEORY AND WHITE HISTORY.

MRS. EDWARDS: THOMAS, IT'S GETTING CLOSE TO SCHOOL BOARD ELECTION TIME. I WOULD LIKE TO START CAMPAIGNING. YOU KNOW, PUT POSTERS UP IN THE NEIGHBORHOOD AND MAYBE EVEN GO AROUND AND TALK TO PEOPLE.

THOMAS SR.:   YOU DON'T HAVE TO GET MY PERMISSION. I'M SURE THAT YOU WILL GET MOST OF THE VOTES IN THE NEIGHBORHOOD. IT'S THE BLACK VOTE THAT WILL MAKE THE DIFFERENCE. YOU WILL HAVE TO GET ENOUGH BLACK VOTES.

MRS. EDWARDS: THAT MEANS I WILL NEED TO GO INTO THE BLACK NEIGHBORHOODS. IT WAS BAD ENOUGH WHEN I WENT TO REGISTER AT THE COURT HOUSE. I WILL NEVER FORGET ALL OF THOSE COLD STARES.

THOMAS SR.:   MR. JOHNSON SAID THAT WE COULD COUNT ON HIS SUPPORT. EVEN HIS WIFE ADMIRED YOU FOR ENTERING THE RACE. THEY CAN HELP US TO GET BLACK VOTES. IF THEY CANNOT, THEN WHO CAN? IF THEY WON'T, WHO WILL?

MRS. EDWARDS: WE TRULY ARE THE MINORITY IN THIS COUNTRY.

THOMAS SR.:   WHAT DO YOU MEAN?

MRS. EDWARDS;   EVEN WHEN IT COMES TO VOTING, WHICH WE ARE FREE TO DO, THERE IS STILL NOT ENOUGH OF US TO WIN. WE ARE STILL DEPENDENT ON THE BLACK MAN. FREEDOM AND INDEPENDENCE ARE NOT EXACTLY THE SAME THING.

FREEDOM AND INDEPENDENCE ARE NOT EXACTLY THE SAME THING. MOST WHITES IN NEW AFRICA DO NOT

WANT TO SEPARATE FROM BLACKS AND FORM AN INDEPENDENT NATION. THAT WOULD BE IMPRACTICAL. THE LOGICAL CONCLUSION OF THIS KIND OF THINKING WOULD BE THE RETURN OF NEW AFRICAN WHITES TO THE THEIR HOMELAND OF EUROPE. HOME FOR MOST WHITES IN THE COUNTRY IS CONSIDERED TO BE NEW AFRICA, NOT EUROPE. MOST CAN TRACE THEIR FAMILIES BACK TO ALMOST FOUR-HUNDRED YEARS OF SLAVERY IN THIS COUNTRY.

THE WHITE MAN WANTS FREEDOM IN TERMS OF EQUAL RIGHTS, EQUAL ECONOMIC OPPORTUNITIES AND ABOVE ALL, EQUAL RESPECT. THAT MEANS AN INTEGRATED SOCIETY, NOT A SEPARATE ONE. IT DEFINITELY DOES NOT MEAN ONE LOCATED ON ANOTHER CONTINENT. THE DESIRED TYPE OF SOCIETY WOULD HAVE BLACKS AND WHITES ATTENDING THE SAME SCHOOL. NEIGHBORHOODS WOULD BE RACIALLY MIXED. SOCIALLY, THERE WOULD BE MUTUAL RESPECT BETWEEN THE RACES. BLACKS WOULD NO LONGER HAVE A PATRONIZING ATTITUDE IN THEIR RELATIONS WITH WHITES. INTERRACIAL DATING AND EVEN MARRIAGE WOULD BE RESPECTED AS RIGHTS OF INDIVIDUAL CHOICE. WHITES WOULD HOLD POSITIONS OF AUTHORITY WITHOUT ANY MISGIVINGS ON THE PART OF BLACKS. WHITE SELF-RESPECT BASED ON A SENSE OF IMPROVED STATUS WOULD RESULT IN LESS WHITE ON WHITE CRIME, LESS STREET GANG FIGHTING, AND MORE OF THE 'VIRTUES" ASSOCIATED WITH MIDDLE CLASS VALUES. THIS IS THE IDEAL THAT ASPIRING WHITES HAVE FOR TRUE FREEDOM IN THE UNITED STATES OF NEW AFRICA.

THIS TYPE OF IDEALISM WILL NOT BE ACHIEVED SIMPLY BY LAWS AND POLICIES THAT DISCOURAGE DISCRIMINATION. WHITE SELF-RESPECT DEPENDS JUST AS MUCH ON HOW WHITES TREAT EACH OTHER AS IT DOES ON HOW THEY ARE TREATED BY BLACKS. THE CRIME AND GANG FIGHTING OF THE INNER CITY IS DIRECTLY RELATED TO THE LACK OF MUTUAL SELF-RESPECT THAT EXISTS AMONG WHITES THEMSELVES.

THIS LACK OF RESPECT IS ITSELF A RESULT OF THE LEGACY OF SELF-CONTEMPT THAT HAD IT'S ORIGIN IN THE FACT THAT WHITES WERE ONCE SLAVES OF BLACKS.

THE STIGMA OF ENSLAVEMENT OF FAIR SKINNED EUROPEANS HAD OVER THE CENTURIES RESULTED IN A COLLECTIVE ATTITUDE THAT INTELLIGENCE AND BEAUTY WERE THE OPPOSITE OF WHITE SKIN, STRAIGHT HAIR, LONG NOSES, AND THIN LIPS. THIS ATTITUDE BECAME THE PREVAILING ONE BECAUSE THOSE WHO POSSESSED THE POLITICAL, SOCIAL, AND ECONOMIC POWER WERE BLACK. **THOSE WHO HAVE THE POWER DO NOT NORMALLY MALIGN THEMSELVES.** IT ONLY MAKES SENSE THAT FREE WHITE MEN REDEFINE THE PHYSICAL STANDARDS FOR SUCH THINGS AS INTELLIGENCE AND BEAUTY. IF WHITES ARE TO HAVE SELF-RESPECT, THEN THEY MUST SEE WHITE SKIN, STRAIGHT HAIR, LONG NOSES, AND THIN LIPS AS ATTRIBUTES OF BEAUTY AND NOT OF SHAME.

HOWEVER, AS MRS. EDWARDS ONCE EXPLAINED TO THOMAS JR., TRADITION IS HARD TO CHANGE. WHITE WOMEN HAVE BEEN CURLING THEIR HAIR FOR A LONG TIME TO MAKE IT LOOK MORE LIKE THAT OF BLACK WOMEN. EVEN SOME WHITE MEN CURL THEIR HAIR. AMONG THOSE WHITES WHO HAPPEN TO BE BORN WITH KINKY OR NEAR KINKY HAIR, THE TERM "GOOD HAIR" IS A POSITIVE DESCRIPTIVE. THERE HAVE EVEN BEEN SOME WHO WERE SO OBSESSED WITH TRYING TO LOOK BLACK THAT THEY HAVE UNDERGONE FACIAL SURGERY AND EXTREME TANNING TO OBTAIN A NEGROID APPEARANCE.

THE IRONY OF IT ALL IS THAT WHITES INTERPRET FREEDOM AS BEING ABLE TO PURSUE THE EDUCATIONAL, SOCIAL AND ECONOMIC ATTAINMENTS OF MIDDLE CLASS BLACK NEW AFRICA. HOWEVER, FREEDOM ON THE OTHER HAND MUST ALSO MEAN ACCEPTANCE OF WHITE PHYSICAL ATTRIBUTES AND EUROPEAN CULTURAL HISTORY. WHITE PEOPLE WILL NEVER TRULY BE FREE AS LONG AS THEIR MINDS ARE

ENSLAVED BY THE NOTION EXPRESSED IN THAT OLD RHYTHMIC VERSE....
"IF YOU'RE BLACK, YOU'RE ON THE RIGHT TRACK.
IF YOU'RE BROWN, STICK AROUND.
IF YOU'RE WHITE, GET OUT OF SIGHT."

THOMAS JR.: I THINK I OVERSLEPT. WHAT'S FOR BREAKFAST?

MRS. EDWARDS: BREAKFAST? SON, IT'S ALMOST NOON! THERE IS NOTHING LEFT FOR BREAKFAST.

THOMAS SR.: WHEN PEOPLE GET HOME AS LATE AS YOU DID LAST NIGHT, THEY USUALLY SLEEP PASS BREAKFAST. QUITE A BIT OF STUDY AT THE LIBRARY, HUH? THAT QUANTUM THEORY MUST REQUIRE A LOT OF READING.

THOMAS JR.: YEAH. I GUESS IT DOES. DAD, DO YOU THINK THAT MR. JOHNSON WOULD HELP TO GET WHITE HISTORY TAUGHT IN THE SCHOOLS?

THOMAS SR.: SON, HE IS ALREADY STICKING HIS NECK OUT BY SUPPORTING YOUR MOTHER'S RUN FOR THE SCHOOL BOARD. HE IS AN OPEN MINDED AND LIBERAL BLACK MAN. I'M SURE HE WOULD BE WILLING TO LISTEN TO YOU.

THOMAS JR.: COULD YOU TALK TO HIM ABOUT....

THOMAS SR.: NO, SON! THE MAN HAS DONE ENOUGH FAVORS FOR ME. WHITE HISTORY IS YOUR AGENDA. I AGREE

WITH YOU. IT IS IMPORTANT. BUT, YOU'RE THE ONE WHO SHOULD TALK TO MR. JOHNSON.

THOMAS JR.: I GUEST YOU'RE RIGHT. BUT, I DON'T WANT TO SEEM LIKE A BEGGAR.

THOMAS SR.: SON, YOU'RE ONLY BEGGING IF YOU ASK HIM WITHOUT HAVING PRIDE IN YOURSELF TO BEGIN WITH, I KNOW YOU SON. YOU HAVE PRIDE. BUT, A LITTLE HUMILITY IS GOOD FOR PRIDE.

PHASE 25

MUTUAL RESPECT

"PRIDE GOES BEFORE A FALL". THOMAS JR. DOES NOT INTEND TO FAIL IN HIS ENDEAVOR TO GET WHITE HISTORY TAUGHT IN THE SCHOOLS. IF HE MUST SWALLOW HIS PRIDE AND ENDURE THE HUMILITY OF ASKING A BLACK MAN TO HELP HIM, THEN THAT LESSON IN HUMILITY HE WILL PATIENTLY LEARN. THE LESSON FOR THOMAS JR. FOCUSES ON A SINGLE WHITE INDIVIDUAL. BUT, IT IS A LESSON THAT ALL WHITE NEW AFRICANS SHOULD LEARN. ESPECIALLY THOSE LIKE THOMAS JR. WHO SEE EURO-CENTRISM AS A MUCH NEEDED DEVELOPMENT IN THEIR PROGRESS. THE LOGIC OF PRACTICALITY MUST TEMPER THE SENTIMENTS OF IDEALISM. THE EURO-CENTRIC IDEAL OF SCHOOLS TEACHING EUROPEAN HISTORY IS DEPENDENT ON THE COOPERATION OF THOSE WHO DOMINATE THE DECISION MAKING PROCESS....BLACKS.

WHITE PRIDE, LIKE INDIVIDUAL PRIDE AND HUMAN EMOTION IN GENERAL, MUST BE TEMPERED BY REASON. THIS IS NOT A CASE OF "EITHER ONE OR THE OTHER". IN NATURE, EXTREMISM IS MORE OFTEN THE EXCEPTION THAN THE RULE. OPPOSITES ARE USUALLY MUTUALLY DEPENDENT NOT MUTUALLY EXCLUSIVE. THIS MEANS THAT ONE LACKS FUNCTIONALITY WITHOUT THE OTHER. IN THE EVERYDAY WORLD OF TYPICAL HUMAN EXPERIENCE, THERE ARE AN ABUNDANCE OF EXAMPLES OF THIS TYPE OF RELATIONSHIP. THE GENDER DISTINCTIONS OF MALE AND FEMALE IS A GOOD EXAMPLE OF MUTUALLY DEPENDENT OPPOSITES. IT IS THE UNION OF THE TWO THAT RESULTS IN MORE OF EITHER SEX. IT IS THE ALTERNATING CONTRAST OF DAY AND NIGHT THAT PROVIDES FOR ONE MEASURE OF

TIME. THE OPPOSING MAGNETIC FORCES PRODUCE THE ROTATION MOTION OF A GENERATOR.

EMOTION AND REASON GO HAND IN HAND. TOO MUCH OF EITHER CAN BE CAUSE FOR DISASTER. THE WHITES OF NEW AFRICA KNOW THE EFFECTS OF BLACK EXTREMISM. IT WAS THIS VERY MENTALITY THAT FORCED A SECOND CLASS CITIZENSHIP UPON WHITES WHO HAD BEEN FREED FROM LEGALIZED SLAVERY ONE-HUNDRED YEARS AGO. IT WAS THIS MENTALITY THAT PRODUCED THE NEGATIVE ENVIRONMENT IN WHICH GENERATIONS OF WHITES REFERRED TO THEMSELVES AS "PECKERWOODS". **UNRESTRAINED RACIAL PRIDE EASILY TURNS INTO RACISM. BUT, HUMILITY WITHOUT SELF-RESPECT IS A PRESCRIPTION FOR SLAVERY.** THOMAS JR. IS NOT A SLAVE. HE IS NOT WITHOUT SELF-RESPECT. HE KNOWS THE VALUE OF HUMILITY.

MR. JOHNSON: HELLO. YES, THIS IS MR. JOHNSON. THOMAS? OH, YES…. THOMAS JR.… THOMAS EDWARD'S SON. WELL, I CERTAINLY WASN'T EXPECTING A PHONE CALL FROM YOU. WHAT CAN I DO FOR YOU?

THOMAS JR.: IT IS KIND OF DIFFICULT TO EXPLAIN OVER THE PHONE. I NEED YOUR HELP WITH SOMETHING.

MR. JOHNSON: WELL SON, YOU ARE WELCOME TO COME BY THE HOUSE THIS AFTERNOON IF YOU WANT TO TALK IN PERSON.

THOMAS JR.: YEAH. I THINK YOU'RE RIGHT. WE NEED TO TALK IN PERSON.

MR. JOHNSON: COME ON OVER. I WILL BE HOME ALL AFTERNOON.

MARY:	THOMAS!
THOMAS JR.:	ARE YOU SURPRISED?
MARY:	WHAT ARE YOU....
THOMAS JR.:	AREN'T YOU GOING TO LET ME IN THE HOUSE?
MARY:	MY MOM AND DAD ARE HERE!
THOMAS JR.:	NO PROBLEM. I'M HERE TO SEE YOUR DAD. DON'T WORRY, IT DOESN'T CONCERN YOU. HE IS EXPECTING ME. NOW, ARE YOU GOING TO LET ME IN?
MARY:	OKAY. COME IN. DAD! IT'S MR. EDWARDS' SON.
MR. JOHNSON:	TELL HIM TO COME INTO THE FAMILY ROOM.
MARY:	WHAT IS THIS ALL ABOUT THOMAS?
THOMAS JR.:	HISTORY.
MARY:	HISTORY? NOW I GET IT. WHITE HISTORY. YOU'RE REALLY SERIOUS ABOUT THIS. WELL, HE'S WAITING ON YOU.

MR. JOHNSON:	COME ON IN AND HAVE A SEAT THOMAS. DE JA VU! IT WAS JUST A SHORT WHILE AGO THAT I SAID THOSE SAME WORDS TO YOUR DAD.

YOU REMIND ME A LOT OF HIM. YES, HE AND I HAD A PRIVATE DISCUSSION THAT LED TO SOME MAJOR CHANGES IN MY FACTORY. IF YOU'RE ANYTHING LIKE YOUR DAD, I KNOW THAT THIS WILL BE A DISCUSSION ABOUT AN IMPORTANT MATTER.

THOMAS JR.: I THINK IT IS IMPORTANT. MR. JOHNSON, YOU ARE DIFFERENT THAN A LOT OF BLACK MEN THAT I HAVE MET. YOU ARE SINCERE ABOUT WANTING TO MAKE THINGS BETTER FOR WHITES IN THIS COUNTRY. MOST OF THE BLACKS THAT I HAVE MET SEEM TO PREFER THINGS THE WAY THEY ARE. IT'S LIKE THEY HAVE AN ADVANTAGE AND THEY DON'T WANT TO LOSE IT. WHY ARE YOU SO DIFFERENT?

MR. JOHNSON: WELL, THOMAS I GUESS I'M JUST NOT AFRAID. FEAR HAS A LOT TO DO WITH PREJUDICE. MANY OF THOSE BLACKS THAT YOU ARE TALKING ABOUT ARE SIMPLY JUST AFRAID. THEY ARE AFRAID OF CHANGE. THEY ARE USED TO THE COMFORT OF FEELING THAT THEY ARE BETTER THAN WHITES. WITHOUT ANY EFFORT OF THEIR OWN, THEY CAN CLAIM THAT THEY ARE BETTER THAN SOMEONE ELSE. OVER THE YEARS THAT I HAVE OWNED MY BUSINESS, I'VE HAD TO RELY ON A LOT OF PEOPLE AS EMPLOYEES. I FOUND THAT SKIN COLOR ALONE DOESN'T DETERMINE WHETHER SOMEONE WILL BE A GOOD EMPLOYEE. PEOPLE LIKE YOUR DAD

HAVE CONVINCED ME OF THAT. THIS COUNTRY CANNOT AFFORD TO EXCLUDE VALUABLE PEOPLE. BUT, YOU DID NOT COME HERE JUST TO DISCUSS ME.

THOMAS JR.: NO, I DID NOT. MR. JOHNSON, ONE OF THE PROBLEMS WE WHITES HAVE IS NEGATIVE ATTITUDES ABOUT OURSELVES. IN SCHOOL, THEY TEACH US ONLY NEGATIVE THINGS ABOUT OUR PAST. IT'S ALWAYS ABOUT SLAVERY AND NOTHING ELSE. THERE ARE MANY MORE POSITIVE THINGS ABOUT OUR HISTORY IN THIS COUNTRY AND EUROPE.

MR. JOHNSON: FOR YOUR AGE, YOU ARE A VERY SERIOUS THINKER. YOU WILL DO WELL IN COLLEGE.

THOMAS JR.: I INTEND TO. BUT, MANY OTHERS WILL NOT. MANY OF US WILL NOT FINISH HIGH SCHOOL. SOME ARE SO DOWN ON THEMSELVES THAT THEY DO NOT CARE ABOUT HIGH SCHOOL. SOME HAVE EVEN JOINED GANGS AND WASTE THEIR TIME FIGHTING AND KILLING EACH OTHER. TEACHING US ABOUT WHITE HISTORY IS NOT THE COMPLETE ANSWER. BUT, IT IS PART OF THE SOLUTION.

MR. JOHNSON: WHY DON'T YOU JUST ASK THE TEACHERS TO TEACH IT?

THOMAS JR.: THEY CANNOT MAKE THAT DECISION THEMSELVES AND NEITHER CAN THE PRINCIPAL. THE SCHOOL BOARD HAS

TO MAKE THAT DECISION. THEY USUALLY ARE NOT VERY CONCERNED ABOUT THE NEEDS OF WHITES.

MR. JOHNSON: YOUR MOTHER IS RUNNING FOR THE BOARD. I THINK SHE HAS A GOOD CHANCE OF WINNING. I AM NOT THE ONLY SENSIBLE BLACK PERSON IN THIS TOWN. I AM SURE SHE WILL GET THEIR VOTES.

THOMAS JR.: BUT, SHE WOULD ONLY BE ONE PERSON OUT OF SEVEN ON THE BOARD. THE ONLY WHITE PERSON.

MR. JOHNSON: IF ENOUGH BLACKS VOTE FOR HER, THE OTHER BOARD MEMBERS WILL TAKE HER AND WANT SHE SUPPORTS SERIOUS. WE NEED TO MAKE THE WHITE HISTORY ISSUE PART OF HER CAMPAIGN. YOU SHOULD HELP WITH THAT SINCE YOU KNOW WHY IT IS SO IMPORTANT. I PROMISED TO HELP YOUR MOTHER. THIS HISTORY ISSUE GIVES US SOMETHING THAT WE CAN TAKE TO THE PUBLIC AND SHOW THE NEED FOR CONSTRUCTIVE CHANGE. MANY PEOPLE UNDERSTAND THAT THIS SOCIETY HAS TO CHANGE. HISTORY CAN BE A WAY TO EVEN EDUCATE THE VOTERS. THOMAS, YOU HAVE MY SUPPORT. BUT, REMEMBER, THIS ELECTION EFFORT WILL ALSO RELY ON YOUR KNOWLEDGE OF HISTORY. ARE YOU UP TO IT?

THOMAS JR.: YES. AND, I WILL NOT BE ALONE.

MR. JOHNSON:	GOOD! THE MORE PEOPLE INVOLVED, THE BETTER THE CHANCE FOR SUCCESS. YOU KNOW, BLACKS ALSO NEED TO LEARN ABOUT WHITE HISTORY. MARY! WOULD YOU COME HERE FOR A MOMENT?
MARY:	YES, DAD?
MR. JOHNSON:	MARY, YOU MET THOMAS AT THE DINNER WE HAD HERE WITH HIS FAMILY. WOULD YOU HELP WITH HIS MOTHER'S ELECTION CAMPAIGN BY WORKING WITH HIM ON MAKING PEOPLE AWARE OF THE NEED FOR WHITE HISTORY IN THE SCHOOLS?
MARY:	WELL...I GUESS. WHAT DO WE HAVE TO DO?
MR. JOHNSON:	MAYBE THE TWO OF YOU COULD GET TOGETHER WITH EACH OF YOUR FRIENDS AND COME UP WITH SOME IDEAS. ALL OF YOU COULD MEET HERE IN OUR HOUSE OR AT THOMAS' HOUSE. BLACK AND WHITE KIDS WORKING TOGETHER WOULD SET A GOOD EXAMPLE FOR OTHER KIDS AND THEIR PARENTS.
MARY:	IT SOUNDS LIKE A GOOD IDEA. I AM SURE JOYCE WOULD NOT MIND HELPING. THOMAS, DO YOU HAVE A FRIEND...ER...I MEAN FRIENDS WHO WOULD HELP.
THOMAS JR.:	YEAH, THERE ARE A FEW I CAN COUNT ON.

MR. JOHNSON: GOOD! GOOD! COME ON THOMAS, I'LL WALK YOU TO THE FRONT DOOR. TELL YOUR MOM AND DAD THAT WE ARE ALL LOOKING FORWARD TO HAVING AN EDWARDS ON THE SCHOOL BOARD.

PHASE 26

AFROS

"BLACK AND WHITE TOGETHER, WE SHALL OVERCOME". THERE IS AN OPTIMISTIC RING TO THAT PHRASE. WHAT WOULD THE WORLD BE LIKE IF RACIAL PREJUDICE AND DISCRIMINATION WERE NO LONGER A PROBLEM? SURELY, IN NEW AFRICA, A COUNTRY WITH A LEGACY OF RACIAL MISTREATMENT OF THE WHITE MAN, THIS QUESTION WOULD BE ANSWERED POSITIVELY. THERE WOULD BE NO MORALE PROBLEMS IN COMPETITIVE SITUATIONS WHERE A PERSON OF ONE RACE LOSES TO A PERSON OF ANOTHER RACE. THE PETTY EVERYDAY "ONE-UPMANSHIP" SOCIAL COMPETITION BETWEEN PEOPLE OF DIFFERENT RACES WOULD NO LONGER INTERFERE WITH THE PARTICULAR BUSINESS AT HAND.

THE MAJOR SOCIAL PROBLEM OF ECONOMIC DISPARITY BETWEEN THE RACES WOULD DISAPPEAR AS WHITES TAKE ADVANTAGE OF A TRULY OPEN SOCIETY AND MOVE UP THE LADDER OF SUCCESS BASED ON THEIR WORTH AS INDIVIDUALS AND NOT THEIR RACE OR COLOR. WHITES WOULD NO LONGER BE BURDENED WITH A NEGATIVE SELF-CONCEPT, CONSTANTLY REINFORCED BY THE STEREOTYPING OF FORMAL MIS-EDUCATION AND INFORMAL MEDIA PORTRAYAL. BOYS AND GIRLS OF ALL COLORS AND RACES WOULD LOOK TO THE FUTURE AND ASPIRE WITHOUT THE BARRIERS PRESENTED BY FALSE PERCEPTIONS OF COLOR AND RACE.

THIS IDEALISTIC PICTURE OF A SOCIETY WITHOUT RACIAL PREJUDICE AND DISCRIMINATION IS A DREAM THAT MANY WHITES AND PROGRESSIVE MINDED BLACKS SHARE. BUT, THIS DREAM IS SHATTERED BY THE "NIGHTMARE" ENVISIONED BY THOSE ULTRA-

CONSERVATIVE BLACKS WHO HAVE NO MISGIVINGS ABOUT THEIR BELIEF THAT BLACKS SHOULD BE SUPERIOR TO WHITES AND THAT THE SOCIAL STRUCTURE OF NEW AFRICA SHOULD REFLECT THAT BELIEF. ALTHOUGH, THESE EXTREMIST ARE THEMSELVES A MINORITY AMONG BLACKS, THEY INDIRECTLY FEED ON THE PREJUDICES AND FEARS OF BLACKS WHO ARE INCLINED TO BE MORE MODERATE IN THEIR ACTIONS.

THE MOST RADICAL AND OUTSPOKEN OF THESE ULTRA-CONSERVATIVES ARE THE "AFROS". THEY ARE A SECRETIVE GROUP THAT DRAWS HEAVIEST FROM TEENAGERS AND YOUNG UNEMPLOYED ADULT BLACKS. MANY OF THESE ARE THEMSELVES SOCIAL DEVIATES WHO HAVING FAILED TO LIVE UP TO BLACK MIDDLE CLASS SOCIAL EXPECTATIONS OF INDIVIDUAL SUCCESS, HAVE RESORTED TO VICTIMIZING WHITES AS SCAPEGOATS FOR THEIR OWN SHORTCOMINGS. THEY DRAW ATTENTION TO THEMSELVES BY WEARING THEIR HAIR IN UNUSUALLY LARGE NATURAL MOUNDS OF KINKINESS. THEY ALSO FREQUENTLY DRESS IN BLACK TO SYMBOLIZE RACIAL PURITY AND SOLIDARITY.

THIS GROUP CAN TRACE IT'S ORIGIN BACK TO THE YEARS SHORTLY AFTER THE FREEING OF THE SLAVES IN 1865. THESE AFRO FORERUNNERS CALLED THEMSELVES THE "ALL AFRICAN ASSOCIATION". UNTIL THE 1960'S, THE "A.A.A." WAS PRIMARILY AN ADULT GROUP COMMITTED TO PREVENTING WHITES FROM UTILIZING THE RIGHTS OF CITIZENSHIP THAT SHOULD HAVE COME WITH THE END OF SLAVERY. THIS WAS ACCOMPLISHED BY OUTRIGHT ACTS OF TERRORISM AND VIOLENCE DESIGNED TO "KEEP PECKERWOODS IN THEIR PLACE". SOME HAVE ESTIMATED THAT AT LEAST 100 WHITES WERE MURDERED EACH YEAR FROM 1865 TO 1900 BY THE A.A.A. MANY OF THESE KILLINGS WERE BY LYNCH MOBS LED BY THE A.A.A.

TODAY IN NEW AFRICA, THE OLD ALL AFRICAN ASSOCIATION AND IT'S UNCHECKED AGGRESSION AGAINST WHITES HAS BEEN GREATLY DIMINISHED.

WHAT REMAINS ARE SCATTERINGS OF LOOSELY AFFILIATED GROUPS OF TEENAGERS AND YOUNG ADULTS WHO CALL THEMSELVES "AFROS". UNPUNISHED MURDERING OF WHITES IS A THING OF THE PAST. BUT, THESE BLACK GANGS HAVE BEEN RESPONSIBLE FOR ISOLATED ASSAULTS ON WHITES. MANY OF THEIR MEMBERS HAVE BEEN RECRUITED FROM PREDOMINATELY BLACK HIGH SCHOOLS. AS STRANGE AS IT MAY SEEM, VERY FEW CONFRONTATIONS HAVE OCCURRED BETWEEN THE AFROS AND WHITE GANG MEMBERS. THE WHITES OF THE BLUES AND REDS HAVE PRIMARILY BEEN PREOCCUPIED WITH FIGHTING EACH OTHER.

THE AFROS ARE THE GROUP THAT WILL SEEK TO SHATTER THE DREAM OF BROTHERHOOD BETWEEN BLACKS AND WHITES. BUT, THEY WILL NOT BE ALONE IN THIS ENDEAVOR. THEY WILL BE ENCOURAGED BY THE FEAR AND APATHY OF MIDDLE CLASS BLACKS. THEY WILL ALSO HAVE AS UNWITTING PARTNERS, WHITE EXTREMIST WHO BELIEVE THAT SEPARATION OF THE RACES IS THE SOLUTION TO RACIAL PROBLEMS.

JOYCE: SOMEONE WROTE IT WITH A BLACK MARKER ON MY LOCKER. I HAD JUST RETURNED TO THE LOCKER FROM MY THIRD HOUR MATH CLASS.

MARY: JOYCE, I BET IT WAS ONE OF THE AFROS. LOOK AT THEM SITTING OVER THERE AT THAT TABLE TOGETHER. EVERYDAY THEY EAT LUNCH TOGETHER AT THAT SAME TABLE. THEY THINK THEY ARE SO TOUGH. HOW DID THEY FIND OUT ABOUT PRETTY BOY AND THOMAS?

JOYCE: I DON'T KNOW. I'M SCARED. YOU KNOW HOW MUCH THEY HATE

	WHITES. WHAT IF THEY TRY TO HURT PRETTY AND THOMAS...OR EVEN US?
MARY:	MAYBE WE HAD BETTER TALK TO THE PRINCIPAL. LOOK, ONE OF THEM IS WALKING TOWARD US!
JOYCE:	IT'S JIMMY WILLIAMS!
JIMMY W.:	I GUESS YOU GOT THE MESSAGE. NOW, WHY WOULD TWO ATTRACTIVE BLACK GIRLS BE SNEAKING AROUND WITH A COUPLE OF STRINGY-HAIRED PECKERWOODS? LET ME GUESS. THEY WANT TO SEE HOW BIG A PECKERWOOD'S DICK IS.
MARY:	SHUT UP! I CAN GUESS HOW BIG YOURS IS. IT'S PROBABLY ABOUT AS BIG AS YOUR BRAIN... "MR. TINY".
JIMMY W.:	LOOK BITCH. IF YOU KNOW WHAT'S GOOD FOR YOU, YOU WILL STOP SEEING THAT PECKERWOOD. THAT GOES FOR YOU TOO, JOYCE.
JOYCE:	AND JUST WHAT ARE YOU GOING TO DO IF WE DO NOT?
MARY:	YOU DO NOT SCARE US.
JIMMY W.:	OH, I DON'T? I SUPPOSE THAT RICH DADDY OF YOURS IS GOING TO PROTECT HIS LITTLE GIRL. YOU TELL DADDY THAT WE ARE WATCHING HIM TOO. "LIKE FATHER...LIKE DAUGHTER". PECKERWOOD LOVERS! MY LUNCH IS GETTING COLD. I WILL SEE YOU TWO LATER.

JOYCE: MARY. WE HAVE GOT TO TALK TO THE PRINCIPAL.

MARY: I'M TALKING TO MY DAD.

JOYCE: WHAT ARE YOU GOING TO TELL HIM? DO YOU WANT HIM TO KNOW THAT WE HAVE BEEN DATING WHITE BOYS? I KNOW YOUR DAD LIKES WHITE PEOPLE, BUT DOES HE LIKE THEM THAT MUCH?

MARY: LET'S TALK TO THE PRINCIPAL.

PRINCIPAL ANDREWS: GIRLS, YOU ARE MAKING SOME STRONG ACCUSATIONS AGAINST JIMMY WILLIAMS AND HIS FRIENDS. I REALLY NEED TO HEAR HIS SIDE OF THE STORY.

MARY: DO YOU REALLY THINK THAT HE IS GOING TO ADMIT TO THREATENING US? WHAT ABOUT THE WRITING ON JOYCE'S LOCKER?

PRINCIPAL A.: ANYONE COULD HAVE DONE THAT. IT WOULD JUST BE YOUR WORD AGAINST HIS. BESIDES, WHY WOULD JIMMY AND HIS FRIENDS WHAT TO HARASS YOU GIRLS?

JOYCE: BECAUSE WE DATED WHITE BOYS.

PRINCIPAL A.:	BLACK GIRLS AND WHITE BOYS. THAT COMBINATION USUALLY LEADS TO TROUBLE. IT'S NOT MY BUSINESS TO TELL YOU GIRLS WHO TO DATE. BUT, BOTH OF YOU ARE OLD ENOUGH TO UNDERSTAND THAT THERE IS A LOT OF PREJUDICE AGAINST WHITES IN THIS CITY. MANY YEARS BEFORE EITHER OF YOU WERE BORN, A WHITE MAN COULD BE LYNCHED FOR JUST STARING AT A BLACK WOMAN. I SUPPOSE YOUR PARENTS DON'T MIND THAT YOU ARE DATING WHITE BOYS? HMMM....NO COMMENT.
MARY:	WELL, SOMEONE DID WRITE ON JOYCE'S LOCKER! WHAT IF SOMETHING ELSE ALSO HAPPENS?
PRINCIPAL A.:	JUST LET ME KNOW ABOUT IT.
MARY:	BUT, ARE YOU GOING TO DO ANYTHING?
PRINCIPAL A.:	WELL, I WILL NEED PROOF.
MARY:	YEAH, SURE. LET'S GO TO CLASS, JOYCE. WE WILL NOT GET MUCH HELP HERE.
PRINCIPAL A.:	YOUNG LADY, THAT TYPE OF ATTITUDE AND LACK OF RESPECT IS WHY YOU ARE HAVING PROBLEMS IN THE FIRST PLACE.

MARY: I WALKED ACROSS THE STUDENT PARKING LOT TO MY CAR AND THERE IT WAS, UNDER THE WIPER. IT'S A NOTE THAT HAS 'PECKERWOOD LOVER' PRINTED ON IT. I WAS SCARED TO DEATH. I JUST SAT HERE IN THE CAR, SHAKING LIKE A LEAF, WAITING FOR YOU.

JOYCE: LET ME SEE IT. THOSE BASTARDS! JIMMY WILLIAMS AND HIS GANG! I HATE THEM! THEY DO NOT CARE WHO THEY HURT. THEY HAVE EVEN GOT OTHER STUDENTS STARING AT ME. I DON'T KNOW IF I CAN TAKE THIS MUCH LONGER. WHAT ARE WE GOING TO DO?

MARY: IF WE TELL OUR PARENTS, THEN THEY WILL FIND OUT ABOUT THOMAS AND PRETTY BOY. I AM SO NERVOUS, I CAN HARDLY DRIVE.

JOYCE: LET'S GO TO YOUR HOUSE AND DECIDE WHAT TO DO. WILL YOUR MOM AND DAD BE THERE?

MARY: YES, BUT WE CAN USE MY BEDROOM. THEY NEVER COME IN THERE. I AM SO NERVOUS!

JOYCE: DON'T HAVE A WRECK BEFORE WE GET TO YOUR HOUSE. WE HAVE ENOUGH TO WORRY ABOUT.

MARY: OH, MY GOD! LOOK! WHY ARE ALL OF THOSE PEOPLE IN MY FRONT YARD?

IS SOMEONE HURT? WHAT IS GOING ON?

JOYCE: I DON'T KNOW. LOOK! THERE IS YOUR DAD. LET'S FIND OUT WHAT IS HAPPENING.

MARY: DAD! DAD! WHAT'S WRONG? IS MOM OKAY?

MR. JOHNSON: MARY! YOUR MOM IS OKAY. SHE IS UPSET, BUT OKAY. SHE IS IN THE HOUSE. SOME ONE WROTE ON OUR FRONT DOOR WITH SPRAY PAINT. THEY WROTE "PECKERWOOD LOVER". WE HAD CALLED THE POLICE. THEY JUST LEFT A FEW MINUTES AGO.

MARY: WHY ARE ALL OF THESE PEOPLE HERE?

MR. JOHNSON: FOLKS, WE APPRECIATE YOUR CONCERN. NO ONE IS HURT. WE ARE ALL OKAY. PLEASE GO HOME. MY FAMILY AND I WOULD LIKE TO HAVE SOME PRIVACY. COME MARY....AND YOU TOO JOYCE, LET'S GO INSIDE.

MARY: MOM! ARE YOU OKAY?

MRS. JOHNSON: YES, I AM OKAY HONEY. I AM JUST A LITTLE NERVOUS. WHO COULD HAVE DONE SUCH A THING? WE INVITE A WHITE FAMILY OVER FOR DINNER, AND WE GET A THREAT ON OUR DOOR!

MR. JOHNSON: LET US NOT JUMP TO CONCLUSIONS. WE DO NOT KNOW WHY THIS

HAPPENED. AFTER ALL, IT IS WELL KNOWN BY NOW THAT I AM SUPPORTING THE FIRST WHITE PERSON TO EVER RUN FOR SCHOOL BOARD IN THIS CITY.

MRS. JOHNSON: WELL, LOOK WHO IS JUMPING TO CONCLUSIONS NOW.

MR. JOHNSON: MARY, I NEED TO SPEAK TO YOUR MOTHER ALONE.

MARY: JOYCE AND I WILL GO TO MY ROOM.

JOYCE: MARY, WHAT IF SOMETHING LIKE THIS HAS HAPPENED AT MY HOUSE?

MARY: MAYBE YOU HAD BETTER PHONE HOME TO CHECK ON THINGS. USE MY PHONE.

JOYCE: HELLO, MOM? IS EVERYTHING OKAY? OH... NOTHING. I WAS JUST CURIOUS. I AM AT MARY'S. I WILL BE HOME SOON. BYE.

MARY: WELL?

JOYCE: EVERYTHING IS OKAY. BUT, I HAVE TO GET HOME SOON. WHAT ARE WE GOING TO DO ABOUT ALL OF THIS?

MARY: I DON'T KNOW. I WONDER WHAT MY MOM AND DAD ARE TALKING ABOUT DOWN STAIRS. IF THEY KNOW THAT I AM THE CAUSE OF ALL OF THIS ......

JOYCE: HEY, YOU DID NOT WRITE ON THE DOOR. WE DATED TWO WHITE GUYS. YOUR FOLKS ARE NOT BIGOTS. THEY EVEN INVITED THOMAS AND HIS FAMILY TO YOUR HOUSE. WHY DON'T YOU JUST TELL THEM ABOUT EVERYTHING.

MARY: ME?! WHAT ABOUT YOU? WHY DON'T YOU JUST TELL YOUR PARENTS? YOU ARE JUST AS AFRAID AS I AM. WHAT IF THE AFROS DO SOMETHING AT YOUR HOUSE? JOYCE, I DO NOT KNOW HOW MY PARENTS WILL FEEL ABOUT ME DATING A WHITE BOY, AND YOU DO NOT KNOW ABOUT YOURS EITHER. I THINK WE BOTH HAD BETTER JUST NOT SAY ANYTHING ABOUT THOMAS AND PRETTY BOY. AND, LET'S PRAY THAT THE AFROS DO NOTHING ELSE.

PHASE 27

WHAT YOU SEE, IS WHAT YOU GET

"WHAT YOU SEE, IS WHAT YOU GET". THAT PARTICULAR PIECE OF STREET JARGON IS, IN A NUTSHELL, A BASIC TENET OF QUANTUM THEORY. THE "UNCERTAINTY PRINCIPLE" (WERNER HEISENBERG) WHICH IS DERIVED FROM THE STUDY OF ELECTRONS AND OTHER SUB-ATOMIC PARTICLES RECOGNIZES THAT BOTH THE VELOCITY AND THE POSITION OF SUCH A PARTICLE CAN NOT BE SIMULTANEOUSLY MEASURED. AN OBSERVER ATTEMPTING TO MEASURE BOTH AT THE SAME TIME IS ONLY PRESENTED WITH UNCERTAINTY ABOUT EITHER. WHEN THE OBSERVER FOCUSES ON ONE OR THE OTHER, ACCURACY OF MEASUREMENT IS OBTAINED FOR ONE, BUT DENIED FOR THE OTHER.

BEFORE THE FOCUSED OBSERVATION OF THE OBSERVER, THE VELOCITY AND THE POSITION OF THE ELECTRON EXIST ONLY AS A RANGE OF POSSIBILITIES. FOCUS NARROWS THE RANGE TO ONE MEASURABLE "REALITY." QUITE LITERALLY, WHAT YOU SEE IS WHAT YOU GET. THIS RELATIONSHIP BETWEEN THE OBSERVER AND THE OBSERVED MAKES BOTH MUTUALLY DEPENDENT WITHIN A COMMON SYSTEM. THE POWER OF THE OBSERVING MIND IS THE ESSENTIAL ELEMENT IN THE RELATIONSHIP.

THE PRECEDENCE OF MIND OVER MATTER IS QUITE EVIDENT IN THE SUB-ATOMIC WORLD. IT IS NOT AS EVIDENT IN THE "NORMAL" SIZE WORLD OF EVERYDAY HUMAN EXPERIENCE. BUT, BOTH WORLDS ARE ACTUALLY ONE WORLD. ONE CAN NOT EXIST WITHOUT THE OTHER. THE SUB-ATOMIC PROCESSES WITHIN THE HUMAN BRAIN THAT GIVE RISE TO SOMETHING CALLED MIND, ARE THE CONNECTING LINK BETWEEN THE TWO WORLDS. THE ABILITY OF MAN TO ACTUALIZE THAT

161

WHICH THE MIND IMAGINES IS THE PRACTICAL APPLICATION OF "MIND OVER MATTER." WHETHER THIS OCCURS WITHIN THE INSTANTANEOUS TIME FRAME OF SUB-ATOMIC PARTICLES OR THE DAYS, MONTHS, AND YEARS OF NORMAL EVERYDAY HUMAN EXPERIENCE, THE SAME PRINCIPLE APPLIES. MENTAL FOCUS BRINGS INTO EXISTENCE AN OBSERVABLE "REALITY." WHAT YOU SEE, IS WHAT YOU GET.

THOMAS JR. HAS FOCUSED ON A GOAL. THE ACTUALIZATION OF IT SEEMS TO PRODUCE, AS ADDITIONAL BENEFITS, OTHER DESIRABLE SOCIAL CHANGES. THE GOAL IS **THE TEACHING OF WHITE HISTORY AS AN ESSENTIAL ELEMENT OF HISTORY COURSES TAUGHT AT THE SCHOOLS.** THE OTHER BENEFITS FROM THIS EFFORT ARE: (1.) THE FIRST WHITE PERSON TO SEEK ELECTION TO THE SCHOOL BOARD. (2.) A MUCH NEEDED SENSE OF WHITE PRIDE AND RESPECT AMONG WHITE STUDENTS. (3.) A DEVELOPING POSITIVE SENSE OF COMMUNITY WITHIN WHITE NEIGHBORHOODS. (4.) THE BEGINNINGS OF A SHARED SENSE OF COMMUNITY BETWEEN BLACKS AND WHITES AS THEY COOPERATE ON EFFORTS THAT ARE MUTUALLY BENEFICIAL.

HOWEVER, AS WITH OUR PHYSICS MODEL (USING THE VELOCITY AND POSITION OF THE ELECTRON), COMPETING WITH THOMAS' POSITIVE FOCUS IS A NEGATIVE POSSIBILITY. THE COMPETITION IS BETWEEN THE COLLECTIVE MINDS OF THOSE INDIVIDUALS WHO SUPPORT THE TYPE OF CHANGE THAT THOMAS DESIRES AND THE COLLECTIVE MINDS OF THOSE WHO OPPOSE IT. BUT, THIS IS NOT CLEARLY A BLACK AND WHITE ISSUE. EACH COLLECTIVE OF MINDS CONTAINS PHYSICAL BODIES THAT ARE BLACK AS WELL AS WHITE. WHAT YOU SEE MAY BE WHAT YOU GET. HOWEVER, AS IN MOST COMPETITION, WHOEVER GETS THERE FIRST IS THE WINNER.

PRINCIPAL J: THOMAS, SON YOU NEVER CEASE TO
                AMAZE ME. THE FIRST TIME WHEN
                YOU WERE SENT TO MY OFFICE FOR
                CHALLENGING MS. MAYFIELD AND
                WEARING YOUR HAIR LONG, I KNEW
                THEN THAT THERE WAS SOMETHING
                SPECIAL ABOUT YOU. I DID NOT LIKE
                YOU... BUT I KNEW YOU WERE
                DETERMINED AND HAD A VISION. I
                HAD A VISION ONCE WHEN I WAS
                YOUNG. I THOUGHT THAT I HAD LOST
                THAT VISION FOREVER. NOW, I MIGHT
                BE ABLE TO SEE IT AGAIN THROUGH
                YOUR EFFORTS. I AM TRULY AMAZED.
                MR. JOHNSON, THE MOST
                INFLUENTIAL MAN IN THIS TOWN, HAS
                COMMITTED HIMSELF TO ` HELPING
                YOUR MOTHER GET ELECTED TO THE
                SCHOOL BOARD AND TO GETTING THE
                **FACTS OF WHITE HISTORY INCLUDED
                WITHIN THE HISTORY COURSES
                TAUGHT AT THE SCHOOLS.**

THOMAS JR.:   MR. JOHNSON ALSO THINKS THAT IT
                WOULD BE A GOOD IDEA IF HIS
                DAUGHTER AND I, AND OTHER BLACK
                AND WHITE KIDS WOULD WORK
                TOGETHER ON PROMOTING MY
                MOTHER'S RUN FOR THE SCHOOL
                BOARD.

PRINCIPAL J.:   THAT IS AN EXCELLENT IDEA. WE
                HAVE NO BLACK STUDENTS AT
                WASHINGTON HIGH AND THERE ARE
                ONLY A HANDFUL OF WHITES AT
                EGYPTIAN HIGH. YOUNG BLACKS AND
                WHITES WORKING TOGETHER IS A
                MUCH NEEDED MODEL FOR THE
                FUTURE OF OUR SOCIETY.

THOMAS JR.:   I WOULD LIKE PERMISSION TO TALK TO STUDENTS ABOUT HELPING WITH THIS.

PRINCIPAL J.:   WELL, YOU HAVE MY PERMISSION. WHY DON'T YOU START WITH MS. MAYFIELD'S HISTORY CLASS? AFTER ALL, THAT IS WHERE ALL OF THIS BEGAN.

MS. MAYFIELD: CLASS, THOMAS WOULD LIKE TO DISCUSS AN IDEA THAT HE HAS.

THOMAS JR.:   WE NEED **WHITE HISTORY TAUGHT WITHIN THE HISTORY COURSES OF THE SCHOOLS.** THE SCHOOL BOARD HAS TO MAKE THE FINAL DECISION. WE NEED A WHITE PERSON ON THE BOARD. MY MOTHER IS RUNNING FOR THE SCHOOL BOARD. SHE WILL NEED THE VOTES OF BLACKS AS WELL AS WHITES TO BE ELECTED. WHAT IF A GROUP OF STUDENTS FROM OUR SCHOOL WORKED WITH A GROUP OF BLACK STUDENTS FROM EGYPTIAN HIGH TO MAKE CAMPAIGN SIGNS AND TO DO OTHER THINGS TO HELP HER ` GET ELECTED?

REGGIE: THOMAS. WE HARDLY EVER ASSOCIATE WITH THE BLACKS FROM EGYPTIAN HIGH. WHAT MAKES YOU THINK THAT ANY OF THEM WOULD BE INTERESTED IN HELPING TO GET WHITE HISTORY IN THE SCHOOLS AND TO GET YOUR MOTHER ELECTED?

BETTY: REGGIE, THE ANSWER TO THAT QUESTION IS "MARY JOHNSON." HAVE YOU HEARD ABOUT IT? THOMAS HAS HIS EYES ON A BLACK GIRL. A "HIGH AND MIGHTY" BLACK GIRL! THE DAUGHTER OF "MR. BUSINESS-MAN" HIMSELF....MR. J. J. JOHNSON!

SARAH: WHAT'S THE MATTER, THOMAS? ARE WE WHITE GIRLS GOOD ENOUGH FOR YOU?

REGGIE: YEAH MAN. I THOUGHT YOU WERE ALL ABOUT WHITE PRIDE.

MS. MAYFIELD: OKAY, CLASS. THOMAS IS NOT HERE TO DISCUSS HIS PERSONAL LIFE. HE IS ASKING YOU ABOUT WORKING WITH STUDENTS FROM EGYPTIAN HIGH ON A COMMON GOAL.

BETTY: MS. MAYFIELD, WHY ARE WHITE MEN SO ANXIOUS TO HAVE A BLACK WOMAN?

MS. MAYFIELD: I DON'T WANT TO TALK ABOUT THAT!

SARAH: THOMAS, DO YOU WANT TO TALK ABOUT THAT?

THOMAS JR.: I KNOW THIS MAKES ME LOOK LIKE A HYPOCRITE, BUT LET ME TRY TO EXPLAIN.

BETTY: LET'S SEE IF HE CAN TALK HIS WAY OUT OF THIS.

165

THOMAS JR.: I'M NOT APOLOGIZING FOR DATING A BLACK GIRL. I MET HER WHEN MY FAMILY WAS INVITED TO THEIR HOUSE FOR DINNER. WE WENT OUT ONE NIGHT WITH ONE OF HER FRIENDS AND ONE OF MINE. I'M NOT PREJUDICE AGAINST BLACKS. SURE, I KNOW ABOUT THE HISTORY OF HOW EUROPEANS WERE ENSLAVED AND MISTREATED IN THIS COUNTRY. I KNOW ABOUT RACISM AND DISCRIMINATION. BUT, NOT ALL BLACKS ARE BAD. MR. JOHNSON IS A DECENT MAN. HE HAS A GOOD FAMILY. IF THE RACISM IN THIS COUNTRY IS GOING TO END, IT WILL TAKE GOOD AND DECENT PEOPLE OF EACH RACE TO CHANGE IT. IT'S JUST AS WRONG FOR US TO BE PREJUDICED AGAINST BLACKS AS IT IS FOR THEM TO BE PREJUDICED AGAINST US.

MS. MAYFIELD: WELL SAID.

BETTY: YEAH. HE REALLY HAS A WAY WITH WORDS. I WONDER WHAT WORDS HE USED WITH MARY JOHNSON.

REGGIE: BETTY, I THINK THAT YOU ARE JEALOUS THAT HE DID NOT USE THOSE WORDS WITH YOU.

BETTY: PECKERWOOD, PLEASE!

MS. MAYFIELD: THERE IS THAT WORD AGAIN. I THOUGHT WE WERE BEGINNING TO DISCIPLINE OURSELVES TO NOT USE IT.

REGGIE: I AGREE WITH THOMAS. WE, THE STUDENTS, ARE THE FUTURE OF THIS COUNTRY. MAYBE IT IS UP TO US TO START MAKING SOME CHANGES. THOMAS, I WILL WORK WITH THE BLACK STUDENTS.

MS. MAYFIELD: I'M PROUD OF YOU REGGIE. NOW, WHAT ABOUT THE REST OF YOU. IS HAVING WHITE HISTORY AND A WHITE SCHOOL BOARD MEMBER MORE IMPORTANT THAN WHO DATES WHOM AND WHAT COLOR THEY ARE?

SARAH: WELL, I GUESS YOU ARE RIGHT. I WILL HELP.

MS. MAYFIELD: BETTY?

BETTY: I STILL THINK YOU SHOULD HAVE A WHITE GIRL FRIEND, THOMAS. BUT, I WILL HELP. I WILL TRY TO PUT MY FEELINGS...I MEAN PREJUDICES ASIDE.

PHASE 28

THE CHILDREN OF NEANDERTHAL

FEELINGS OR PREJUDICE? BETTY SEEMS TO BE UNCERTAIN ABOUT WHICH ONE IS RESPONSIBLE FOR HER NEGATIVITY TOWARDS THOMAS' PROPOSAL AND HIS AFFAIR WITH MARY JOHNSON. ACTUALLY, BOTH ARE PLAYING AN EQUAL ROLE IN HER MOTIVATION. IN HER HEART, SHE KNOWS THAT REGGIE WAS RIGHT. SHE DOES HAVE GREAT ADMIRATION FOR THOMAS BECAUSE OF WHAT HE HAS TRIED TO ACCOMPLISH. THAT ADMIRATION HAS BLOSSOMED INTO A TEENAGE "CRUSH". YES, SHE IS PERSONALLY DISAPPOINTED BY THOMAS' ATTRACTION TO MARY JOHNSON. THE FACT THAT MARY IS BLACK MAKES THAT DISAPPOINTMENT EVEN MORE POINTED. THE DISAPPOINTMENT POINTS DIRECTLY TO HER OWN SUBCONSCIOUS RACIAL BIAS AND CAUSES IT TO SURFACE. HOLDING BACK HER FEELINGS AND PREJUDICES, SHE HAS ONLY GRUDGINGLY AGREED TO COOPERATE.

PREJUDICE IS NOT UNIQUE TO ANY ONE RACIAL GROUP. WHITES, DUE TO THEIR GENERALLY LOWER SOCIO-ECONOMIC AND POLITICAL STATUS, HAVE TRADITIONALLY BEEN VICTIMS OF RACIAL PREJUDICE IN THE UNITED STATES OF NEW AFRICA. BUT, MANY WHITES HAVE COME TO HARBOR IRRATIONAL IDEAS ABOUT BLACKS. THE MOST PREVALENT OF THESE BEING THE NOTION THAT BLACKS IN GENERAL THINK OF THEMSELVES AS BETTER THAN WHITES. FOR SOME WHITES, THIS NOTION MANIFESTS ITSELF IN A BASIC MISTRUST OF BLACKS.

THERE IS EVEN A SMALL MINORITY OF WHITES WHO HAVE REJECTED ALL OF THE VALUES IDENTIFIED WITH THE DOMINATE BLACK CULTURE. THESE ARE THE EXTREME WHITE NATIONALIST. SOME OF THESE HAVE

GONE SO FAR AS TO CALL FOR SETTING UP A WHITE STATE WITHIN THE COUNTRY OR FOR WHITES TO MIGRATE TO EUROPE. THESE EXTREMIST ARE NOT DISCRETE IN EXPRESSING THEIR OUTRIGHT HATRED OF BLACKS. THEY HAVE REDEFINED THEIR OWN SELF-CONCEPTS BY EQUATING WHITE WITH GOOD AND BLACK WITH BAD. BOTH SEXES WEAR THEIR HAIR AT LEAST SHOULDER LENGTH AND LONGER. MANY OF THE MEN GROW FULL BEARDS. THE MOST NOTORIOUS OF THESE EXTREMIST GROUPS CALLS ITSELF "THE CHILDREN OF NEANDERTHAL". AMONG THIS GROUP, EVEN SUCH TRITE AFRICAN TRADITIONS AS WHITE CATS BEING SYMBOLS OF BAD LUCK IS REVERSED. THEY ACTUALLY TEACH THEIR CHILDREN THAT **BLACK** CATS SYMBOLIZE BAD LUCK. ALTHOUGH THEY DO NOT CLAIM ANY STATE-LIKE TERRITORY WITHIN THE BORDERS OF NEW AFRICA, THE ORGANIZATION CLAIMS MEMBERS THROUGHOUT THE COUNTRY. THE ORGANIZATION ITSELF IS SIMILAR TO A RELIGIOUS SECT. THE NATIONAL LEADER HAS THE TITLE OF "GRAND REVEREND".

THE GRAND REVEREND WILL PERIODICALLY BRING THE FOLLOWERS TOGETHER IN SOME SELECTED CITY FOR A REVIVAL TYPE MEETING. BEING A MINORITY WITHIN A MINORITY, THIS TYPE OF PUBLIC EXPOSURE IS CRUCIAL FOR KEEPING THE GROUPS AGENDA ALIVE. THE AGENDA APPEARS TO BE MOSTLY EMOTIONAL. THE ORGANIZATION LACKS THE POLITICAL SOPHISTICATION AND ORGANIZATION FOR ANY REAL IMPACT ON THE GOVERNMENTAL POWER STRUCTURE. THE GRAND REVEREND HIMSELF IS AN INDIVIDUAL WITH EXTRAORDINARY ORATORY SKILLS. CRITICS SIMPLY SAY THAT HE HAS A BIG MOUTH. HE DEFINITELY HAS THE ABILITY TO AROUSE THE EMOTIONS OF THOSE WHOM HE SPEAKS TO. TOO OFTEN, THESE ARE NEGATIVE EMOTIONS THAT TEND TO MAKE AN ADVERSARIAL SITUATION OUT OF MOST ISSUES THAT INVOLVE THE TWO RACES.

HOWEVER, TO THE TRUE BELIEVER THIS AGITATION IS THE "SUBSTANCE OF THINGS HOPED FOR". THE

EXTREMISTS WISTFULLY BUT TRULY HOPE FOR A REVERSAL OF THE ROLES BETWEEN THE RACES. THE PROMISED LAND IS A NATION WHERE WHITES ARE DOMINANT SOCIALLY, POLITICALLY, AND ECONOMICALLY. GIVEN THE REALITY OF LIFE IN NEW AFRICA, THE AGENDA OF THE CHILDREN OF NEANDERTHAL CAN PROBABLY BEST BE DESCRIBED AS "EVIDENCE OF THINGS NOT YET SEEN".

IT IS ONLY NATURAL THAT THE LOCAL CHAPTER OF THE CHILDREN SHOULD INVITE THE GRAND REVEREND TO TOWN. THE REVIVAL OF WHITE PRIDE IN THE COMMUNITY AND THE RENEWED INTEREST IN WHITE HISTORY PROVIDE THE PERFECT SETTING FOR THE REVEREND AND HIS CHILDREN TO PREACH THE WORDS OF WHITE EXTREMISM. HOWEVER, THE TRUE BELIEVERS ARE NOT THE ONLY ONES WHO ARE READY TO HEAR WHAT THE GRAND REVEREND HAS TO SAY.

A FEW HUNDRED WHITES GATHER WITHIN THE LARGE CIRCUS-LIKE TENT JUST OUTSIDE THE CITY LIMITS. AMONG THOSE IN ATTENDANCE ARE THE DOZEN LOCAL FAITHFUL FOLLOWERS WHO ARE ON THE STAGE WITH THE REVEREND. THEY ARE ALL MEN. EACH ONE IS WEARING A WHITE ROBE. EACH HAS A FULL BEARD. ALL PROFESS THE BELIEF IN THE POSITIVE VALUE OF BEING WHITE. BUT, THE HISTORICAL REALITY OF BLACK-MASTER AND WHITE-SLAVE INTERBREEDING, REVEALS A RANGE OF SHADES OF "WHITE" SKIN. ON ONE END OF THE SPECTRUM ARE THE BLONDE HAIRED, BLUE-EYED AND FAIR SKINNED SUCH AS THE REVEREND HIMSELF. ON THE OTHER END ARE THE TAN COLORED, CURLY HAIRED AND SLIGHTLY NEGROID IN FACIAL FEATURE ONES WHO ARE LIKE PRETTY BOY IN APPEARANCE.

ALSO IN ATTENDANCE ARE THE VARIED INDIVIDUALS IN THE AUDIENCE. MANY ARE WHITES WHO HAVE HAD A MEMORABLE BAD EXPERIENCE WITH BLACKS OR WHO FEEL THAT THEY HAVE A PERSONAL GRIEVANCE AGAINST BLACKS. BETTY OVERSTREET, THOMAS' FELLOW HISTORY STUDENT AND SECRET ADMIRER,

SITS AS A REPRESENTATIVE OF THIS GROUP. MOST OF THOSE PRESENT ARE THE CURIOUS WHO SIMPLY WANT TO KNOW FOR THEMSELVES THE TRUTH ABOUT THE CHILDREN OF NEANDERTHAL. THOMAS JR., SITTING AT A FRONT ROW SEAT, CAN BE COUNTED AMONG THIS GROUP. ABSENT FROM ATTENDANCE ARE THOSE WHITES WHO OUT OF FEAR OF HOW BLACKS MIGHT REACT, DO NOT WANT TO BE SEEN AT SUCH AN EVENT. PRINCIPAL JACKSON CAN BE COUNTED AMONG THIS GROUP.

THE RUMBLING OF VOICES THROUGHOUT THE AUDIENCE SUDDENLY GROWS QUIET. THE GRAND REVEREND RISES FROM HIS SEAT, STANDS AT THE PODIUM AND WITH ARMS STRETCHED OUT, BEGINS TO SPEAK.

REVEREND: BROTHERS AND SISTERS! I WELCOME YOU TO THIS GATHERING OF THE FAMILY. THE WORD "FAMILY" IS INDEED APPROPRIATE. FOR IN REALITY, ALL WHITES ARE THE DESCENDANTS OF NEANDERTHAL. WHEN I SPEAK OF NEANDERTHAL, I AM REFERRING TO OUR PRE-HISTORIC EUROPEAN ANCESTORS.

IN THIS COUNTRY THE BLACK MAN HAS DEFINED BLACK AS GOOD AND WHITE AS BAD. BUT, BROTHERS AND SISTERS, I AM HERE TO TELL YOU THAT IS A LIE! WHITE ` IS GOOD AND BLACK IS **EVIL**! WHAT RACE HAS KILLED OR ENSLAVED OTHERS THROUGHOUT THE WORLD? WHAT RACE HAS RAPED AND FORCED IT'S BLOOD INTO THE FAMILIES OF OTHER RACES?

WHITE IS BEAUTIFUL! EVERYBODY, SAY IT LOUD AND TOGETHER! **WHITE IS BEAUTIFUL!**

OKAY! OKAY! NOW, THAT IS THE FRAME OF MIND THAT WE NEED TO HAVE, WE MUST REJECT WHAT THE BLACK MAN HAS TAUGHT US. WE MUST RE-TEACH OURSELVES. WHITE SKIN IS BEAUTIFUL. STRAIGHT HAIR IS BEAUTIFUL. LONG NOSES AND THIN LIPS ARE BEAUTIFUL. WE MUST PRESERVE THE PHYSICAL QUALITIES OF OUR RACE. WE OF THE CHILDREN DO NOT BELIEVE IN RACE MIXING. OUR RACE HAS BEEN TAINTED ENOUGH BY THE BLACK MAN. RACE MIXING HAPPENS AS A RESULT OF SOCIAL MIXING. THOSE AMONG US WHO PRACTICE INTER-RACIAL SOCIALIZING ARE NOTHING BUT TRAITORS. WE MUST CLEANSE OURSELVES OF THE BLACK MAN'S INFLUENCE.

THERE ARE THOSE IN THIS COMMUNITY WHO SEEK TO ENCOURAGE THE INTERRACIAL SOCIALIZING THAT WILL LEAD TO MORE RACE MIXING. I SAY TO THOSE MISGUIDED BROTHERS AND SISTERS, BEWARE!

LOOK AT WHAT HAS HAPPENED TO US SINCE WE WERE BOUGHT TO THIS COUNTRY AS SLAVES. WE HAVE ADOPTED CUSTOMS THAT REINFORCE NEGATIVE SELF-CONCEPTS ABOUT OURSELVES. MOST OF OUR WOMEN

AND SOME OF OUR MEN ROUTINELY CURL THEIR NATURALLY BEAUTIFUL STRAIGHT HAIR. WHY? BECAUSE THE BLACK MAN HAS SAID THAT KINKY IS THE STANDARD FOR HAIR BEAUTY. MANY OF YOU BELIEVE THAT BECAUSE YOUR SKIN IS TANNED, THAT YOU ARE BETTER THAN THE PERSON SITTING NEXT TO YOU WHO HAS FAIR SKIN. WHY? BECAUSE THE BLACK MAN HAS SAID:

"IF YOU'RE BLACK, YOU'RE ON THE RIGHT TRACK.
IF YOU'RE BROWN, STICK AROUND.
IF YOU'RE WHITE, GET OUT OF SIGHT".

TO HELL WITH WHAT THE BLACK MAN SAYS! ALL OF US ARE WHITE. WE WILL NOT LET THE BLACK MAN DIVIDE US!

SOME OF YOU, NO DOUBT, ADMIRE THAT SO-CALLED ENTERTAINER BY THE NAME OF JACKIE MICHAELS. THE SAME JACKIE MICHAELS WHO CURLS HIS HAIR, HAD HIS SKIN DARKENED, AND WHO HAD FACIAL SURGERY TO MAKE HIMSELF LOOK LIKE A BLACK MAN. NONE OF YOU SHOULD ADMIRE THAT TRAITOR. HE IS OF THE SAME MOLD AS THOSE SOUTHERN EUROPEANS OF THE PAST WHO HELPED TO ENSLAVE THEIR OWN WHITE NORTHERN EUROPEAN ` BROTHERS. HE AND THEY SOLD OUT FOR PERSONAL GAIN. WHY? BECAUSE THE BLACK MAN HAS DICTATED THAT BLACK IS GOOD AND WHITE IS BAD.

BROTHERS AND SISTERS, I AM HERE TO TELL YOU THAT THE TRUTH WILL SET YOU FREE. THE TRUTH IS THAT WHITE IS GOOD AND BLACK IS **EVIL**! IF THE DEVIL IS ANY COLOR, IT MUST BE BLACK. WHITE CATS ARE NOT BAD LUCK. BLACK CATS MEAN BAD LUCK! WE SHOULD NOT WEAR WHITE CLOTHING AT FUNERALS. WE SHOULD WEAR BLACK CLOTHING.

NOW, I KNOW THAT SOME OF YOU ARE FRIGHTENED BY WHAT I HAVE SAID. THERE ARE SOME OF YOU WHO THINK THAT I AM A FANATICAL PECKERWOOD. WELL, I AM NOT A PECKERWOOD. I **AM** FANATICAL ABOUT BEING WHITE. THOSE BOOT-LICKING, BLACK-ASS-KISSING MEMBERS OF OUR RACE ARE THE TRUE PECKERWOODS. IF YOU BELIEVE WHAT THE BLACK MAN HAS TAUGHT US, YOU ARE A PECKERWOOD! IF YOU WANT TO SOCIALIZE AND INTERBREED WITH THE BLACK MAN, YOU ARE A PECKER-WOOD! YOU THINK I'M CRAZY? **PECKERWOOD, PLEASE!**

WHITE IS BEAUTIFUL! EVERYBODY, REPEAT AFTER ME! WHITE IS BEAUTIFUL!

PHASE 29

WHITE POWER

PRINCIPAL JACKSON: MS. MAYFIELD, DID YOU READ THE PAPER THIS MORNING?

MS. MAYFIELD: YES, I DID.

PRINCIPAL J.: THAT FANATIC GRAND REVEREND IS GOING TO STIR UP TROUBLE BETWEEN THE RACES. THIS IS WORST THAN ANYTHING THAT THOMAS JR. EVER DID.

MS. MAYFIELD: THOMAS HAS BEEN A POSITIVE INFLUENCE. HE IS EVEN TRYING TO GET BLACK AND WHITE KIDS TO WORK TOGETHER. IF ANY OF OUR STUDENTS ATTENDED THAT NEANDERTHAL MEETING AND WERE IMPRESSED, IT COULD LEAD TO PROBLEMS. THOSE NEANDERTHALS PREACH HATRED.

PRINCIPAL J.: THOSE FOOLS DON'T SEEM TO UNDERSTAND THAT BLACKS ARE THE MAJORITY AND THEY HAVE THE POWER. ALL OF THEIR BAD-MOUTHING OF BLACKS WILL NOT CHANGE THE STATUS QUO. IF TOO MANY WHITES ACCEPT THEIR IDEAS, IT WILL LEAD TO VIOLENCE BETWEEN THE RACES. VIOLENCE CAN ONLY RESULT IN

175

	TRAGEDY FOR WHITES. WE MUST BE ON GUARD AND QUICKLY DISPEL ANY NOTIONS OF WHITE SUPERIORITY.
MS. MAYFIELD:	ISN'T IT IRONIC. WE ONCE SAW THOMAS JR. AS A THREAT BECAUSE OF HIS IDEAS ABOUT WHITE PRIDE. BUT NOW, THE NEANDERTHALS MAKE HIM SEEM VERY MODERATE.
PRINCIPAL J.:	LET'S NOT BE NAÏVE. WHAT THIS COMMUNITY IS FACING RIGHT NOW IS PARTIALLY THOMAS' FAULT. HE STARTED THIS WHITE PRIDE STUFF. THE NEANDERTHALS WOULD NOT BE MAKING THE NEWS TODAY IF HE HAD NOT PAVED THE WAY FOR THEM WITH ALL OF THIS WHITE PRIDE BUSINESS. ONE THING LEADS TO ANOTHER.
MS. MAYFIELD:	SURELY, YOU'RE NOT BLAMING THOMAS FOR WHAT THE NEANDERTHALS ARE SAYING.
PRINCIPAL J.:	NOT ALL TOGETHER. BUT, HE DOES SHARE SOME RESPONSIBILITY. AT THIS MOMENT, I WOULD SAY THAT HE IS SIMPLY THE LESSER OF TWO EVILS. UNFORTUNATELY, THE COMMUNITY NEEDS HIM. HE IS NEEDED IF FOR NO OTHER REASON THAN TO PROVIDE AN ALTERNATIVE TO THE NEANDERTHALS. AT LEAST HIS

BRAND OF WHITE PRIDE DOESN'T LABEL BLACKS AS THE DEVIL. AND, THE COOPERATION BETWEEN HIS FAMILY AND THE JOHNSON'S IS A MODEL OF WHAT IS NEEDED IN THIS TOWN.

MS. MAYFIELD, I BELIEVE THIS TOWN IS HEADING TOWARD A CLIMATIC CHANGE. IT WILL EITHER BE FOR THE BETTER OR FOR THE WORST. IF IT IS FOR THE BETTER, THOMAS WILL BE A HERO. IF IT IS FOR THE WORST, THEN HE WILL PROBABLY BE THE SCAPEGOAT FOR MOST OF THE BLAME.

WHAT IS THE EXACT INSTANCE OF A QUANTUM UNIT OF MEASUREMENT THAT DISTINGUISHES ONE UNIT FROM THE NEXT? THAT VERY THOUGHT PROVOKING QUESTION IS FUNDAMENTAL TO A BASIC PROBLEM OF PHYSICS. THE PROBLEM IS UNDERSTANDING THE CONNECTIVE STRUCTURE OF THE UNIVERSE WHERE INFINITY PRESENTS ITSELF AS AN INSURMOUNTABLE OBSTACLE TO EXACTNESS. WHERE DOES ONE STOP WHEN SUBDIVIDING FRACTIONS INTO SMALLER AND SMALLER NUMERICAL MEASUREMENTS? AT WHAT POINT DOES ONE UNIT OF SOMETHING BECOME ANOTHER UNIT WHEN BOTH CAN BE INFINITELY DIVIDED? WHERE DOES ONE COLOR IN THE SPECTRUM END AND ANOTHER BEGINS? MATTER AS OPPOSE TO SPACE? EXISTENCE AND NON-EXISTENCE?

THIS BASIC PROBLEM OF QUANTUM PHYSICS IS APPLICABLE TO THE MUCH LARGER WORLD OF HUMAN EXPERIENCE AND EVENTS. THE ELUSIVE QUANTITY (OR QUALITY) IS ANALOGOUS TO A CLIMAX. THE CLIMAX WOULD BE THE HIGHEST POINT IN THE ACCUMULATION OF A SERIES THAT RESULTS IN A NEW QUANTITY OR

QUALITY OF MEASUREMENT. THIS WOULD BE THE PROVERBIAL "STRAW THAT BREAKS THE CAMEL'S BACK".

WITHIN THE CONTEXT OF PRINCIPAL JACKSON'S PERCEPTION OF AN IMPENDING CHANGE IN THE COMMUNITY, THE "STRAW" IS THE UNKNOWN CLIMATIC EVENT. THE OTHER UNKNOWN IS THE RESULT OR HOW THE REALITY OF RACE RELATIONS WITHIN THE COMMUNITY WILL BE CHANGED BY THE EVENT. WILL IT BE NEGATIVE AS SYMBOLIZED BY THE PHRASE "THE STRAW THAT BREAKS THE CAMEL'S BACK". OR, WILL IT TAKE THE POSITIVE FORM OF "THE STRAW THAT COMPLETES THE BUNDLE"?

PRINCIPAL JACKSON CORRECTLY UNDERSTANDS THAT HIS COMMUNITY AND TOWN ARE NEAR THE "FORK IN THE ROAD". THE PREVIOUSLY TRAVELED ROAD IS COMING TO AN END. ONE PATH OF THE FORK PROMISES A SOCIETY IN WHICH THE RACES FIND COMMON GROUND FOR THEIR MUTUAL BENEFIT. THE OTHER THREATENS WITH A BATTLEGROUND OF MUTUAL DEMISE.

BETTY: I'M TELLING YOU GUYS, THE GRAND REVEREND SPEAKS THE TRUTH. WE SHOULD NOT SOCIALIZE WITH THE BLACKS. I DON'T CARE WHAT THOMAS SAYS. THEY ARE OUR ENEMIES. YOU SHOULD HAVE BEEN THERE. THE REVEREND TOLD IT LIKE IT IS. WHITE IS GOOD. BLACK IS **EVIL**!

THOMAS JR.:   I WAS THERE. I DISAGREE WITH YOU.

BETTY: YOU?! YOU WOULD DISAGREE. YOU JUST DON'T WANT TO GIVE UP YOUR LITTLE BLACK BITCH.

MS. MAYFIELD: NOW, THAT IS ENOUGH. IT'S TIME FOR THE CLASS TO BEGIN. BETTY, THAT TYPE OF LANGUAGE IS NOT APPROPRIATE!

REGGIE (R.G.M. #1): MS. MAYFIELD, BETTY MAY BE RIGHT. WHY SHOULD WE ALWAYS SUCK-UP TO THE BLACKS. WE CAN ACCOMPLISH THINGS ON OUR OWN. THOMAS, MAN, I RESPECT WHAT YOU HAVE TRIED TO DO AT THIS SCHOOL FOR WHITE PRIDE. I MEAN…WHITE HISTORY AND ALL OF THAT IS IMPORTANT. BUT, I'M TIRED OF ALWAYS BEING DEPENDENT ON BLACKS. I THINK WE SHOULD INVITE THE GRAND REVEREND TO OUR SCHOOL AND HEAR WHAT HE HAS TO SAY.

THOMAS JR.: REGGIE, I'VE HEARD WHAT HE HAS TO SAY. HE IS PREACHING HATE.

BETTY: BLACKS HAVE BEEN PREACHING HATRED AGAINST US FOR YEARS.

THOMAS JR.: DOES THAT MAKE IT RIGHT FOR US TO DO IT? DON'T LET HATE BLIND YOU TO THE TRUTH.

BETTY: THOMAS, **LOVE** CAN BLIND TOO. I DON'T THINK YOU CAN SEE PASS MARY JOHNSON. WE DON'T NEED BLACK PEOPLE. WE NEED EACH OTHER. WE NEED **WHITE POWER!**

REGGIE: YEAH. I LIKE THOSE WORDS. **WHITE POWER!**

THOMAS JR.:   REGGIE, I THOUGHT YOUR FAVORITE COLOR WAS **RED!**

MS. MAYFIELD: NO! NO! I WILL NOT ALLOW THIS CLASS TO BECOME A BREEDING GROUND FOR HATE.

BETTY: **WHITE POWER!**

REGGIE: **WHITE POWER!**

BETTY: **WHITE POWER!**

PHASE 30

NIGGER, PLEASE

AS SCHOOL BOARD ELECTION DAY NEARS, A FEELING OF FOREBODING SEEMS TO BE BUILDING UP THROUGHOUT THE TOWN. EMOTIONS ARE RUNNING HIGH AND REASON APPEARS TO HAVE RETREATED. WITHIN THE BLACK COMMUNITY, THE AFROS HAVE ORGANIZED TO OPPOSED THE POSSIBLE ELECTION OF A WHITE SCHOOL BOARD MEMBER. LATE NIGHT PHONE THREATS HAVE BEEN MADE ON A REGULAR BASIS TO THE JOHNSON HOUSEHOLD. MARY JOHNSON CONTINUES TO RECEIVE NASTY NOTES AND "HATE STARES" FROM SOME OF HER FELLOW STUDENTS. LEAFLETS ARE CIRCULATING THROUGH THE BLACK SUBURBS CONDEMNING ALL FORMS OF RACIAL INTERMIXING AND CALLING FOR BLACK VOTER TURN OUT TO INSURE THE ELECTION OF ANOTHER ALL BLACK SCHOOL BOARD.

MOST BLACKS DO NOT SUBSCRIBE TO THE RACIAL EXTREMISM CHARACTERIZED BY THE AFROS. BUT, THERE IS A CONCERN (AND IN THE MINDS OF SOME A FEAR) THAT THE ESTABLISHED AND FAMILIAR WAY OF DOING THINGS IS BEING THREATENED. THE FAMILIARITY OF THE STATUS QUO IS PREFERABLE TO THE UNKNOWN THAT ACCOMPANIES CHANGE. FOR THE LAST FEW YEARS BLACKS HAVE READ ABOUT AND SEEN TELEVISION COVERAGE OF THE GANG VIOLENCE THAT PLAGUES THE WHITE NEIGHBORHOODS. THIS HAS ONLY SUPPORTED THE NEGATIVE WHITE STEREOTYPE THAT MANY BLACKS ALREADY HAVE. THE FACT THAT THE GRAND REVEREND IS IN TOWN PREACHING HIS BRAND OF HATRED, CAUSES MORE THAN A FEW BLACKS TO BE ALARMED BY THE NEW SPIRIT OF RACIAL PRIDE THAT HAS EMERGED IN THE WHITE COMMUNITY. WHERE

WHITE PRIDE SIMPLY MAKES BLACKS CONCERNED, WHITE POWER MAKES THEM FEARFUL.

IN THE WHITE COMMUNITY, THERE ARE ALSO THOSE WHO ARE FEARFUL. CONSERVATIVE WHITES ARE EMBARRASSED BY THE LONG STRINGY HAIR OF THOSE RECLAIMING WHITE PRIDE. THEY ARE FRIGHTENED ALMOST TO THE POINT OF HYSTERIA BY THE BELIEFS OF THE CHILDREN OF NEANDERTHAL. WHITES LIKE PRINCIPAL JACKSON HAD LONG AGO LEARNED TO ASSUME A SUBORDINATE ATTITUDE IN THEIR SOCIAL CONTACT WITH BLACKS. DURING THE SLAVE ERA, WHITES HAD TO REFRAIN FROM LOOKING DIRECTLY INTO THE EYES OF A BLACK PERSON WHEN TALKING TO THE PERSON. THAT CUSTOM IS YET PRACTICED BY WHITES LIKE PRINCIPAL JACKSON. THERE ARE A FEW WHITES FOR WHOM THE IDEA OF VOTING AS A BLOC TO ELECT A WHITE SCHOOL BOARD MEMBER IS ITSELF A FORM OF RADICALISM. IN THEIR VIEW, SUCH ACTION IS A DIRECT CHALLENGE TO THE SELF-CONTEMPT THAT THEY HAD LONG AGO FOUND COMFORT IN.

IN CONTRAST TO THE FEARFUL WITHIN THE WHITE COMMUNITY, THERE ARE THOSE WHO ARE DETERMINED TO BE FEARLESS IN THEIR REJECTION OF THE STATUS QUO. IRONICALLY, THESE STUDENTS OF HATE SHARE A COMMON GROUND WITH THEIR BLACK COUNTERPARTS. THEY ARE OPPOSED TO THE CANDIDACY OF MRS. EDWARDS. THEIR OPPOSITION IS NOT BECAUSE SHE IS WHITE, BUT BECAUSE BLACKS ARE PLAYING A MAJOR ROLE IN HER CAMPAIGN. THE EMOTIONALISM OF WHITE POWER SEEKS TO REPLACE THE COOL, REASONED PRAGMATISM OF THE TYPE OF WHITE PRIDE THAT WAS INITIALLY PROMOTED BY THOMAS JR.

SINCE HIS CLASSROOM CONFRONTATION WITH BETTY AND REGGIE, THOMAS JR. HAS FOUND HIS SCHOOL HERO STATUS DIMINISHED. TO THE DISMAY OF PRINCIPAL JACKSON AND MS. MAYFIELD, THE WORDS "WHITE POWER" AND THE RAISED CLENCHED FIST ARE FREQUENTLY HEARD AND SEEN ON CAMPUS. REGGIE AND BETTY HAVE BECOME THOMAS' RIVAL STUDENT

LEADERS. THE STUDENT BODY FINDS ITSELF SEPARATING INTO TWO COMPETING FACTIONS. EVEN THE ASININE FIGHTING BETWEEN THE BLUES AND REDS HAS TAKEN A BACK SEAT TO THE RIVALRY BETWEEN WHITE MILITANTS AND WHITE MODERATES. REGGIE HAS EFFECTIVELY PERSUADED THE REDS TO END THEIR CONFRONTATIONS WITH THE BLUES AND TO TAKE UP THE WHITE POWER CAUSE. ODDLY ENOUGH, BLUE GANG MEMBER NUMBER ONE HAS BEFRIENDED THOMAS JR. THE BLUES CONSIDER THEMSELVES TO BE WHITE MODERATES ON THE RACIAL ISSUE. IRONICALLY, IN THIS NEW STATE OF AFFAIRS, THE REDS AND BLUES ARE STILL ON OPPOSING SIDES.

THOMAS JR. WEARILY CONTEMPLATES THE POSSIBLE OUTCOMES OF ALL OF THESE RECENT DEVELOPMENTS. WILL WHITE AND BLACK EXTREMIST POLARIZE THE COMMUNITY TO THE POINT WHERE THE SCHOOL BOARD ELECTION BECOMES A WHITE VERSUS BLACK CONTEST? WILL THOMAS BE ABLE TO GRADUATE FROM A HIGH SCHOOL THAT IS NOT TORN BY GANG, RACIAL OR POLITICAL ISSUES? WHAT WILL BECOME OF HIS EFFORTS TO HAVE **WHITE HISTORY INCLUDED WITHIN THE MATERIALS USED TO TEACH HISTORY COURSES?** WILL HE AND MARY JOHNSON CONTINUE TO SEE EACH OTHER? ALL OF THESE QUESTIONS SWIRL THROUGH THOMAS' MIND. THEY HAVE MADE HIS FRIDAY NIGHT'S SLEEP A RESTLESS ONE. THEY ARE STILL WITH HIM THIS BRIGHT SATURDAY MORNING ON THE WEEKEND PRIOR TO THE TUESDAY SCHOOL BOARD ELECTION. THE QUESTIONS ARE UPPERMOST IN HIS MIND AS HE ENTERS THE BARBERSHOP AND TAKES A SEAT TO AWAIT HIS TURN IN LINE. HE IS ALMOST OBLIVIOUS TO THE GREETINGS FROM THE BARBER AND THE OTHER CUSTOMERS. FATIGUE SOON TAKES IT'S TOLL AS HE DRIFTS OFF INTO A DREAMY SLEEP.

IF MIND AND MATTER CAN BE CATEGORIZED AS DIFFERENT REALMS OF ONE REALITY, THEN THE SEMI-CONSCIOUS WORLD OF DREAMS WOULD BE A SPECIAL REGION IN THE MIND REALM. THIS WOULD BE A REGION WHERE THE IMAGINATION HAS NO BOUNDARIES. SPACE, TIME, MATTER AND THE OTHER LIMITATIONS ON THE PHYSICAL WORLD WOULD BE AS ELUSIVE AS THE INFINITELY DIMINISHING FRACTION OF TIME AND SPACE THAT DISTINGUISHES ONE QUANTUM UNIT FROM ANOTHER.

IN THE WORLD OF DREAMS THE VAST DISTANCES OF SPACE CAN BE TRAVELED INSTANTANEOUSLY. IN THE WORLD OF DREAMS MATTER CAN TAKE ANY SHAPE OR FORM. IN THE WORLD OF DREAMS THERE CAN BE MANY "REALITIES". IN THE WORLD OF DREAMS ONE CAN DREAM WITHIN A DREAM...WITHIN A DREAM. IN THE WORLD OF DREAMS ONE CAN AWAKE FROM ONE DREAM AND BE IN ANOTHER.

BARBER: BOY, WAKE UP! THIS ISN'T A MOTEL.

PRETTY BOY: YEAH **NIGGER**, AND IT'S NOT YOUR HOME EITHER. YOU COME IN HERE ALL "UPPITY" AND IGNORING EVERYBODY. AS THOUGH YOU DIDN'T SEE ME... AS PRETTY AS I AM, SITTING HERE GETTING MY HAIR **"FRIED, DIED, AND LAID TO THE SIDE"**!

THOMAS JR.:   MAN! I JUST HAD A CRAZY DREAM. I DREAMED THAT WE WERE ALL **WHITE**!

BARBER: WHITE?! BOY, WHAT HAVE YOU BEEN SMOKING?

THOMAS JR.:   I HAVEN'T BEEN SMOKING ANYTHING. EVERYTHING WAS THE REVERSE OF WHAT IT IS NOW. BLACK PEOPLE

WERE THE MAJORITY. WHITE PEOPLE USE TO BE SLAVES. THIS COUNTRY WAS CALLED THE **UNITED STATES OF NEW AFRICA!**

PRETTY BOY: NIGGER, AS **BLACK** AS YOU ARE, IF YOU TURNED WHITE, IT WOULD ONLY BE IN A DREAM! YOU'RE TALKING LIKE A CRAZY MAN. WHITE SLAVES?! THE UNITED STATES OF NEW AFRICA?!

"NIGGER, PLEASE"!

EPILOGUE

THE PREFACE OF THIS BOOK EXPLAINS IT'S INTENTION TO ENCOURAGE SERIOUS INDIVIDUAL REFLECTION ON SOCIAL MATTERS PERTAINING TO RACE. BY REVERSING THE TRADITIONAL ROLES PLAYED BY BLACKS AND WHITES, IT IS HOPED THAT INDIVIDUALS OF ALL GROUPS WILL GAIN A BROADER PERSPECTIVE FOR MAKING RATIONAL CHOICES FOR THEIR ACTIONS THAT IMPACT SOCIETAL PROBLEMS OF RACE. IT IS ALSO HOPED THAT THOSE WHO PRESENTLY HAVE AN ADVANTAGE DUE TO THE FACT THAT THEY ARE MEMBERS OF THE SOCIO-ECONOMICALLY DOMINATE GROUP, WILL TEMPER THEIR ACTIONS AFFECTING OTHER GROUPS WITH A FORETHOUGHT. THAT FORETHOUGHT IS SIMPLY THE **GOLDEN RULE.**

HOWEVER, THE GOLDEN RULE IS APPLICABLE TO THE DISADVANTAGED AS WELL AS THE ADVANTAGED. THIS DOES NOT END WITH THE OBVIOUS CONCLUSION THAT DIFFERENT GROUPS AND INDIVIDUALS SHOULD TREAT EACH OTHER WITH MUTUAL RESPECT. BEFORE THERE CAN BE MUTUAL RESPECT, THERE MUST BE SELF-RESPECT. FOR BLACKS, WHO WERE THE VICTIMS OF **INSTITUTIONALIZED SELF-CONTEMPT** IN THE FORM OF SLAVERY, SEGREGATION, FORMAL AND INFORMAL MIS-EDUCATION, THIS IS A VERY CRUCIAL MATTER.

THE COMPOUNDING OF NEGATIVE INDIVIDUAL CHOICES IN SUCH AREAS AS GANGS AND DRUGS IS A HINDRANCE TO THE PROGRESS OF BLACKS AS A GROUP. BUT, AT THE ROOT OF ALL OF THESE PROBLEMS IS THE FAILURE TO DEVELOP A **GROUP MIND-SET** THAT PLACES AT THE TOP OF ITS VALUES LIST THE **WELL-BEING OF THE GROUP** ITSELF. SUCH A MINDSET WOULD REJECT INDIVIDUAL GAIN MADE AT THE EXPENSE OF THE GROUP. THE **TRIBALISM** OF GANGS, CLASS AND COLOR IS REDUCED IN DIRECT

PROPORTION TO THE GROWTH OF A POSITIVE GROUP MIND-SET. THE **QUANTUM** IN THIS CASE IS EACH INDIVIDUAL MIND.

YES, **A MIND IS A TERRIBLE THING TO WASTE.** THAT CATCHY SLOGAN IS PRIMARILY DIRECTED AT THE IMPORTANCE OF FORMAL EDUCATION. FORMAL EDUCATION IS GENERALLY DIRECTED AT USEFULNESS FROM A CAREER STANDPOINT. HOWEVER, AN EDUCATED, CAREER TRAINED MIND CAN BE JUST AS WASTED AS THE OPPOSITE. THIS IS PARTICULARLY THE CASE WHEN THAT "EDUCATED" MIND HAS NOT LEARNED TO VALUE **LESSON NUMBER ONE.** THE WELL-BEING OF THE GROUP IS LESSON NUMBER ONE. THIS IS NOT LIMITED TO ONE RACIAL GROUP. ULTIMATELY, IT ENCOMPASSES ALL OF MANKIND. EACH GROUP OF HUMANITY MAY WELL REPRESENT ONE PARTICULAR UNIT OF QUANTUM MEASUREMENT OF THE **WAVE FUNCTION.** TOGETHER, ALL INDIVIDUALS (BLACK, WHITE, BROWN AND YELLOW) REPRESENT THE **WAVE** ITSELF.

Eddie J. Thomas

About the Author

I am a middle school teacher who has taught for 31 years. During those 31 years I have encountered hundreds of teenage personalities from all racial backgrounds. As a new teacher in 1971, I was intrigued by the attitudes about race that I discovered among my students. Having gone to high school and college during the Civil Rights and Black Pride movements of the 1960's. I expected to see black and white students with much more rational attitudes about race. I was disappointed in 1971. I am disappointed in 2002, but more optimistic.

SUGGESTED READING

THESE ARE JUST A FEW OF THE BOOKS THAT HAVE BEEN INSTRUMENTAL IN SHAPING MY IDEAS AND THOUGHTS.

THE BIBLE

JAMES H. BREASTED, THE DAWN OF CONSCIENCE, (CHARLES SCRIBNER'S SONS, NY, 1933).

BARBARA LOVETT CLINE, MEN WHO MADE A NEW PHYSICS.

PAUL DAVIES, GOD AND THE NEW PHYSICS, (SIMON AND SCHUSTER).

CHEIKH ANTA DIOP, THE AFRICAN ORIGIN OF CIVILIZATION: MYTH OR REALITY. (LAWRENCE HILL AND CO., NY, 1974).

JOHN HOWARD GRIFFIN, BLACK LIKE ME, (HOUGHTON MIFFLIN CO., 1960).

PAUL R. GROSS AND NORMAN LEVITT, HIGHER SUPERSTITION: THE ACADEMIC LEFT AND IT'S QUARRELS WITH SCIENCE.

ALEX HALEY, THE AUTOBIOGRAPHY OF MALCOLM X, (GROVE PRESS, INC, NY, 1966).

WERNER HEISENBERG, PHYSICS AND BEYOND, (HARPER AND ROW, 1971).

DRUSILLA DUNJEE HOUSTON, WONDERFUL ETHIOPIANS OF THE ANCIENT CUSHITE EMPIRE: BOOK 1, (UNIVERSAL PUBLISHING CO., OK, 1926).

DONALD JOHANSON AND JAMES SCHREEVE, <u>LUCY'S CHILD</u>, (EARLY MAN PUBLISHING, INC., 1989).

KENNETH R. PELLETIER, <u>TOWARD A SCIENCE OF CONSCIOUSNESS</u>, (DELA CORTE PRESS, NY, 1978).

JEAN PAUL SATRE, <u>EXISTENTIALISM AND HUMAN EMOTIONS</u>, (PHILOSOPHY LIBRARY, 1957).

EDMUND SINNOT, <u>MATTER, MIND, AND MEN</u>, (HARPER BROTHERS, 1957).

MICHAEL TALBERT, <u>BEYOND THE QUANTUM</u>, (MACMILLAN PUBLISHING CO., NY).

CHANCELLOR WILLIAMS, <u>DESTRUCTION OF BLACK CIVILIZATION</u>, (THIRD WORLD PRESS, CHICAGO, 1987).

CARTER G. WOODSON, <u>THE MIS-EDUCATION OF THE NEGRO</u>, (AFRICA WORLD PRESS, INC., 1990).

www.ingramcontent.com/pod-product-compliance
Lightning Source LLC
Chambersburg PA
CBHW030317290526
45785CB00001B/397